Office for
National Statistics

United Kingdom Health Statistics

No 3
2008 Edition

Editors: Claire Collins
Victoria Chenery
David Sweet

Office for National Statistics

palgrave
macmillan

ISBN 978-0-230-21096-7
ISSN 1475–0821

A National Statistics publication

National Statistics are produced to high professional standards as set out in the National Statistics Code of Practice. They are produced free from political influence. Not all the statistics contained within this publication are national statistics because it is a compilation from various sources.

About us

The Office for National Statistics

The Office for National Statistics (ONS) is the executive office of the UK Statistics Authority, a non-ministerial department which reports directly to Parliament. ONS is the UK government's single largest statistical producer. It compiles information about the UK's society and economy which provides evidence for policy and decision-making and in the allocation of resources.

The Director of ONS is also the National Statistician.

Palgrave Macmillan

This publication first published 2008 by Palgrave Macmillan, Houndmills, Basingstoke, Hampshire RG21 6XS and 175 Fifth Avenue, New York, NY 10010, USA

Companies and representatives throughout the world.

Palgrave Macmillan is the global academic imprint of the Palgrave Macmillan division of St. Martin's Press, LLC and of Palgrave Macmillan Ltd. Macmillan® is a registered trademark in the United States, United Kingdom and other countries. Palgrave is a registered trademark in the European Union and other countries.

A catalogue record for this book is available from the British Library.

10 9   8   7   6   5   4   3   2   1
17 16 15 14 13 12 11 10 09 08

Contacts

This publication

For information about the content of this publication, contact the Editor, email: ukhs@ons.gsi.gov.uk

Other customer and media enquiries

ONS Customer Contact Centre
Tel: 0845 601 3034
International: +44 (0)845 601 3034
Minicom: 01633 812399
Email: info@statistics.gsi.gov.uk
Fax: 01633 652747

Post: Room 1015, Government Buildings, Cardiff Road, Newport, South Wales NP10 8XG
www.statistics.gov.uk

Publication orders

To obtain the print version of this publication, contact Palgrave Macmillan, tel: 01256 302611
www.palgrave.com/ons

Copyright and reproduction

Printing

This book is printed on paper suitable for recycling and made from fully managed and sustained forest sources. Logging, pulping and manufacturing processes are expected to conform to the environmental regulations of the country of origin.

Printed and bound in Great Britain by Hobbs the Printer Ltd, Totton, Southampton

Typeset by Curran Publishing Services Ltd, Norwich, Norfolk

Contents

Page

List of tables

4: Health-related behaviour

5: Preventive healthcare

Page

List of figures and maps

x

Page

Foreword

I am delighted to introduce the third edition of *United Kingdom Health Statistics*, which contains updated and extended information on health and care for the UK and constituent countries. *United Kingdom Health Statistics* provides a ready reference for the comparison of key figures between the four constituent countries of the UK, and between the UK as a whole and other nation states.

United Kingdom Health Statistics is developed with the guidance of a steering group representing the Department of Health and the NHS Information Centre for Health and Social Care, the Scottish Government Health Department, the Welsh Assembly Government and the Department of Health, Social Services and Public Safety in Northern Ireland, and ONS.

The compilation of the data for this edition has been accompanied by a collaborative programme of improvements to the cross-UK comparability of the figures. As a result, this edition contains 11 new tables, while a further 23 tables have been revised as a result of harmonisation in methods or definitions between the countries. New and updated material has focussed particularly on the high priority areas of hospital waiting times, patient activity and healthy lifestyles.

We have also sought to improve the timeliness of the information, although this remains a challenge. Forty-eight of the 67 tables and three maps in this edition contain data up to 2006, and six contain data as recent as 2007.

This publication follows previous editions in being based primarily on published figures which have appeared in a range of sources including *Health Statistics Quarterly, Population Trends, Regional Trends* and in statistical reports of government and health service organisations in the four countries. Some data have also been published as part of the OECD publication *Health at a Glance* which compares key health and healthcare measures across the OECD countries. In some cases, figures have been recalculated or presented in different ways from the originals to aid cross-UK comparison, and we have drawn attention to this where necessary.

United Kingdom Health Statistics reflects both the strong UK role which is being played by ONS under the auspices of the new UK Statistics Authority, and the close collaborative relationships which continue with government departments and the devolved administrations. I am grateful to everyone involved in preparing this publication, and for their commitment to making coherent, high quality UK health statistics accessible to both specialist users and the wider public.

Karen Dunnell

Karen Dunnell

National Statistician

Acknowledgements

We are grateful to many colleagues within ONS and in organisations in all four countries of the UK who have contributed to this publication by providing data or finished tables; advising on content; commenting on wording or checking drafts; drafting sections of text; constructing charts; and in a host of other ways. Because of the large number of people involved, we have listed organisations rather than individuals. We apologise for any omissions from the list which follows:

Breast Test Wales
Care and Social Services Inspectorate for Wales
Central Services Agency, Northern Ireland
Cervical Screening Wales
Child & Adolescent Health Research Unit, University of Edinburgh
Commission for Social Care Inspection
Communicable Disease Surveillance Centre
Communicable Disease Surveillance Centre Northern Ireland
Communicable Disease Surveillance Centre Wales
Department for Transport
Department for Work and Pensions
Department of Health
Department of Health, Social Services and Public Safety, Northern Ireland.
Department of Public Health and Health Professionals, Welsh Assembly Government
Department for Environment, Food and Rural Affairs
Drinking Water Inspectorate
European Monitoring Centre on Drugs and Drug Addiction
Eurostat
General Register Office for Scotland
Health & Safety Executive
Health and Safety Executive of Northern Ireland
Health Behaviour in School-aged Children (HBSC) Study
Health Protection Agency
Health Protection Scotland (formerly SCIEH)
HM Treasury
Infant Feeding Survey, British Market Research Bureau
Information Services Division, NHS in Scotland
Institute of Child Health (London)
National Cancer Intelligence Centre
National Public Health Service Wales
NHS Information Centre for Health and Social Care
Northern Ireland Cancer Registry
Northern Ireland Statistics and Research Agency
Office for National Statistics
Scottish Cancer Registry
The Scottish Government
Welsh Cancer Intelligence and Surveillance Unit

Steering Group

Paul Allin	Office for National Statistics
Jennifer Bishop	Information Services Division, NHS in Scotland
Myer Glickman	Office for National Statistics
Sue Leake	Welsh Assembly Government
Tracy Power	Department of Health, Social Services and Public Safety, Northern Ireland
Cleo Rooney	Office for National Statistics
Julie Stroud	The Information Centre for Health and Social Care
Richard Wilmer	Department of Health, England

Symbols and conventions

Reference years

For most tables, the most recent year or a run of recent years is shown. When comparable data are available for a relatively long period of time, census years or an evenly spread representative selection of years are shown for the earlier period.

Because of differences in data collection and processing and publication schedules, the year of the most recent available data may differ between countries. Consequently, as comparability between the countries has been given priority, there are differences between tables in the most recent year presented.

Rounding of figures

In tables where figures have been rounded to the nearest final digit, there may be apparent discrepancies between the sum of constituent items and the total as shown.

Provisional data

Some data, usually for the most recent available year, may be provisional. These have been indicated in the footnotes.

Survey data

Many of the tables present the results of household surveys, which are subject to sampling error. Care should therefore be taken in drawing conclusions about differences between countries on the basis of these data.

Calendar and non-calendar years

Unless otherwise stated, figures are for calendar years (1 January–31 December). In some tables figures are for financial years (1 April–31 March) and these are shown as, for example, 2005/06.

Figures based on some data sources are presented as three year averages; in these cases, titles and labels normally refer to the central year of the three.

In a few cases figures are a 'snapshot' as of a specific date, which is shown in the table heading.

Geographical coverage and totals

Whenever possible, data are presented for all four countries of the UK. In some cases data are available only for the three countries of Great Britain. Most tables include totals for the UK or Great Britain as appropriate in addition to figures for the individual countries. Certain tables are presented without such totals, however, either because the data for the individual countries cannot be aggregated for technical reasons (for example concerning weighting of survey data) or because substantive differences (such as in the operation of reporting systems) would make the calculations of totals misleading.

Symbols

The following symbols have been used:

..   not available

Where a number is negligible, that is less than half the final digit shown, it is represented by 0 in the table but explained in a footnote.

People and work

1

This chapter contains key figures on the composition of the population in the four countries of the UK. It provides essential background to help understand the differences between the countries in the measures of health and healthcare presented in this report.

Population

In 2006, 65 per cent of the UK population were aged between 16 and 64 years. The proportion of the population in this age group was largely consistent between the four countries, with Scotland having the highest proportion at 66 per cent and Wales the lowest at 63 per cent (Table 1.1). A similar pattern was seen in the male population (Figure 1.1), with 67 per cent aged between 16 and 64 years in Scotland and 64 per cent in Wales, and in the female population, with 65 per cent in Scotland and 62 per cent in Wales.

Wales had the highest proportion of older people, with 18 per cent of the whole population aged over 65 years compared with 16 per cent in the UK as a whole. This was seen in both the male and female population, with 16 per cent of males over 65 years in Wales compared to the UK figure of 14 per cent, and 20 per cent of the females over 65 years in Wales compared to the UK figure of 18 per cent.

Relatively more women than men were aged over 65 years in all four countries, reflecting greater female life expectancy. This was seen in both the male and female population, with 16 per cent of males over 65 years in Wales compared to the UK figure of 14 per cent, and 20 per cent of

Figure 1.2

Trends in total dependency ratios:[1] 2006–2026; five-yearly projections

United Kingdom

Percentages

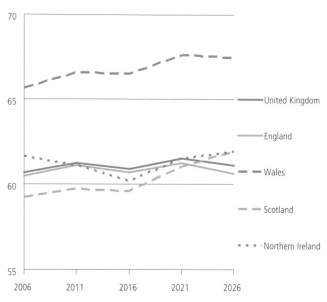

1   Working age and pensionable age populations are based on state retirement age for the given year. Between 2010 and 2020, state retirement age will change from 65 years for men and 60 years for women to 65 years for both sexes. Between 2024 and 2026 state pension age will increase to 66 years for both sexes.

Source: Office for National Statistics

Figure 1.1

Population: by age and sex,[1] 2006

United Kingdom

Percentages

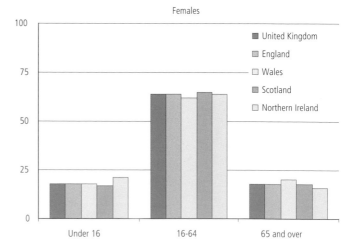

1   Mid-year estimates.

Source: Office for National Statistics

Table 1.1

Population: by age and sex,[1] 2006

United Kingdom

Thousands, percentages

	Thousands														Percentages		
	All ages	0–4	5–9	10–14	15–19	20–24	25–34	35–44	45–59	60–64	65–74	75–84	85–89	90 and over	Under 16	16–64	65 and over
People																	
United Kingdom	60,587	3,496	3,490	3,751	3,996	4,024	7,896	9,262	11,744	3,240	5,029	3416	820	423	19	65	16
England	50,763	2,956	2,922	3,130	3,334	3,362	6,708	7,793	9,777	2,697	4,171	2860	695	360	19	65	16
Wales	2,966	160	172	189	202	196	332	421	592	177	273	186	45	22	19	63	18
Scotland	5,117	269	279	308	329	339	628	790	1,058	280	456	287	63	32	18	66	16
Northern Ireland	1,742	112	117	125	131	127	229	259	316	87	130	84	18	8	22	64	14
Males																	
United Kingdom	29,694	1,790	1,785	1,924	2,060	2,048	3,941	4,587	5,804	1,584	2,379	1,413	273	106	20	66	14
England	24,926	1,513	1,493	1,606	1,720	1,713	3,353	3,875	4,839	1,320	1,981	1,190	233	91	20	66	14
Wales	1,445	82	88	97	105	99	164	205	291	87	130	77	15	5	20	64	16
Scotland	2,469	137	143	157	169	171	310	380	517	135	208	113	20	8	19	67	14
Northern Ireland	853	57	60	64	67	65	113	127	156	42	60	33	6	2	23	65	12
Females																	
United Kingdom	30,893	1,706	1,705	1,827	1,936	1,976	3,956	4,675	5,940	1,656	2,650	2,003	547	317	18	64	18
England	25,837	1,442	1,428	1,523	1,615	1,649	3,356	3,918	4,938	1,377	2,191	1,670	461	270	18	64	18
Wales	1,521	78	84	92	98	97	168	216	301	90	143	109	30	16	18	62	20
Scotland	2,648	131	136	151	160	168	317	410	541	145	247	174	43	25	17	65	18
Northern Ireland	888	55	57	61	64	62	115	132	160	45	69	51	12	6	21	64	16

Figures may not be exact due to rounding.

1 *Mid-year estimates.*

Source: *Office for National Statistics*

the females over 65 years in Wales compared to the UK figure of 18 per cent.

Northern Ireland had a younger population with 22 per cent of the population aged under 16 years compared with 19 per cent for the UK as a whole. The lowest proportion of population under 16 years was in Scotland, at 18 per cent.

An Excel workbook containing the data for Table 1.1 for selected years between 1981 and 2006 can be found on the National Statistics website.

Another way of looking at the age structure of the population is the dependency ratio, that is, the ratio of people of 'dependent' ages – children under 16 years, women over 60 years and men over 65 years – to people of working age – women between 16 and 60 years and men between 16 and 65 years. It can be expressed as a percentage of the number of

people of working age. Projections of population growth and migration can be used to estimate future trends in the dependency ratio. (Figure 1.2)

For the UK in 2006, the total dependency ratio was 60.7 which was made up of a children dependency ratio of 30.6 and an older person dependency ratio of 30.1 (Table 1.2). The total dependency ratios in the four countries ranged from 59.3 in Scotland to 65.7 in Wales. The highest children dependency rate was in Northern Ireland at 35.3 per cent and the lowest children dependency rate was in Scotland at 28.7 per cent. These figures reflect the higher proportion of children in Northern Ireland, and of older people in Wales, relative to the rest of the UK.

For the given years, Northern Ireland has the highest dependency rate of children in all years. In all four countries, the children dependency rate decreased over time from 1971

Table 1.2

Trends in dependency ratios,[1] 1971–2026 (selected years)

United Kingdom

Percentages

											Projections[2]			
	1971	1981	1991	2001	2002	2003	2004	2005	2006	2011	2016	2021	2026
Total dependency														
United Kingdom	71.8	66.8	63.2	62.4	62.0	61.7	61.4	61.1	60.7	61.2	60.9	61.5	61.1
England	71.0	66.4	62.9	62.2	61.8	61.5	61.3	61.0	60.5	61.1	60.7	61.2	60.6
Wales	73.2	69.2	67.9	67.3	66.9	66.4	66.1	65.9	65.7	66.6	66.5	67.6	67.5
Scotland	75.3	66.6	61.3	60.8	60.5	60.2	59.9	59.7	59.3	59.7	59.6	61.0	61.9
Northern Ireland	80.6	76.5	70.1	64.0	63.5	63.1	62.6	62.1	61.6	61.1	60.2	61.5	61.9
Children [3]														
United Kingdom	43.8	37.1	33.2	32.6	32.2	31.8	31.4	31.0	30.6	29.9	30.0	30.5	29.8
England	42.9	36.6	32.9	32.5	32.1	31.8	31.4	31.0	30.6	30.0	30.1	30.7	30.0
Wales	43.4	37.6	34.4	33.7	33.2	32.7	32.2	31.8	31.4	30.2	29.9	30.4	29.7
Scotland	48.2	38.2	32.4	30.8	30.3	29.9	29.9	29.1	28.7	27.5	27.1	27.4	26.8
Northern Ireland	56.6	50.8	44.1	38.6	37.9	37.2	36.4	35.8	35.3	33.5	32.7	33.0	32.2
Pension Age[4] and over														
United Kingdom	28.0	29.7	30.0	29.8	29.8	29.9	30.0	30.1	30.1	31.3	30.9	31.0	31.2
England	28.1	29.9	30.0	29.7	29.7	29.8	29.9	29.9	29.9	31.0	30.6	30.5	30.6
Wales	29.8	31.6	33.5	33.6	33.6	33.7	33.9	34.1	34.3	36.5	36.7	37.3	37.8
Scotland	27.1	28.4	28.9	30.0	30.2	30.3	30.5	30.6	30.6	32.1	32.5	33.6	35.1
Northern Ireland	24.0	25.7	26.1	25.5	25.7	25.9	26.2	26.3	26.4	27.6	27.5	28.5	29.7

Figures may not add exactly due to rounding.

1 *Working age and pensionable age populations are based on state retirement age for the given year. Between 2010 and 2020, state retirement age will change from 65 years for men and 60 years for women to 65 years for both sexes. Between 2024 and 2026 state pension age will increase to 66 years for both sexes.*
2 *2006-based principal projections.*
3 *Children under 16 as a percentage of working population.*
4 *Persons of state pension age as a percentage of the working population.*

Source: Office for National Statistics

Table 1.3

Population: by ethnic group, 2005

United Kingdom

Thousands, percentages

	All ethnic groups	All ethnic minority groups [1]	White	Mixed	Asian or Asian British	Black or Black British	Chinese	Other
	Thousands		Percentages					
United Kingdom	58,692	5,464	90.7	1.0	4.5	2.2	0.4	1.2
England [2]	49,145	5,253	89.3	1.1	5.2	2.6	0.4	1.3
Wales [3]	2,891	73	97.4	0.6	0.8	0.3	0.1	0.8
Scotland [3]	4,965	122	97.5	0.3	1.2	0.1	0.4	0.5
Northern Ireland [3]	1,691	15	99.1	0.2	0.4	0.1	0.2	0.1

1 All ethnic groups except White.
2 Other excludes non-response of 0.1.
3 These estimates are based on very small sample sizes and are subject to a very high degree of sampling variability. They therefore should be treated with caution.

Source: Office for National Statistics

onwards, reflecting the decline in the annual number of births. This decline is projected to continue until 2021 when the projected children dependency for the UK is 30.5 per cent, then falling to 29.8 percent in 2026.

There is considerable difference between the countries of the UK in the proportion of the population made up of ethnic minority groups. In 2005, Northern Ireland had the highest proportion of the population classified as White at 99.1 per

cent, compared with 90.7 per cent in the UK as a whole (Table 1.3).

In all countries the largest ethnic minority was Asian or Asian/British, ranging from 0.4 per cent of the population in Northern Ireland to 5.2 per cent in England. The smallest ethnic group for England and Wales was Chinese but for Scotland and Northern Ireland it was Black or Black British.

Table 1.4

Size of households, 2007[1]

United Kingdom

Percentages, persons

Size of household [2,3]	United Kingdom	England	Wales	Scotland	Northern Ireland
One person	29.0	28.7	29.7	32.3	27.8
Two people	35.3	35.3	35.6	35.4	31.7
Three people	15.7	15.7	15.4	16.3	14.9
Four people	13.5	13.7	13.5	11.8	14.7
Five people	4.6	4.6	4.7	3.4	7.8
Six or more people	1.8	2.0	1.2	0.8	3.1
All households (thousands)	25,046	20,866	1,264	2,237	680
Average household size (persons)	2.4	2.4	2.3	2.2	2.5

1 Calendar quarter April to June.
2 Households are defined as: A single person, or a group of people living at the same address who have the address as their only or main residence and either share one main meal a day or share the living accomodation (or both).
3 Household size is calculated according to survey response and represents the number of usual residents.

Source: Office for National Statistics

Households

Surveys define a household as a single person, or a group of people living at the same address, who share their living accommodation or normally have at least one daily meal together. A family is defined in terms of the 'nuclear family' of a couple (or a single person) with or without children, but not extending to more than two generations. A household can contain more than one family.

In 2007, Scotland had the highest proportion of one person households at 32.3 per cent (Table 1.4). Northern Ireland had the lowest proportion of one person households at 27.8 per cent and two person households at 31.7 per cent, but had the highest proportion of households with four or more people.

This resulted in Northern Ireland having the largest average household size at 2.5 people and Scotland the smallest at 2.2 people. This compares to the UK average household size of 2.4 people.

Scotland had the highest proportion of one person households consisting of people under pensionable age, at 16.7 per cent compared with 14.4 per cent for the UK as a whole (Table 1.5). Wales had the highest proportion of one person households consisting of people over pensionable age, at 16.3 per cent compared with 14.6 per cent for the UK as a whole.

Northern Ireland had the lowest proportion of family households with no children, with 24.6 per cent compared with 28.7 per cent for the UK as a whole. The highest per cent of households with no children was for Wales at 29.7 per cent and also the highest per cent of lone parent households with dependent children at 7.4 per cent compared with 7.1 per cent for the whole of the UK.

Table 1.5

Composition of households, 2007[1]

United Kingdom

Percentages

Household composition	United Kingdom	England	Wales	Scotland	Northern Ireland
One person					
Under pensionable age [2]	14.4	14.3	13.4	16.7	14.2
Over pensionable age [3]	14.6	14.4	16.3	15.6	13.6
Two or more unrelated adults	3.1	3.2	2.3	3.0	2.1
Single family households[4]					
Couple [5]					
No children	28.7	28.9	29.7	27.8	24.6
1–2 dependent children [6]	18.1	18.2	17.2	17.1	18.0
3 or more dependent children [6]	3.5	3.6	3.2	2.2	6.5
Non-dependent children only	6.3	6.2	6.9	6.4	9.0
Lone parent					
Dependent children [6]	7.1	7.1	7.4	6.9	6.9
Non-dependent children only	3.0	3.0	2.5	3.6	4.0
Multi-family households	0.8	0.8	0.9	0.5	0.9
All households[7] (thousands)	25,046	20,866	1,264	2,237	680

Note: Percentages may not add to 100 due to rounding.

1 Calendar quarter April to June.
2 Men aged 16-64 and women aged 16-59.
3 Men aged 65 and over and women aged 60 and over.
4 Other individuals who were not family members may also be included.
5 Excluding same-sex couples and civil partnerships.
6 May also include non-dependent children.
7 Includes same sex couples and civil partners. Percentages are calculated based on this total.

Source: Office for National Statistics

Table 1.6

Adult population of working age: by sex and socio-economic classification,[1,2] 2005

United Kingdom

Thousands

Social Class	United Kingdom	England	Wales	Scotland	Northern Ireland
People					
Higher managerial and professional	10.9	11.4	7.7	9.7	6.7
Lower managerial and professional	22.2	22.4	20.3	22.0	19.1
Intermediate occupations	10.1	10.1	9.7	10.3	9.2
Small employers and own account workers	7.6	7.7	7.6	5.9	8.8
Lower supervisory and technical	8.8	8.7	10.2	9.6	7.9
Semi-routine occupations	12.8	12.6	14.1	13.7	14.2
Routine occupations	9.3	9.0	10.5	10.8	10.5
Never worked and long term unemployed	18.4	18.2	20.0	17.9	23.7
All persons (100%)	36,455	30,533	1,750	3,123	1,050
Men					
Higher managerial and professional	15.1	15.7	10.4	13.3	8.9
Lower managerial and professional	20.3	20.6	18.6	19.2	16.5
Intermediate occupations	5.2	5.2	5.0	5.6	5.2
Small employers and own account workers	11.0	11.1	11.2	8.6	15.0
Lower supervisory and technical	12.1	11.9	14.0	13.3	10.6
Semi-routine occupations	9.6	9.4	10.4	10.2	10.4
Routine occupations	11.3	10.9	12.7	13.9	14.0
Never worked and long term unemployed	15.5	15.2	17.8	15.9	19.2
All men (100%)	18,721	15,692	898	1,593	539
Women					
Higher managerial and professional	6.6	6.9	4.8	5.9	4.3
Lower managerial and professional	24.1	24.3	22.1	24.9	21.7
Intermediate occupations	15.2	15.3	14.7	15.2	13.5
Small employers and own account workers	4.0	4.1	3.8	3.2	2.3
Lower supervisory and technical	5.3	5.3	6.2	5.7	4.9
Semi-routine occupations	16.2	15.9	18.0	17.4	18.1
Routine occupations	7.2	7.1	8.2	7.7	6.7
Never worked and long term unemployed	21.4	21.3	22.2	20.0	28.5
All women (100%)	17,735	14,842	852	1,530	511

1 Men aged 16–64, women aged 16–59.
2 Based on the National Statistics Socio-Economic Classification (NS SEC).

Source: Office for National Statistics

Socio-economic status, qualifications and economic activity

The socio-economic status of adults of working age in the UK can be classified using the National Statistics Socio-Economic Classification (NS SEC) based on occupation and employment status (Table 1.6, Figure 1.4).

In 2005, England had the highest proportion of people in managerial and professional classes (33.8 per cent altogether); Northern Ireland had the lowest proportion (25.8 per cent). Scotland had the highest proportion of routine occupations of 10.8 per cent compared with the UK average of 9.3 per cent. Northern Ireland had the highest proportion of the population classed as 'never worked or long term unemployed' at 23.7 per cent, compared with the UK average of 18.4 per cent.

The proportion of women in higher managerial and professional posts was 6.6 per cent in the UK compared with 15.1 per cent of men in similar posts. However, the proportion of women in lower managerial and professional post was 24.1 per cent compared with 20.3 per cent of men. The proportion of women who had never worked or were long-term unemployed was 21.4 per cent compared to 15.5 per cent of men.

In 2005, 23.7 per cent of the working age population in Northern Ireland had no qualifications compared with 15.3 per cent of the UK as a whole (Table 1.7, Figure 1.3). England and

Scotland had the lowest proportion of the population with no qualifications each with 14.8 per cent. Scotland had the highest proportion of the population with GCE A level or equivalent with 28.6 per cent, but also had the lowest proportion with GCSE grades A-C or equivalent with 17.3 per cent compared with the UK figure of 22.5 per cent. England had the highest proportion of the population with a degree or equivalent with 18.9 per cent compared with 14.8 per cent of the population of Northern Ireland, which was the lowest.

The unemployment rate was higher in England at 5.4 per cent (Table 1.8, Figure 1.4) than in the other UK countries; the overall UK unemployment rate was 5.3 per cent with Northern Ireland having the lowest rate at 4.9 per cent. Male unemployment in Scotland was highest at 6.2 per cent compared with a UK proportion of 5.8 per cent. Female unemployment in Northern Ireland was lowest at 3.7 per cent compared with a UK proportion of 4.8 per cent.

Scotland had the highest percentage of economically active people at 63.6 per cent and Wales had the lowest proportion of economically active people at 58.6 per cent. The proportion of economically active people in the UK was 62.9 per cent.

An Excel workbook containing the data for Table 1.8 for the years 2004–2006 inclusive can be found on the National Statistics website.

Figure 1.3

Population of working age with no qualifications,[1] 2005

United Kingdom

Percentages

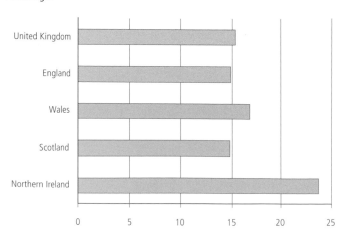

1   Men aged 16–64 and women aged 16–59.

Souce: Office for National Statistics

Figure 1.4

Employment rate,[1] 2006

United Kingdom

Percentages

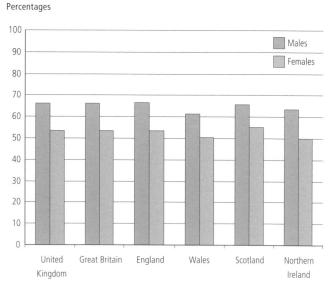

1   Total employment as a percentage of all people aged 16 and over.

Source: Office for National Statistics

Table 1.7

Population of working age: by highest qualification,[1] 2005

United Kingdom   Thousands, percentages

	No qualifications	GCSE grades A–C or equivalent	GCE A level or equivalent [2]	Higher education [3]	Degree or equivalent	Other qualifications	Total (100%)
United Kingdom	15.3	22.5	23.2	8.3	18.4	12.3	28,273
England	14.8	23.0	22.5	7.6	18.9	13.2	22,394
Wales	16.7	25.5	22.8	8.9	15.3	10.7	1,734
Scotland	14.8	17.3	28.6	13.0	17.8	8.6	3,106
Northern Ireland	23.7	22.5	24.4	8.2	14.8	6.4	1,039

1 Men aged 16–64 and women aged 16–59.
2 Includes recognised trade apprenticeship.
3 Excluding degree or equivalent.

Souce: Office for National Statistics

Table 1.8

Unemployment and economic activity, 2006

United Kingdom   Rates

	Unemployment rate (ILO definition) [1]	Employment rate [2]	Employment rate [3]	Percentage economically active [4-6]
	All aged 16 and over		Working age	All aged 16 and over
People				
United Kingdom	5.3	59.6	74.1	62.9
Great Britain	5.3	59.7	74.3	63.0
England	5.4	59.9	74.3	63.3
Wales	5.2	55.5	71.1	58.6
Scotland	5.2	60.3	75.7	63.6
Northern Ireland	4.9	56.6	68.7	59.5
Males				
United Kingdom	5.8	66.2	78.3	70.2
Great Britain	5.8	66.2	78.5	70.3
England	5.7	66.5	78.7	70.6
Wales	5.8	61.2	74.3	65.0
Scotland	6.2	66.0	78.3	70.3
Northern Ireland	5.8	63.8	73.3	67.7
Females				
United Kingdom	4.8	53.5	69.6	56.2
Great Britain	4.8	53.6	69.8	56.3
England	4.9	53.6	69.6	56.4
Wales	4.5	50.3	67.8	52.7
Scotland	4.1	55.1	73.1	57.5
Northern Ireland	3.7	49.9	63.8	51.9

1 Total unemployed (ILO definition) as a percentage of all economically active persons.
2 Total in employment as a percentage of all people aged 16 and over.
3 Total in employment as a percentage of all people of working age (16–64 for males, 16–59 for women).
4 Including people on government-supported training and employment programmes and unpaid family workers.
5 Population in private households, student halls of residence and NHS accomodation.
6 Total economically active (either in employment or ILO unemployed) as a percentage of all aged 16 and over.

Source: Office for National Statistics

Disability

England had the lowest proportion of disabled people of working age (16 to 59/64 years) at 14.8 per cent compared with the UK proportion of 15.2 per cent (Table 1.9). The proportion was lowest in England for men, at 15.6 per cent and women at 14.0 per cent. Wales had the highest proportion of disabled people of working age at 20.0 per cent. For children under five years the lowest proportion was seen in Wales for both boys at 3.2 per cent and girls at 1.7 per cent.

Table 1.9

Disabled people[1] (including those with longstanding limiting illnesses) as a percentage of the population: by age and gender, 2005–06

United Kingdom
Percentages

	Disabled children/ Young people[2]		Disabled people								
	Less than 5	5–15+[3]	16–24[3]	25–34	35–44	45–54	55–64	65–74	75+	16–59/64
All persons										
United Kingdom	3.5	6.9	7.0	9.2	13.2	20.3	30.0	41.0	57.0	15.2
England	3.6	6.7	6.9	9.1	13.0	19.6	29.0	39.7	56.1	14.8
Wales	2.4	9.2	7.9	11.5	15.5	27.4	39.0	51.2	69.2	20.0
Scotland	3.9	8.0	7.1	9.1	13.5	21.9	30.3	44.7	58.2	15.8
Northern Ireland	3.5	6.0	7.6	9.5	14.1	24.1	41.7	48.3	55.4	17.6
Men										
United Kingdom	3.9	8.4	7.1	10.0	13.4	19.7	29.4	41.4	55.6	16.0
England	4.0	8.2	6.8	10.0	13.2	19.1	28.4	40.1	54.8	15.6
Wales	3.2	10.0	9.8	13.5	17.2	23.2	38.6	51.8	70.6	21.4
Scotland	3.4	9.9	8.2	8.5	12.8	21.2	29.3	45.3	54.1	16.2
Northern Ireland	4.3	7.4	6.2	9.2	15.1	25.9	39.9	48.0	57.0	18.6
Women										
United Kingdom	3.1	5.3	6.9	8.5	13.1	20.9	30.5	40.6	57.8	14.4
England	3.1	5.1	7.0	8.3	12.9	20.1	29.5	39.3	56.9	14.0
Wales	1.7	8.4	5.8	9.6	13.9	30.8	39.5	50.6	68.2	18.5
Scotland	4.4	5.9	6.0	9.6	14.1	22.5	31.2	44.2	60.7	15.4
Northern Ireland	2.7	4.5	9.0	9.9	13.2	22.4	43.4	48.5	54.4	16.5

1 People defined as disabled are those who have physical or mental disability that limits their activities in any way.
2 A child/young person is defined as someone aged under 16, and aged 16 to 18 year old who is in full-time non-advanced education and living at home.
3 There may be some overlap between the '5–15+' and the '16–24' age groups for reasons explained in note 2. A person will not be in both groups.

Source: Department for Work and Pensions

Additional notes

Table 1.3 – Ethnic group

The information presented here is based on the Labour Force Study (LFS) output classifications introduced in spring 2001. The classification is based on six categories: White, Mixed, Asian or Asian British, Black or Black British, Chinese or Other ethnic minority group.

Table 1.4, 1.5 – Households and families

A household is a single person, or a group of people living at the same address, who have the address as their only or main residence and either share one main meal a day or share the living accommodation (or both). Families are defined as married or co-habiting couples, either with or without their never-married children (of any age), who have no children of their own, or a lone parent with such children. Most household surveys do not consider a person living alone to form a family. A family could also consist of a grandparent (or grandparents) with grandchildren, if there are no apparent parents of the grandchildren usually resident in the household (note: this definition differs slightly to that used in the census). A household can contain one or more families and also household members other than those belonging to a nuclear family.

Table 1.6 – Socio-economic classification

The National Statistics Socio-economic Classification (NS-SEC) replaced Social Class based on Occupation (SC, formerly Registrar General's Social Class) and Socio-economic Groups (SEG) in 2001. The information required to create the NS-SEC is occupation coded to the unit groups of the Standard Occupational Classification 2000 (SOC 2000) and details of employment status (such as whether the respondent is an employer, self-employed or an employee, and whether they are a supervisor and the number of employees at their workplace).

Table 1.7 – Educational qualifications

Data presented here are LFS data based on the International Standard Classification of Education (ISCED 97). Further information on this classification system can be found in the LFS User Guide, Volume 5, Classifications, 2004. Comparisons of examination results for England, Wales and Northern Ireland with those of Scotland are not straightforward because of the different education and examination systems. The following should be used as a guideline:

- Five or more GCSEs at grades A* - C = Five or more SCE S grades at levels 1-3

- One to four GCSEs at grades A* -C = One to four SCE S grades at levels 1-3

- GCSEs at grades D-G only = SCE S grades at levels 4-7 only

- Two or more GCE A level passes at A-E = Three or more SCE H grade passes at A-C

Table 1.8 – Unemployment and economic activity

The International Labour Office (ILO) defines unemployed people as people without a job who were available to start work within two weeks and had either looked for work in the previous four weeks or were waiting to start a job they had already obtained.

The unemployment rate is the total number of people in employment as a percentage of all persons of working age (16–64 for males, 16–59 for women).

Table 1.9 – Disabled people

The definition of disability used in this report includes those with longstanding limiting illnesses. Limited Long-Standing Illness is defined as an illness, disability or infirmity that is longstanding (has troubled someone over a period of time or is likely to) and limits their activities in any way.

Disabled people, including children and young people, are those who have a physical or mental disability that limits their activities in any way. A child/young person is defined as someone aged 16 and under, and aged 16-18 who is in full-time non-advanced education and living at home.

Pregnancy and childbirth

Chapter 2

DATA

Download data by clicking the online pdf

www.statistics.gov.uk/
downloads/theme_health/
ukhs3/

This chapter contains key statistics about fertility, pregnancy and the health of babies.

Fertility

The age-specific fertility rate (ASFR) is the number of births to mothers of a specified age group per 1,000 women of that age in that year. It is a useful measure for comparing births to women of different ages. The total fertility rate (TFR) is a summary measure of the fertility of women of childbearing age (15-44 years) at one point in time, independent of the age structure of the population, and so is useful for looking at trends over a number of years.

In 2006, women aged 30-34 years and 25-29 years had the highest age-specific fertility rates in the UK as a whole (104.6 and 100.1 births per 1,000 women) (Table 2.1). Fertility was highest at ages 25-29 years in Wales and at 30-34 years in the other countries of the UK. The highest fertility rate of any age group was 119.2 births per 1,000 women, for women aged 30-34 in Northern Ireland.

Wales had the highest proportion of births outside marriage at 53.0 per cent, and Northern Ireland had the lowest at 38.0 per cent. The proportion of births outside marriage was 43.7 per cent in the UK as a whole.

An Excel workbook containing the data for Table 2.1 for all years from 1991 to 2006 inclusive can be found on the National Statistics website.

The UK total fertility rate declined over a period of 30 years, from 2.41 births per woman aged 15-44 in 1971 to a low of 1.63 in 2001 (Table 2.2). It then rose again to reach 1.84 in

Figure 2.1

Total fertility rate, 2006

United Kingdom

Births per 1,000 women

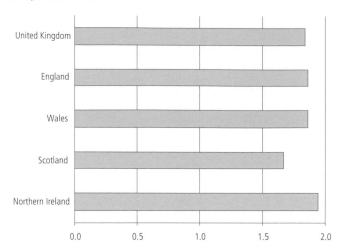

Source: Office for National Statistics; General Register Office for Scotland; Northern Ireland Statistics and Research Agency

2006, when Northern Ireland had the highest TFR at 1.94 and Scotland had the lowest at 1.67 (Table 2.2, Figure 2.1). Throughout the period, Northern Ireland had the highest fertility rate, despite having had the largest fall over time. England had the lowest fertility from 1971 to 1981, while Scotland had the lowest rates for all subsequent years.

Conceptions

The conception rate is the number of pregnancies that result in a live or still birth, or a legal abortion under the 1967 Abortion Act, per 1,000 women of the relevant age.

Table 2.1

Age specific fertility rates (ASFR), total fertility rate (TFR), and percentage of live births outside marriage, 2006

United Kingdom

Rates, percentages

	Age specific fertility rates (per 1,000 population)[1,2]							TFR	% outside marriage
	All age[3]	under 20[4]	20-24	25-29	30-34	35-39	over 40[5]		
United Kingdom	59.7	26.4	72.0	100.1	104.6	53.4	11.1	1.84	43.7
England	60.3	26.3	72.9	100.3	105.0	54.3	11.6	1.86	43.0
Wales	58.1	31.5	78.2	106.7	99.4	45.1	8.4	1.86	53.0
Scotland	52.8	25.8	61.9	90.2	97.1	47.8	8.7	1.67	47.7
Northern Ireland	62.5	22.5	63.6	112.0	119.2	58.2	11.3	1.94	38.0

1 ASFRs are produced for England and Wales to exclude births to women usually resident outside England and Wales. These births are, however, included in the UK total. Scotland exclude births where age is not stated. Data for England and Wales based on occurences, Scotland and Northern Ireland on registrations.
2 ASFRs are the number of live births to mothers of a particular age per 1,000 women in that age group.
3 Fertility rates for women of all ages are based on the female population aged 15-44.
4 Fertility rates for women of age under 20 are based on the female population aged 15-19.
5 Fertility rates for women of aged over 40 are based on the female population aged 40-44.

Source: Office for National Statistics; General Register Office for Scotland; Northern Ireland Statistics and Research Agency

Table 2.2

Trends in total fertility rate,[1,2] 1971-2006 (selected years)

United Kingdom   Total fertililty rate

	United Kingdom	England	Wales	Scotland	Northern Ireland
1971	2.41	2.37	2.44	2.53	3.13
1976	1.74	1.70	1.78	1.79	2.68
1981	1.82	1.79	1.87	1.84	2.59
1986	1.78	1.76	1.86	1.67	2.45
1991	1.82	1.81	1.88	1.69	2.16
1992	1.79	1.79	1.87	1.67	2.08
1993	1.76	1.76	1.84	1.62	2.01
1994	1.74	1.75	1.79	1.58	1.95
1995	1.71	1.71	1.77	1.55	1.91
1996	1.73	1.73	1.81	1.56	1.95
1997	1.72	1.73	1.81	1.58	1.93
1998	1.71	1.72	1.78	1.55	1.90
1999	1.68	1.69	1.72	1.51	1.86
2000	1.64	1.65	1.68	1.48	1.75
2001	1.63	1.63	1.66	1.49	1.80
2002	1.64	1.65	1.64	1.48	1.77
2003	1.71	1.73	1.73	1.54	1.81
2004	1.77	1.78	1.78	1.60	1.87
2005	1.78	1.79	1.81	1.62	1.87
2006	1.84	1.86	1.86	1.67	1.94

1   Total fertility rate is a measure of the fertility of women of childbearing age (15-44 years) at one in point in time.
2   Figures for England and Wales each exclude births to women usually resident outside England and Wales. These births are, however, included in the totals for the UK. Births to non-resident mothers in Northern Ireland are excluded from the figures for Northern Ireland, and for the UK.

Source: Office for National Statistics; General Register Office for Scotland; Northern Ireland Statistics and Research Agency

For conceptions leading to abortions, age at conception is estimated by subtracting recorded gestation from the woman's date of birth at abortion. Similarly, conceptions leading to maternities age is estimated using gestation collected for stillbirths, and 38 weeks gestation is assumed for live births.

In 2005, within Great Britain, England had the highest conception rate at 76.3 per 1,000 women and Scotland had the lowest at 63.1 (Table 2.3). Wales had the highest conception rate for women aged under 20 years (63.1 per 1,000 women) while England had the highest rates for women aged 30 years and over. For all countries, the conception rate was highest in the 25-29 age group. In absolute numbers, there were more conceptions in the 30-34 age group than in the 25-29 age group in Scotland.

England had the highest proportion of conceptions leading to abortion for all ages combined, at 22.4 per cent, as well as in each age group. In Great Britain the proportions were highest for women under 20 and were lowest in all countries for women aged 30-34 years.

Abortions

The abortion rate is the number of abortions that are legally performed under the 1967 Abortion Act per 1,000 women of the relevant age.

Mother's age at abortion as shown in Table 2.4 is calculated using the woman's date of birth (provided on the abortion notification form) and the date of abortion. Figures are based on number of legal abortions that were performed in Great Britain on residents of England, Wales and Scotland.

Comparable data are not available for Northern Ireland, where the 1967 Act does not apply. A number of abortions to women resident in Northern Ireland are performed in Great Britain but not included in these figures.

The overall abortion rate in Great Britain in 2006 was 17.2 per 1,000 women. Rates of abortion were highest among women aged 20 to 24 in all countries. England had the highest abortion rates for women in all age groups, with an overall abortion rate of 17.5 per 1,000 women compared with 14.5 per 1,000 in Wales and 14.4 in Scotland.

Excel workbooks containing the data for Tables 2.3 for all years from 1991 to 2006 inclusive can be found on the National Statistics website.

Birthweight

The proportion of babies who are of low birthweight (under 2,500g) or very low birthweight (1,500g) is important because low birthweight babies have an increased risk of infant death compared to babies of normal birthweight, and low birthweight is associated with continuing health problems in childhood.

Between 1996 and 2004, the proportion of low birthweight babies in the UK remained fairly constant, ranging from 7.4 per cent in 1996 and 1998 to a maximum of 7.6 per cent in 2002 and 2003. The proportion of very low birthweight babies was between 1.2 and 1.3 per cent throughout the same period (Table 2.5 and 2.6).

In Wales, Northern Ireland and Scotland the highest proportions of low and very low birthweight babies were among those born to women under 20 years old, while in England the highest proportion was in babies of women over 40 years old.

Table 2.3

Conceptions by age and outcome, 2004-05[1]

Great Britain   Numbers, rates, percentages

	All ages	under 16	under 18	under 20	20-24	25-29	30-34	35-39	40 & over
Numbers									
England	800,901	7,473	39,804	96,201	175,476	201,192	200,033	105,380	22,619
Wales	40,930	457	2,521	6,111	10,009	10,105	9,136	4,607	962
Scotland [4]	70,683	707	3,993	9,045	14,810	16,574	18,422	9,774	2,058
Rates per 1,000 women [2]									
England	76.3	7.8	41.3	59.9	108.9	125.7	112.9	53.7	11.6
Wales	71.0	7.9	43.6	63.1	106.8	128.4	100.3	43.4	8.8
Scotland [4]	63.1	7.5	25.3	40.6	91.9	112.8	103.4	47.5	10.0
Percentage ending in abortion [3]									
England	22.4	57.5	46.8	40.7	28.9	18.2	13.3	17.8	32.9
Wales	19.1	50.8	38.6	33.7	23.6	13.7	11.2	15.9	29.2
Scotland [4]	18.8	56.7	43.2	38.1	26.2	14.3	9.8	13.1	21.1

1 Data for England and Wales are for 2005. Data for Scotland is for 2004, and is therefore not directly comparable.
2 Rates for all ages, under 16, under 18, under 20 and 40 and over are based on female populations aged 15-44, 13-15, 15-17, 15-19 and 40-44 respectively.
3 For further notes on abortion rates, see table 2.4.
4 These figures differ from the figures routinely published by ISD (Scotland) because the latter include spontaneous abortions (miscarriages).

Source: Office for National Statistics; Information Services Division, NHS in Scotland

Table 2.4

Legal abortions by age, 2006

Great Britain   Numbers, rates

	All ages[1]	under 16	under 18	under 20	20-24[2]	25-29	30-34	35-39	40 and over
Numbers									
Great Britain	206,818	4,352	20,225	44,732	59,298	42,827	29,761	21,273	8,927
England[3]	185,307	3,749	17,615	39,122	52,816	38,770	27,126	19,281	8,192
Wales[3]	8,430	241	1,004	2,164	2,524	1,626	1,027	793	296
Scotland[4]	13,081	362	1,606	3,446	3,958	2,431	1,608	1,199	439
Rates per 1,000 women[5]									
Great Britain	17.2	4.0	18.1	23.9	31.0	22.9	15.1	9.4	3.9
England[3]	17.5	3.9	18.3	24.2	32.0	23.7	15.7	9.9	4.2
Wales[3]	14.5	4.1	17.4	22.1	26.1	20.0	11.8	7.5	2.7
Scotland[4]	14.4	3.8	17.0	21.6	23.6	15.8	9.8	6.0	2.1

1 Includes age not stated.
2. In England and Wales there were 30 records with no known age. These were included in the 20-24 age band.
3. Figures include abortions to residents of England and Wales, performed in England and Wales only. Abortions to residents of England and Wales performed outside England and Wales are excluded.
4. Figures include abortions performed in Scotland. Abortions to residents of Scotland, performed outside Scotland, are excluded.
5. Rates for all ages, under 16, under 18, under 20 and 40 and over are based on female populations aged 15-44, 13-15, 15-17, 15-19 and 40-44 respectively.

Source: Information Services Division, NHS in Scotland; Department of Health

Figure 2.2

Live births: by birthweight, 2006[1]

United Kingdom

Percentages

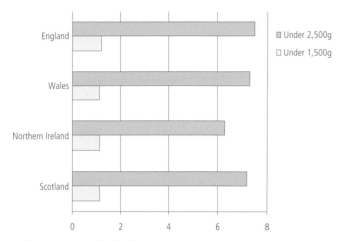

1 Data for Scotland is for 2004.

Source: Office for National Statistics; Northern Ireland Statistics and Research Agency; Information Services Division, NHS in Scotland

In 2006, England had the highest proportion of low birthweight babies (the latest Scottish data available are for 2004), at 7.5 per cent, as well as the highest proportion of very low birthweight babies at 1.2 per cent (Figure 2.2). The percentages in England were higher than in other countries for most of the time period.

Excel workbooks containing the data for Tables 2.5 and 2.6 for all years from 1996 to 2006 inclusive can be found on the National Statistics website.

Infant and perinatal mortality

In 2006, Wales had the lowest neonatal and infant mortality rates (deaths under four weeks and under one year of age) in the UK, at 2.8 and 4.1 per 1,000 live births respectively. Wales also had the lowest perinatal mortality rate (stillbirths and deaths under one week) along with Northern Ireland, both at 6.9 per 1,000 live and stillbirths (Table 2.7). The data for England and Wales reported separately cover deaths of residents of those countries only. The data for England, Wales and Elsewhere, Scotland and Northern Ireland covers deaths of non residents as well as residents.

Infant mortality in the UK has fallen considerably over the past 30 years, from 17.9 deaths per 1,000 live births in 1971 to 5.0 in 2006 (Table 2.7). Neonatal mortality (deaths under four weeks) and perinatal mortality (stillbirths and deaths under one week) have also declined considerably over this period.

Northern Ireland had the highest infant mortality rate (IMR) in 1971, at 22.7 deaths per 1,000 live births and although it had fallen considerably, it remained the highest in 2006 at 5.1 deaths per 1,000 live births (Figure 2.3). The rates for England were equal to or below the UK rates for all years. Northern Ireland had the highest perinatal mortality in the UK at the start of the period. The pattern of perinatal mortality across countries was less clear from 1991; however Wales had the lowest rate in most years. Because infant deaths are now relatively uncommon, variations from year to year in smaller populations may sometimes be due to chance.

Figure 2.3

Infant, neonatal and perinatal mortality rates, 2006

United Kingdom

Rates

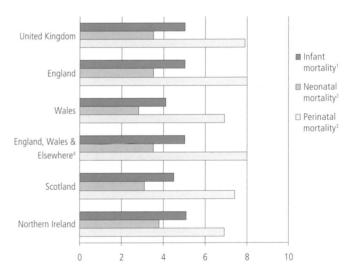

1 Deaths under one year, per 1,000 live births.
2 Deaths under four weeks per 1,000 live births.
3 Stillbirths and deaths under one week per 1,000 live and stillbirths.
4 'England, Wales & Elsewhere' covers both Residents and Non-Residents, comparable with Scotland and Northern Ireland data. The separate 'England' and 'Wales' categories cover Residents Only.

Source: Office for National Statistics; General Register Office for Scotland; Northern Ireland Statistics and Research Agency

Table 2.5

Live births by birthweight and mother's age: 2006[1]

United Kingdom

Percentages, numbers

Birthweight (grams)	Mother's age [2]							Number of births
	Under 20	20-24	25-29	30-34	35-39	40 and over	All ages	
England [3]								
Under 2500	8.7	8.0	7.2	6.9	7.6	9.0	7.5	47,629
Under 1500	1.5	1.3	1.2	1.1	1.3	1.6	1.2	7,848
2500-2999	20.2	19.4	17.0	15.4	15.2	16.3	16.9	107,321
3000-3499	38.2	36.7	36.0	34.7	33.8	32.9	35.4	225,342
3500-3999	24.9	26.3	28.2	30.0	29.7	28.7	28.4	180,480
4000 and over	7.0	8.7	10.5	12.1	12.8	12.1	10.8	68,844
Not stated	0.9	1.0	1.0	0.9	0.9	1.1	1.0	6,132
Number of births	42,418	120,221	163,909	180,733	105,701	22,766	635,748	
Wales [3]								
Under 2500	9.5	7.6	6.5	7.0	7.0	8.6	7.3	2,445
Under 1500	1.6	1.1	0.9	1.2	1.1	1.2	1.1	378
2500-2999	18.6	18.0	15.1	14.6	14.3	15.2	15.8	5,330
3000-3499	37.8	36.7	36.0	34.0	33.6	33.4	35.4	11,899
3500-3999	26.2	28.0	30.6	31.2	30.5	30.3	29.7	10,002
4000 and over	7.7	9.7	11.5	12.9	14.3	12.2	11.5	3,878
Not stated	0.2	0.1	0.2	0.3	0.3	0.3	0.2	74
Number of births	3,086	7,576	8,668	8,612	4,756	930	33,628	
Northern Ireland								
Under 2500	9.0	7.4	5.9	5.2	7.0	7.1	6.3	1,491
Under 1500	1.7	1.4	1.0	0.8	1.3	1.6	1.1	270
2500-2999	19.3	16.0	12.7	11.3	11.7	15.0	13.2	3,094
3000-3499	35.6	35.8	33.0	32.8	32.0	32.3	33.4	7,854
3500-3999	28.4	30.5	34.3	34.7	32.0	29.6	32.9	7,734
4000 and over	7.7	10.2	14.0	16.1	17.2	16.0	14.2	3,345
Not stated	0.0	0.0	0.0	0.0	0.0	0.0	0.0	3
Number of births	1,430	3,989	6,384	7,116	3,844	749	23,512	
Scotland [4]								
Under 2500	9.6	7.6	6.9	6.7	7.2	7.9	7.2	3,723
Under 1500	1.5	1.1	1.1	1.0	1.2	1.0	1.1	581
2500-2999	18.9	17.9	15.4	14.6	14.0	15.4	15.6	8,035
3000-3499	36.6	34.8	35.1	33.3	32.6	31.1	34.1	17,504
3500-3999	26.8	29.2	30.1	31.2	30.8	30.1	30.1	15,461
4000 and over	8.1	10.5	12.6	14.2	15.3	15.6	12.9	6,624
Not stated	..	..	..	..	..	..	..	11
Number of births	3,961	9,496	12,568	15,282	8,470	1,581	51,358	

The categories 'under 2,500g' and 'under 1,500g' are not exclusive.

1 *Data for England and Wales are based on occurrences. Data for Northern Ireland and Scotland are based on registrations. Data for England, Wales and Northern Ireland is for 2006, data for Scotland is for 2004 and is therefore not directly comparable.*
2 *Figures exclude births to mothers whose age was not known.*
3 *Figures for England, Wales and Northern Ireland exclude births to non-residents of each country.*
4 *Figures for Scotland differ from the counts of births routinely published by the Registrar General for Scotland because birthweight data are not available for births outside hospital.*

Source: Office for National Statistics; Northern Ireland Statistics and Research Agency; Information Services Division, NHS in Scotland.

Table 2.6

Trends in birthweight,[1] 1996-2006

United Kingdom   Percentages, numbers

Birthweight (grams)	1996	1997	1998	1999	2000	2001	2002	2003	2004	2005	2006
United Kingdom											
Under 2500	7.4	7.5	7.4	7.5	7.5	7.5	7.6	7.6	7.5	..	..
Under 1500	1.2	1.2	1.2	1.3	1.2	1.3	1.3	1.3	1.2	..	..
2500-2999	17.2	16.5	16.6	16.6	16.3	16.6	16.8	16.9	16.8	..	..
3000-3499	37.2	35.6	35.7	35.6	35.5	35.6	35.5	35.5	35.5	..	..
3500-3999	30.0	28.7	28.9	28.8	29.0	28.8	28.7	28.6	28.7	..	..
4000 and over	11.4	11.0	1.1	11.2	11.5	11.3	11.3	11.2	11.3	..	..
Not stated	0.2	0.2	0.1	0.3	0.2	0.2	0.2	0.2	0.2	..	..
Number of births	706,484	730,842	716,177	698,746	678,407	667,488	667,812	694,596	713,277		..
England											
Under 2500	7.3	7.5	7.5	7.6	7.6	7.6	7.7	7.7	7.6	7.5	7.5
Under 1500	1.2	1.2	1.2	1.3	1.2	1.3	1.3	1.3	1.2	1.2	1.2
2500-2999	16.8	16.9	16.8	16.8	16.5	16.9	17.1	17.2	17.1	17.0	16.9
3000-3499	36.1	36.0	35.9	35.8	35.7	35.7	35.6	35.6	35.7	35.6	35.4
3500-3999	28.7	28.6	28.6	28.5	28.8	28.5	28.5	28.3	28.4	28.5	28.4
4000 and over	10.8	10.8	11.0	11.0	11.2	11.1	11.0	11.0	11.0	11.0	10.8
Not stated	0.2	0.2	0.1	0.3	0.2	0.2	0.2	0.2	0.2	0.4	1.0
Number of births	614,184	608,202	602,111	589,468	572,826	563,744	565,709	589,851	607,184	613,028	635,748
Wales											
Under 2500	6.9	7.0	7.2	7.4	7.5	7.5	7.4	7.3	7.2	6.8	7.3
Under 1500	1.1	1.2	1.1	1.3	1.2	1.2	1.2	1.2	1.2	1.2	1.1
2500-2999	16.0	16.2	16.2	16.3	15.7	16.1	16.4	16.8	16.5	16.2	15.8
3000-3499	35.7	36.0	35.3	35.7	36.0	35.8	35.6	35.7	34.9	35.5	35.4
3500-3999	29.8	29.5	29.7	29.0	28.9	28.9	28.8	28.8	29.0	29.5	29.7
4000 and over	11.3	11.2	11.6	11.5	11.8	11.7	11.8	11.4	12.3	11.8	11.5
Not stated	0.2	0.1	0.1	0.1	0.1	0.1	0.1	0.1	0.1	0.1	0.2
Number of births	34,894	34,520	33,438	32,111	31,304	30,616	30,205	31,400	32,325	32,593	33,628
Scotland[3]											
Under 2500	6.8	6.9	7.0	7.1	7.0	7.3	7.4	7.6	7.2	..	..
Under 1500	1.0	1.0	1.0	1.0	1.1	1.1	1.2	1.2	1.1	..	..
2500-2999	15.9	15.8	16.1	15.7	15.6	15.5	15.8	15.5	15.6	..	..
3000-3499	35.2	34.9	34.6	34.2	34.1	34.4	34.4	34.2	34.1	..	..
3500-3999	30.1	30.2	29.9	30.4	30.1	30.1	29.7	30.1	30.1	..	..
4000 and over	12.0	12.2	12.4	12.6	13.2	12.7	12.8	12.6	12.9	..	..
Not stated	0.0	0.0	0.0	0.0	0.0	0.0	0.0	0.1	0.0	..	..
Number of births	57,406	58,605	56,768	54,174	52,567	51,337	50,448	51,605	51,358	..	..
Northern Ireland											
Under 2500	5.6	5.8	5.7	6.2	6.0	6.0	6.3	5.9	5.9	6.0	6.3
Under 1500	1.0	1.1	1.1	1.0	1.1	1.1	1.2	1.1	1.1	1.2	1.1
2500-2999	13.5	13.3	13.4	13.7	12.9	13.6	13.2	13.2	12.6	13.0	13.1
3000-3499	34.7	34.6	34.4	34.4	33.2	34.2	34.2	34.2	33.7	34.0	33.4
3500-3999	32.3	32.1	32.5	31.7	33.2	32.6	32.6	32.8	33.0	32.7	32.9
4000 and over	13.7	14.1	14.0	14.0	13.5	13.7	13.7	13.9	14.8	14.4	14.2
Not stated	0.0	0.0	0.0	0.0	0.0	0.0	0.0	0.0	0.0	0.0	0.0
Number of births	24,358	24,039	23,860	22,993	21,710	21,791	21,450	21,740	22,410	22,393	23,512

All Ages includes births where the birthweight was not stated.

1 Figures for England and for Wales exclude births to women usually resident outside England and Wales. (407 in 1996, 373 in 1997, 352 in 1998, 292 in 1999, 311 in 2000, 272 in 2001, 208 in 2002, 218 in 2003, 212 in 2004, 214 in 2005 and 255 in 2006), however these are included in the total count for England and Wales combined.
2 Figures for Scotland and Northern Ireland differ from the counts of births routinely published by the Registrar General for Scotland and the Northern Ireland Statistics Research Agency. These figures are based on occurences provided by their hospital systems and not by their registration systems (registrations).

Source: Office for National Statistics; Information Services Division, NHS in Scotland; Northern Ireland Statistics and Research Agency; Child Health System, Department of Health, Social Services and Public Safety, Northern Ireland

Table 2.7

Trends in infant, neonatal and perinatal mortality rates, 1971-2006 (selected years)

United Kingdom

Rates per thousand

	Mortality rates								
	1971	1981	1991	2001	2002	2003	2004	2005	2006
Infant mortality[1]									
United Kingdom	17.9	11.2	7.4	5.5	5.3	5.3	5.1	5.1	5.0
England	17.5	10.9	7.3	5.4	5.3	5.3	5.1	5.0	5.0
Wales	18.4	12.6	6.6	5.4	4.7	4.1	4.9	4.3	4.1
England, Wales & Elsewhere [2]	..	11.1	7.4	5.5	5.3	5.3	5.1	5.0	5.0
Scotland	19.9	11.3	7.1	5.5	5.3	5.1	4.9	5.2	4.5
Northern Ireland	22.7	13.2	7.4	6.0	4.6	5.2	5.3	6.1	5.1
Neonatal mortality [3]									
United Kingdom	12.0	6.7	4.4	3.7	3.6	3.7	3.5	3.5	3.5
England	11.6	6.6	4.3	3.6	3.6	3.7	3.5	3.4	3.5
Wales	12.3	8.1	4.1	3.4	3.1	3.0	3.1	2.9	2.8
England, Wales & Elsewhere [2]	..	6.7	4.4	3.6	3.6	3.7	3.5	3.4	3.5
Scotland	13.5	6.9	4.4	3.8	3.2	3.4	3.1	3.5	3.1
Northern Ireland	15.9	8.3	4.6	4.4	3.4	3.9	3.6	4.9	3.8
Perinatal mortality[4]									
United Kingdom	22.6	12.0	8.1	8.0	8.2	8.5	8.2	8.0	7.9
England	22.1	11.7	8.0	8.0	8.3	8.5	8.1	8.0	8.0
Wales	24.4	14.1	7.9	7.5	7.7	7.5	8.0	7.4	6.9
England, Wales & Elsewhere [2]	..	11.8	8.0	8.0	8.3	8.5	8.2	8.0	8.0
Scotland	24.5	11.6	8.6	8.5	7.6	8.0	8.1	7.7	7.4
Northern Ireland	27.2	15.3	8.4	8.4	8.7	8.0	8.0	8.1	6.9

1 Deaths under one year per 1,000 live births.
2 'England, Wales and Elsewhere' covers both Residents and Non-Residents, comparable with the Scotland and Northern Ireland figures.
   The separate 'England' and 'Wales' categories cover Residents Only.
3 Deaths under four weeks per 1,000 live births.
4 Stillbirths and deaths under one week per 1,000 live and stillbirths.

Source: Office for National Statistics; General Register Office for Scotland; Northern Ireland Statistics and Research Agency

Additional notes

Table 2.1 – Age-specific fertility rate (ASFR)

The number of births to mothers of a certain age group divided by the number of women in that age group in that year. This is usually expressed as the number of children born per 1,000 women of a certain age.

Table 2.1 – Total fertility rate (TFR)

The sum of the single year age-specific fertility rates of all women aged 15-44 years in a population at one point in time. The TFR estimates the number of children a woman would have if exposed to the age-specific fertility rates for the current year, throughout her child bearing years.

Table 2.1 – Births outside marriage

The number of live births outside marriage per 100 live births. A birth is recorded as occurring inside marriage if the parents were lawfully married to each other:

England and Wales: when the child was conceived or on date of birth

Scotland: on the date of birth

Northern Ireland: at the time of registration of the birth

Tables 2.3, 2.4 – Differences between figures on abortions

The figures for legal abortions are based on abortions reported under the 1967 Abortion Act. Mother's age in Table 2.4 is reported as the date of abortion.

Mother's age at conception for conceptions ending in abortion is based on subtraction of the reported gestation period from the date of abortion. Mother's age in Table 2.3 is reported as the estimated date of conception.

Because of these differences in calculation, the numbers and age distribution of abortions in Tables 2.3 and 2.4 are not directly comparable.

Table 2.4 Legal abortions: by age, 2006

The figures for legal abortions are based on abortions reported under the 1967 Abortion Act. Mother's age in Table 2.4 is reported as the date of the abortion.

Figures on abortions are based on legal abortions under the Abortion Act 1967 to women resident in the relevant country. The figures shown include:

England and Wales: abortions to residents of each country, wherever in Great Britain the abortion was performed

Scotland: abortions to residents of Scotland, performed in Scotland only

The tables therefore exclude abortions:

- to residents in Scotland, performed in England and Wales

- to residents of any country, performed outside Great Britain

- to non-residents of Great Britain, including residents of Northern Ireland

and in addition:

- a small number of abortions performed in Scotland, where place of residence was not recorded or was subject to postcode change

- A small number of abortions performed in Northern Ireland that take place to save the life of the women

Table 2.7 – Stillbirths

In October 1992 the legal definition of a stillbirth was changed, from a baby born dead after 28 completed weeks of gestation to one born dead after 24 completed weeks.

References

1   Macfarlane A, Mugford M, 2000; Birth Counts: statistics of pregnancy and childbirth, 2nd edition. National Perinatal Epidemiology Unit, Oxford.

2

General health and morbidity

Chapter 3

DATA

Download data by clicking the online pdf

www.statistics.gov.uk/ downloads/theme_health/ ukhs3/

This chapter contains a range of key statistics about general health and selected illnesses, including road accident casualties, cancer, occupationally-related illnesses and communicable diseases. Where figures are based on surveys, these may have relatively small sample sizes, so comparisons between the countries and over time should be treated with caution.

Self-assessed general health

Self-assessed general health status is estimated from the General Household Survey in England, Scotland and Wales, and the Continuous Household Survey in Northern Ireland.

In 2006, the proportion of respondents reporting their general health to be good was highest in Scotland in males (69 per cent) and in Wales in females (67 per cent) (Figure 3.1, Table 3.1). The widest disparity between the youngest and oldest adult age groups for reporting their health as good was for males in Scotland, falling from 83 per cent at age 16-24 to 31 per cent of those aged 75 years or over. The highest rates of good health were reported in all countries for children aged 5-15, while self-reported good health was highest at ages 16-34.

Healthy life expectancy

Healthy life expectancy (HLE) is the number of years of life spent in 'good' or 'fairly good' health. Table 3.2 shows HLE at birth and at age 65 years for men and women. Disability-free life expectancy is the number of years lived free from a limiting long-standing illness or disability. These measures are calculated by combining life expectancy with self-assessed general health and limiting long-standing illness data. More information on life expectancy trends and life expectancy at specific ages is included in Chapter 7.

In 2004, UK healthy life expectancy at birth was 67.9 years for males and 70.3 years for females. At birth, healthy life expectancy was highest for males in England at 68.3 years and lowest in Scotland at 65.6 years. For females, healthy life expectancy was highest in England at 70.6 years and lowest in Wales at 68.3 years.

In the UK, healthy life expectancy for males at age 65 years was 12.5 years and for females was 14.5 years. At 65 years, the healthy life expectancy for males was highest in Northern Ireland at 12.8 years and lowest in at Scotland 11.5 years. For females, healthy life expectancy was highest in England at 14.6 years and lowest in Wales at 13.2 years.

Disability-free life expectancy at birth in 2004 for males was 62.3 years and for females was 63.9 years. At age 65 years, disability free life expectancy for males was highest in England at 10.1 years and lowest in Northern Ireland at 8.8 years compared to the UK figure of 9.9 years. Similarly, for females at 65 years, disability free life expectancy was highest in England at 10.8 years and lowest in Northern Ireland at 8.7 years.

General Practice consultations

The figures reported here for England, Scotland and Wales are taken from the General Household Survey, and include

Figure 3.1

Self assessed 'good' or 'fairly good' health: by sex,[1,2] 2006

United Kingdom

Percentages

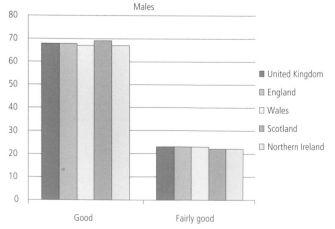

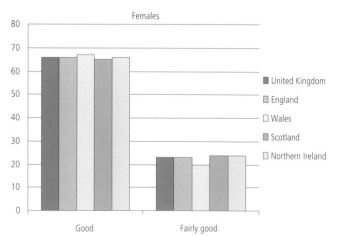

1   All figures in this table are calculated using three-year averages. The year shown is the centre of the three-year period.
2   Health is self-assessed for ages 16 and upward, assessed by the (adult) survey respondent for ages 0-15.

Source: Office for National Statistics; Northern Ireland Statistics and Research Agency

Table 3.1

Self-assessed 'good' or 'fairly good' health: by age and sex, 2006[1,2]

United Kingdom   Percentages

	0-4	5–15	16-24	25-34	35-44	45-54	55-64	65-74	75 and over	All ages	Base
					Good health						
United Kingdom											
Males	81	87	83	76	73	64	53	44	33	68	10059
Females	85	88	78	73	68	62	55	43	33	66	11340
England											
Males	81	87	83	75	73	64	53	45	33	68	8679
Females	84	87	78	73	69	63	54	42	33	66	9743
Wales											
Males	78	95	77	79	73	70	50	40	35	67	525
Females	86	96	81	83	65	60	57	46	33	67	579
Scotland											
Males	79	84	83	78	78	68	54	42	31	69	855
Females	93	86	83	69	66	62	55	46	33	65	1018
Northern Ireland											
Males	86	88	80	76	68	51	45	40	31	67	2256
Females	85	90	74	73	64	53	45	35	28	64	2906
					Fairly good health						
United Kingdom											
Males	15	11	14	20	20	26	30	36	43	23	10059
Females	14	10	18	20	22	23	29	38	39	23	11340
England											
Males	15	11	14	20	21	26	30	36	43	23	8679
Females	14	11	19	20	22	23	30	38	39	23	9743
Wales											
Males	15	5	21	16	17	26	31	39	37	23	525
Females	14	3	17	11	21	24	22	33	40	20	579
Scotland											
Males	19	14	16	20	14	19	29	38	47	22	855
Females	6	13	15	25	23	19	31	40	41	24	1018
Northern Ireland											
Males	12	10	17	19	22	32	32	38	42	22	2256
Females	12	8	22	19	24	31	32	46	40	24	2906

1 *All figures in this table are calculated using three-year averages. The year shown is the centre of the three-year period.*
2 *Health is self-assessed for ages 16 and upward, assessed by the (adult) survey respondent for ages 0-15.*

Source: Office for National Statistics; Northern Ireland Statistics and Research Agency

Table 3.2

Healthy life expectancy and disability-free life expectancy at birth and age 65: by country and sex, 2004

United Kingdom   Years

Country	Healthy life expectancy	Disability-free life expectancy
At birth		
Males		
United Kingdom	67.9	62.3
Great Britain	68.0	62.3
England	68.3	62.6
Wales	66.5	60.6
Scotland	65.6	61.0
Northern Ireland	66.8	59.7
Females		
United Kingdom	70.3	63.9
Great Britain	70.3	64.0
England	70.6	64.2
Wales	68.3	62.2
Scotland	69.6	63.4
Northern Ireland	68.4	60.3
At age 65		
Males		
United Kingdom	12.5	9.9
Great Britain	12.5	9.9
England	12.7	10.1
Wales	11.8	9.3
Scotland	11.5	9.3
Northern Ireland	12.8	8.8
Females		
United Kingdom	14.5	10.7
Great Britain	14.5	10.7
England	14.6	10.8
Wales	13.2	9.6
Scotland	13.9	10.5
Northern Ireland	13.6	8.7

Source: Office for National Statistics

consultations with both NHS and private sector general medical practitioners. They relate to all types of consultation whether at home, at the doctor's surgery or over the phone, in the two weeks preceding the survey. Figures for Northern Ireland are taken from the Continuous Household Survey.

The all-age percentage of males consulting a general medical practitioner in 2006 was 11 per cent in both England and Scotland and 9 per cent in Wales (Table 3.3). Consultation rates for males and females increased with age from ages over 15.

The all-age consultation rate for women in both England and Wales was 15 per cent and in Scotland and Northern Ireland 14 per cent. Consultation rates were generally higher amongst women than men at all ages over 15 years.

Consultation rates for females aged 0-4 showed the greatest variation, ranging from 16 per cent in England to 2 per cent in Scotland, which was only slightly lower than Wales at 3 per cent. The consultation rate for women in Wales aged 45-64 was 14 per cent; this doubled to 28 per cent in women aged over 65 years.

Road accident casualties

The Department of Transport road accident statistics, compiled from police reports, cover all reported accidents involving personal injury.

Between 1999 and 2006 there was a decline in the numbers of road accident casualties in all four countries of the UK, though the rate of decline was slowest in Scotland and Wales. The proportion of reported road accident casualties that were fatalities was fairly constant, with a rate of 1.1 per cent between 1999 and 2002, rising to 1.2 per cent between 2003 and 2006. In 2006, Scotland had the highest proportion of road accident casualties that were killed or seriously injured, at 17.0 per cent of accidents, including the highest proportion of fatalities at 1.8 per cent (Table 3.4, Figure 3.2).

Figure 3.2

Proportion of road accident casualties who were killed or severely injured, 2006

United Kingdom

Percentages

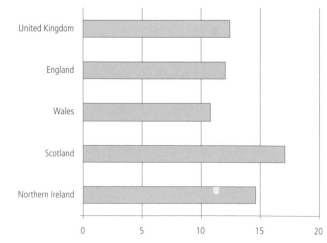

Source: Department for Transport

Table 3.3

General practice consultations:[1] by age and sex, 2006

Great Britain — Percentages

	All ages	0–4	5–15	16–44	45–64	65 and over
Males						
United Kingdom	11	14	6	8	13	20
England	11	15	7	8	14	20
Wales	9	9	4	6	10	18
Scotland	11	9	7	9	14	19
Northern Ireland	10	15	4	6	14	18
Females						
United Kingdom	15	15	6	15	15	21
England	15	16	6	16	15	20
Wales	15	3	2	14	14	28
Scotland	14	2	5	13	16	24
Northern Ireland	14	12	6	12	18	25

1 Percentage of population consulting an NHS or private general practitioner in the 14 days before interview.

Source: Office for National Statistics

Table 3.4

Trends in road accident casualties: by severity, 1994-2006

United Kingdom — Percentages, numbers

	1994-1998 Average	1999	2000	2001	2002	2003	2004	2005	2006
				Percentage of total					
Fatalities									
United Kingdom	1.1	1.1	1.1	1.1	1.1	1.2	1.2	1.2	1.2
England	1.1	1.0	1.0	1.0	1.1	1.2	1.1	1.1	1.2
Wales	1.4	1.3	1.2	1.4	1.0	1.2	1.5	1.4	1.3
Scotland	1.7	1.5	1.6	1.7	1.6	1.8	1.7	1.6	1.8
Northern Ireland	1.2	1.0	1.2	1.1	1.3	1.5	1.5	1.7	1.4
				Percentage of total					
Killed or severely injured									
United Kingdom	14.8	13.2	12.9	13.0	13.1	12.8	12.3	12.0	12.4
England	14.4	12.8	12.6	12.5	12.7	12.5	12.0	11.6	12.1
Wales	13.5	13.0	12.9	12.5	11.4	11.8	11.2	10.4	10.8
Scotland	21.7	19.4	18.9	18.9	18.2	17.5	16.5	16.2	17.0
Northern Ireland	13.8	12.3	13.3	13.9	14.1	13.9	14.0	14.8	14.6
				Numbers					
Total road accident casualties									
United Kingdom	332,427	333,759	335,003	326,451	314,519	300,932	290,347	279,176	267,586
England	282,768	285,126	285,721	279,678	269,020	257,899	248,762	240,484	228,577
Wales	14,856	14,347	14,087	13,775	14,336	14,036	13,687	12,738	12,692
Scotland	22,304	20,837	20,475	19,856	19,249	18,672	18,391	17,795	17,135
Northern Ireland	12,499	13,449	14,720	13,142	11,914	10,325	9,507	8,159	9,182

Source: Department for Transport

Table 3.5

Newly diagnosed cases of cancer: by sex and by cancer site,[1,2] 2004

United Kingdom

Rates per 100,000 population

ICD10 code	Site description	United Kingdom	England	Wales	Scotland	Northern Ireland
Males						
C00-C97 X C44	**All malignancies excluding nmsc[3]**	**401.7**	**394.3**	**449.6**	**446.4**	**393.8**
C00-C14	Lip, mouth & pharynx	10.9	10.3	11.7	16.3	10.9
C15	Oesophagus	14.0	13.7	13.9	17.9	11.2
C16	Stomach	15.3	14.8	18.2	18.0	17.5
C18-20	Colorectal	53.7	52.2	57.9	63.7	59.6
C25	Pancreas	10.1	10.1	11.2	9.9	8.2
C32	Larynx	5.4	5.0	5.6	8.3	5.8
C34	Lung	62.8	60.4	65.0	85.5	61.3
C43	Melanoma of skin	11.4	11.2	11.7	13.0	11.8
C61	Prostate	92.7	93.2	104.9	81.5	83.3
C62	Testis	6.4	6.2	7.2	7.9	7.2
C64	Kidney	10.8	10.6	12.5	12.1	11.8
C67	Bladder	19.9	19.2	34.1	18.0	17.4
C71	Brain	7.7	7.7	8.3	8.0	7.2
C81-C96	Lymphomas and leukaemias	36.2	35.7	41.4	38.3	34.3
C81-C85	Lymphomas	18.1	18.0	18.0	18.8	17.9
C81	Hodgkin's disease	2.8	2.7	3.0	3.0	2.0
C82-C85	Non-Hodgkin's lymphoma	15.3	15.3	15.0	15.8	15.9
C90	Multiple myeloma	5.8	5.6	7.6	5.9	6.6
C91-C95	All leukaemias	11.9	11.6	15.0	13.1	9.5
Females						
C00-C97 X C44	**All malignancies excluding nmsc[3]**	**343.3**	**338.0**	**366.4**	**378.5**	**344.8**
C00-C14	Lip, mouth & pharynx	4.8	4.6	5.1	6.8	4.5
C15	Oesophagus	5.6	5.4	6.3	7.4	4.5
C16	Stomach	6.2	5.9	7.9	7.8	7.2
C18-20	Colorectal	33.7	32.8	35.2	38.9	39.1
C25	Pancreas	7.7	7.6	9.0	8.0	7.2
C34	Lung	35.1	33.2	35.5	52.7	32.6
C43	Melanoma of skin	13.0	12.7	13.2	15.1	14.5
C50	Breast	118.2	118.4	120.8	117.5	110.4
C53	Cervix	8.2	8.0	9.1	9.5	8.1
C54	Uterus	15.6	15.6	16.9	14.3	17.1
C56	Ovary	17.4	17.1	19.5	18.2	20.3
C64	Kidney	5.6	5.4	7.1	6.3	6.7
C67	Bladder	5.8	5.6	9.9	6.0	4.7
C71	Brain	4.9	4.9	5.9	4.6	5.0
C81-C96	Lymphomas and leukaemias	24.2	23.9	26.4	26.0	23.7
C81-C85	Lymphomas	13.1	13.0	12.4	14.0	14.4
C81	Hodgkin's disease	2.0	1.9	1.9	2.4	2.0
C82-C85	Non-Hodgkin's lymphoma	11.1	11.0	10.4	11.6	12.4
C90	Multiple myeloma	3.7	3.7	4.9	3.6	3.4
C91-C95	All leukaemias	7.2	7.0	9.0	8.1	5.8

1 *Figures are directly age-standardised registration rates using European standard population.*
2 *All numbers and rates in this table are calculated as three-year averages.*
3 *Non-melanoma skin cancer (C44).*

Source: National Cancer Intelligence Centre; Office for National Statistics; Welsh Cancer Intelligence and Surveillance Unit; Scottish Cancer Registry; Northern Ireland Cancer Registry

Cancer

Figures on newly diagnosed cases of cancer are taken from the Cancer Registration Statistics. As the risk of cancer varies greatly with age, directly age-standardised registration rates are used to take account of differences in a country's age structure.

In 2004, the male rate for all cancers taken together was highest in Wales with a standardised rate of 449.6 per 100,000 population, compared with 394.3 in England, 393.8 per 100,000 in Northern Ireland and 446.4 in Scotland (Table 3.5).

Registrations of lung cancer among men were approximately a third higher in Scotland than in the other countries of the UK. Less variability between countries was found in other cancer sites. All four UK countries have experienced a fall in numbers of registrations of lung cancer for men between 2001 and 2004, but the scale of difference between Scotland and the other countries remained constant.

Prostate cancer was the most common cancer among men, with a UK rate of 92.7 per 100,000 men; it was also the most common in each country except in Scotland, where cancer of the lung was slightly more frequent. Registrations of male

bladder cancer in Wales, at 34.1, were nearly double the rate of 17.4 in Northern Ireland.

In 2004, the registration of all cancers among women was highest in Scotland with a standardised rate of 378.5 per 100,000, compared with 338.0 in England, 344.8 in Northern Ireland and 366.4 in Wales.

Lung cancer among women showed a similar distribution by country to men, with Scotland experiencing a rate approximately 50 per cent higher than the other countries of the UK. Trends in female lung cancer registrations between 2001 and 2004 showed no notable change.

Breast cancer was the most common cancer among women, with a UK rate of 118.2; it was also the most common in each country. Wales had the highest rate of breast cancer at 120.8 newly diagnosed cases per 100,000 women, and Northern Ireland had the lowest newly diagnosed breast cancer rate at 110.4 cases.

Health and safety at work

The Health and Safety Executive produces statistics on work-related health and safety in England, Scotland and Wales

Table 3.6

Self-reported work-related illness and injuries,[1] 2005-06

Great Britain   Thousands, rates per 100,000 population

	Thousands			Rate per 100 000		
		95% C.I.[2]			95% C.I.	
	central	lower	upper	central	lower	upper
Estimated prevalence and rates of self-reported illness caused or made worse by work, for people ever employed						
			2005/06			
Great Britain	1,958	1,893	2,022	4,540	4,390	4,690
England	1,696	1,636	1,757	4,580	4,410	4,740
Wales	102	87	117	4,630	3,970	5,280
Scotland	160	141	178	4,130	3,660	4,590
Estimated incidence and rates of reportable non-fatal injuries to workers						
			Average 2003/04 - 2005/06			
Great Britain	328	313	344	1,200	1,140	1,250
England	278	264	293	1,180	1,120	1,240
Wales	18	15	22	1,410	1,140	1,680
Scotland	31	27	36	1,300	1,110	1,500

1 Reportable workplace injuries include all those sustained as a result of a non-road traffic accident, resulting in over three days of absence from work.
2 95% C.I.: 95% confidence interval, the range within which we are 95% confident that the true value lies in the absence of bias.

Source: Labour Force Survey (published by the Health and Safety Executive)

derived from a variety of sources. The most broadly based figures are estimates of self-reported ill health and injuries from the Labour Force Survey (LFS). These relate to health conditions which people think have been caused or made worse by their current or past work, and to injuries which meet the criteria to be reportable under the Reporting of Injuries, Diseases and Dangerous Occurrences Regulations (RIDDOR) 1995.

The estimated rates of self-reported illness caused or made worse by work in Great Britain in 2005-06 was 4,540 per 100,000 population. Within Great Britain, Wales had the highest rate of 4,630 per 100,000; Scotland had the lowest rate of 4,130 per 100,000 (Table 3.6).

Reportable workplace injuries include all those sustained as a result of a non-road traffic accident, resulting in over three days of absence from work. In Great Britain, the average estimated incidence rates of reportable non-fatal injuries to workers for 2003/04-2005/06 was 1,200 per 100,000. Wales had the highest rate at 1,410; England had the lowest rate at 1,180 per 100,000 population (Table 3.6).

The Health and Safety Executive also collects data on compensated cases of prescribed industrial diseases, classified into lung related diseases and non-lung related diseases, for the England, Scotland and Wales (Table 3.7). These only cover a limited number of diseases and only count cases assessed for compensation.

In recent years the numbers of cases of most lung diseases (notably those associated with exposure to coal and asbestos) assessed for compensation have increased, while the number of cases of non-lung related diseases generally fell (especially for vibration white finger). These movements are influenced by administrative changes and other factors affecting the take-up of claims (such as publicity campaigns).

The Health and Safety Executive also collects statistics on workplace injuries reported by RIDDOR. For non-fatal injuries these are subject to under-reporting, the effect of which varies between countries and sectors. The injury rate is the number of workplace injuries occurring in a year divided by the employed population in that year, and expressed per 100,000

In the UK, the fatal workplace injury rate was highest in Agriculture, Hunting, Forestry and Fishing where there were 5.6 fatal injuries over 100,000 employees in 2005-06 (Table 3.8).

Reported non-fatal major workplace injuries were highest in extractive and utility supplying industries in all countries except England where the construction industry was highest. There were wide variations between countries, in Scotland the rate of

Figure 3.3

New diagnoses of HIV-infected individuals, 2006[1]

United Kingdom

Rates per million population

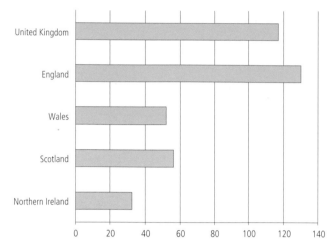

1 Individuals with laboratory reports of infection plus those with AIDS or death reports for whom no matching laboratory report has been received. Reports to the end of June 2007.

Source: Health Protection Agency

non-fatal workplace injury was 143.2 per 100,000 compared with 59.5 per 100,000 in Northern Ireland.

Communicable diseases

Between 1996 and 2006 there was a considerable change in the rate of notifications per 100,000 population of measles, mumps and rubella within the countries in the UK. Measles notifications per 100,000 population fell from 11.8 to 6.6; rubella notifications decreased from 20.1 to 2.3 per 100,000 population in the UK, the fall was seen in all countries (Table 3.9). In contrast, notifications of mumps increased markedly in all countries, with the UK rate rising from 3.8 per 100,000 in 1996 to 21.2 in 2006. Notifications of meningococcal meningitis fell from 2.3 to 1.1 in England and Wales between 1996 and 2006.

Sexually transmitted diseases

Data on sexually transmitted diseases (STDs) are provided by genito-urinary medicine clinics and collated by the Health Protection Agency Centre for infections and NHS National Services Scotland.

The incidence of all STDs per 100,000 population in 2006 was higher in England for men and women than in other parts of the UK (Table 3.10). Between 2000 and 2006 rates of syphilis in men increased eight-fold to 8.8 per 100,000 men in England, and 15-fold to reach 7.5 in Scotland. In women, rates in England increased more than three times to 1.3 in 2006.

Table 3.7

Prescribed industrial diseases,[1,2] 2005

Great Britain

Numbers

Disease	Great Britain	England	Wales	Scotland
Lung diseases (2005)				
Pneumoconiosis[3]				
coal	670	510	155	5
asbestos	820	670	30	95
other	85	65	15	10
Diffuse Mesothelioma	1,535	1,300	45	145
Occupational Asthma	230	205	10	15
Lung cancer with asbestosis / pleural thickening	80	65	..	5
Pleural thickening	415	365	25	15
Chronic Bronchitis and/or emphysema	190	135	40	10
Others	5	5	..	..
Total	4,035	3,320	325	305
Non-lung diseases (2004-5)				
Musculoskeletal[4]	370	325	20	20
Occupational deafness (2005)	255	205	25	25
Vibration white finger	865	610	105	150
Carpal tunnel syndrome	675	495	80	100
Allergic rhinitis	90	65	15	15
Dermatitis	165	125	20	20
Others	65	55	5	5
Total	2,490	1,880	270	335

p Provisional figures.
To avoid the risk of disclosing information about individuals data has been rounded to the nearest five.

1 Figures for Great Britain include a small number of cases not included in England, Wales and Scotland breakdowns. These individuals developed
   industrial diseases from employment in Great Britain, but are currently residing overseas.
2 Figures are for calendar years for Lung diseases and years ending 30th September for Non-Lung diseases, except for occupational deafness where
   calendar year 2005 is shown.
3 Totals for England, Wales, Scotland and Great Britain for 2005 include a small number of pneumoconiosis cases for which the industry group has
   not been coded at the time of publication due to the provisional nature of the data.
4 Mainly upper-limb disorders.

Source: Department for Work and Pensions (published by the Health and Safety Executive)

New diagnoses of gonorrhoea were reported more frequently in men than in women. Trends across time showed rates among men remaining constant in England until 2003 after which there has been a steady decline from 59.8 per 100,000 in 2003 to 46.2 per 100,000 in 2006. Chlamydia was the most common STD in the UK. Trends in diagnoses of chlamydia in men in Scotland showed a greater than two-fold increase between 2000 and 2006, while increases were more modest in England and Northern Ireland.

HIV infection

Deaths of HIV-infected individuals in the UK rose steeply from 1985 to a peak of 36.7 per million population in 1995, before falling because of improvements in treatment to 9.0 per million population in 2005. In 2005 the death rate among of HIV-infected individuals was highest in England with a rate of 9.3 per million population. In England and Wales there was a decrease in the number deaths of HIV-infected individuals; in Scotland the rate has remained constant, averaging 9.6 per million population since 1999 with the exception of a drop to 4.9 per million population in 2004. The rate in Northern Ireland remained low at 0.6 per million (Table 3.11, Figure 3.3).

In the UK as a whole, new diagnoses of HIV more than doubled between 1985 and 2004 from 66.5 per million population to 148.0 per million population. Since then the rate of new diagnoses has decreased with 117.1 per million diagnosed in 2006. In Scotland rates dropped from 60.3 per million in 1985 to 26.9 in 1989 before rising again to 56.1 million in 2006 with a peak rate of 74.6 new diagnoses in 2004.

Table 3.8

Workplace injuries: by severity and industrial sector, 2005-06

United Kingdom

Rate per 100,000 employees, numbers

	Agriculture, hunting, forestry and fishing[1]	Extractive and utility supplying industries	Manufacturing	Construction	Total service industries	All industries
			Fatal injuries			
UK	5.6	3.9	1.4	3.7	0.3	0.6
England	5.7	3.7	1.2	3.3	0.3	0.6
Wales	3.3	2.8	2.6	5.4	0.6	1.1
Scotland	0.0	0.0	1.8	3.8	0.2	0.6
Northern Ireland	15.4	21.0	2.3	7.8	0.2	1.3
			Non-fatal major injuries			
UK	205.8	252.0	180.9	303.4	86.3	109.1
England	223.3	219.5	178.0	302.0	86.0	107.9
Wales	203.1	338.1	17.2	327.5	9.0	117.8
Scotland	110.9	403.8	234.1	372.4	112.6	143.2
Northern Ireland	69.3	167.8	133.5	167.1	39.3	59.5
			Over three day injuries			
UK	389.0	873.8	813.1	622.3	390.9	452.3
England	442.6	880.8	802.3	622.4	394.4	453.6
Wales	255.5	786.1	802.4	628.6	350.3	414.7
Scotland	213.8	1,580.1	993.6	725.7	460.7	552.8
Northern Ireland	154.1	524.3	805.6	456.9	294.4	365.9
		Numbers of 'Total fatal', 'non-fatal major' and 'over three day' injuries				
UK	1,383	1,744	30,379	11,545	105,983	151,034[2]
England	1,170	1,197	25,163	9,490	90,216	127,236
Wales	141	400	2,297	1,236	8,561	12,635
Scotland	41	113	2,101	577	5,353	8,185
Northern Ireland	31	34	818	242	1,853	2,978

p   Provisional figures.

1   Excludes sea-fishing.
2   Includes nine injuries where the country is unable to be identified.

Source: Health and Safety Executive; Health and Safety Executive of Northern Ireland

Of the 51,713 individuals with an HIV infection receiving care at NHS clinics in 2006, in the UK, the probable route of infection was homosexual contact for 41.7 per cent and heterosexual contact for 49.5 per cent (Table 3.12). In Northern Ireland, homosexual contact was associated with almost half of infections (48.8 per cent) and in Wales more than half (51.4 per cent) were associated with homosexual contact. Scotland had the highest proportion with a probable route of infection via injecting drug use at 15.2 per cent, over five times higher than

any other country in the UK. It should be noted, however, that over 90 per cent of all injectors reported in Scotland were diagnosed prior to 2000.

Trends over time between 1997 and 2006 saw a three-fold increase in the number of individuals with HIV infection receiving care from an NHS provider in the UK. In England, Wales and Northern Ireland, a greater than three-fold increase was observed in the same period. In Scotland the increase was two-fold.

Table 3.9

Notifications of selected communicable diseases, 1996 and 2006

United Kingdom   Rates per 100,000 population

	United Kingdom [p]		England and Wales		Scotland [p]		Northern Ireland	
	1996	2006	1996	2006	1996	2006	1996	2006
Measles	11.8	6.6	10.9	6.5	20.7	5.1	11.9	3.0
Mumps	3.8	21.2	3.4	23.9	7.2	55.1	4.0	11.8
Rubella	20.1	2.3	17.7	2.1	48.1	2.9	11.4	1.9
Whooping cough	4.7	4.3	4.6	1.0	3.7	1.2	8.9	1.6
Scarlet fever	10.5	4.3	9.5	3.8	14.7	5.3	28.8	12.2
Dysentery	4.5	2.0	4.5	2.0	3.5	2.1	9.3	0.4
Food poisoning [1]	163.2	130.5	161.9	123.2	201.7	136.5	87.6	84.3
Typhoid and Paratyphoid fevers	0.5	0.6	0.5	0.7	0.3	0.1	0.1	0.1
Hepatitis	4.9	8.3	:	:	:	:	:	:
Viral hepatitis	:	:	4.7	7.0	7.1	19.2	:	:
Infective hepatitis	:	:	:	:	:	:	4.8	2.6
Tuberculosis [2, 3]	10.7	13.2	11.0	13.3	10.0	6.9	4.5	2.8
Malaria	3	1.1	3.2	1.1	1.4	0.4	0.8	0.3
Total meningitis	:	:	5.2	2.6	:	:	:	:
Meningococcal meningitis	:	:	2.3	1.1	:	:	:	:
Meningococcal septicaemia	:	:	2.2	1.1	:	:	4.0	4.3
Ophthalmia neonatorum	:	:	0.5	0.2	:	:	:	:
Meningococcal infection	:	:	:	:	4.0	2.7	:	:
Erysipelas	:	:	:	:	1.7	0.5	:	:
Acute encephalitis/meningitis	:	:	:	:	:	:	6.3	3.3
Gastro-enteritis (children under 2 years)	:	:	:	:	:	:	44.8	41.2

:   Country does not require notification of a certain disease.
p   Provisional figures.

1   Scotland's food poisoning includes 'otherwise ascertained' for the first time in 1995.
2   England and Wales formal notifications of new cases only. The figures exclude chemoprophylaxis.
3   Scotland figures include cases of tuberculosis not notified before death.

Sources: Information Services Division, NHS in Scotland; Communicable Disease Surveillance Centre (Northern Ireland); Health Protection Agency

Table 3.10

New diagnoses[1,2] of selected sexually transmitted infections, by sex and condition, 2000 to 2006

United Kingdom

Rates per 100,000 population

Condition	Country	2000		2001		2002		2003		2004		2005		2006	
		Males	Females	Males	Females	Males	Females	Males	Females	Males	Females	Males	Females	Males	Females
Syphilis	United Kingdom	0.9	0.3	2.2	0.4	3.9	0.5	5.0	0.6	6.8	0.9	8.1	1.4	8.2	1.1
	England	1.0	0.3	2.6	0.4	4.4	0.5	5.5	0.7	7.1	1.0	8.8	1.6	8.8	1.3
	Scotland	0.5	0.1	0.4	0.3	1.1	0.1	2.0	0.2	6.5	0.2	6.0	0.2	7.5	0.2
	Wales	0.4	0.0	0.4	0.1	0.9	0.0	3.1	0.1	2.8	0.0	2.7	0.3	2.0	0.3
	Northern Ireland	0.0	0.0	1.1	0.2	2.4	0.0	1.2	0.0	3.8	1.1	3.4	0.6	3.2	0.3
Gonorrhoea	United Kingdom	53.1	21.7	57.7	23.4	61.7	25.5	59.8	24.8	53.6	21.8	47.1	17.5	46.2	17.5
	England	59.4	24.7	64.8	26.7	69.7	29.2	66.6	28.4	59.5	24.7	51.3	19.5	50.1	19.6
	Scotland	21.7	6.2	22.4	7.0	21.5	6.1	25.1	4.7	24.8	5.6	26.4	6.9	29.2	6.4
	Wales	22.4	10.5	21.3	8.7	21.4	9.3	27.6	11.7	24.9	12.0	26.6	10.0	23.6	9.2
	Northern Ireland	14.5	2.8	15.4	2.4	12.8	1.3	15.2	3.1	12.6	2.2	19.2	2.3	19.3	3.6
Chlamydia	United Kingdom	103.9	127.6	115.7	142.5	133.5	161.1	147.8	173.6	165.1	182.7	176.1	187.1	190.0	187.4
	England	110.6	138.0	122.3	152.7	141.3	172.7	155.3	186.6	173.6	196.5	182.5	197.6	197.5	196.1
	Scotland	72.9	69.9	90.5	92.0	107.7	106.4	131.1	115.3	149.8	123.1	165.7	145.8	177.4	162.5
	Wales	70.2	93.5	79.8	109.2	83.2	114.1	89.2	111.6	93.3	109.8	132.4	133.9	124.8	127.2
	Northern Ireland	58.5	56.0	57.4	54.8	66.1	71.7	77.4	76.2	83.4	85.6	92.7	96.3	117.6	112.0
Herpes	United Kingdom	23.7	36.5	25.0	38.8	24.9	40.2	24.7	39.4	24.6	38.6	25.8	39.8	28.5	43.3
	England	25.7	39.6	26.9	41.8	26.9	43.3	26.3	42.0	26.2	41.2	27.5	42.1	30.2	46.4
	Scotland	14.6	20.7	17.1	25.6	16.4	25.0	20.2	28.6	21.4	28.8	20.6	31.3	23.9	30.4
	Wales	12.4	21.5	14.3	22.6	15.2	25.8	14.2	25.7	11.9	23.9	15.6	27.4	16.2	27.2
	Northern Ireland	13.2	20.1	11.3	19.1	9.5	20.7	7.2	19.1	8.2	17.5	7.8	19.5	10.8	20.8
Warts	United Kingdom	131.2	111.6	133.6	115.4	137.7	115.6	139.1	118.2	145.3	121.5	145.8	124.4	150.8	127.9
	England	133.1	113.8	135.3	117.6	139.9	118.1	141.6	120.4	148.2	124.4	147.0	125.9	152.4	129.6
	Scotland	118.4	91.8	122.2	98.7	123.9	98.8	127.6	102.4	138.6	109.3	140.6	113.6	151.4	120.2
	Wales	118.0	105.9	123.8	106.2	123.9	100.9	118.6	105.9	117.9	96.7	135.6	118.0	131.2	119.9
	Northern Ireland	136.3	115.8	134.3	118.3	138.4	118.6	133.4	122.4	126.1	119.1	143.1	124.8	135.3	115.2

1 Cases seen at Genito-Urinary Medicine Clinics.
2 Rates are calculated using resident population.

Source: Health Protection Agency; Information Services Division, NHS in Scotland; The Communicable Disease Surveillance Centre Wales; The Communicable Disease Surveillance Centre Northern Ireland, Department of Health, Social Services and Public Safety, Northern Ireland

Table 3.11

Trends in new diagnoses of HIV and deaths of HIV-infected individuals,[1] 1985-2006

United Kingdom   Rates per million population

New diagnoses of HIV individuals by year of diagnosis [2,3] 1985-2006

	1985	1986	1987	1988	1989	1990	1991	1992	1993	1994	1995	1996	1997	1998	1999	2000	2001	2002	2003	2004	2005	2006	Total
United Kingdom	66.5	59.1	53.2	41.6	45.8	54.4	58.2	58.5	55.8	54.4	56.2	57.1	57.7	58.8	64.8	80.1	104.8	127.6	147.6	148.0	127.3	117.1	84,952
England	72.1	62.1	57.0	45.1	50.9	60.7	64.0	65.0	61.1	59.9	62.2	62.9	63.6	65.5	72.7	90.8	119.6	144.9	166.8	165.1	141.1	130.0	78,779
Wales	11.3	13.0	13.8	15.5	14.5	15.8	15.8	21.9	17.1	20.1	19.2	14.4	20.1	12.6	14.3	19.9	25.5	32.9	45.7	42.9	41.2	52.0	1,236
Scotland	60.3	70.9	52.7	33.1	26.9	29.1	40.1	32.0	41.6	35.4	34.8	39.5	39.3	37.6	34.6	33.3	36.2	48.1	58.3	74.6	71.1	56.1	4,472
Northern Ireland	10.5	10.4	7.8	8.6	8.5	10.2	16.0	10.0	9.9	11.4	9.7	12.8	7.2	7.1	11.0	13.3	14.7	20.7	24.3	46.0	36.5	32.7	465

Deaths among HIV-infected individuals by year of death [2,3,4] 1985-2005

	1985	1986	1987	1988	1989	1990	1991	1992	1993	1994	1995	1996	1997	1998	1999	2000	2001	2002	2003	2004	2005	2006	Total
United Kingdom[5]	3.3	6.9	9.1	10.4	16.1	19.2	23.9	26.5	33.4	36.5	36.7	31.1	15.7	10.7	9.7	9.6	9.5	10.5	10.9	9.3	9.0	..	16,827
England	3.8	7.6	10.1	11.5	17.6	20.6	25.0	28.6	36.3	39.3	39.2	33.3	16.7	11.2	10.2	10.3	10.2	10.9	11.9	10.3	9.3	..	14,808
Wales	0.5	4.0	1.8	3.1	6.2	5.7	8.8	6.6	12.7	12.3	10.5	7.9	5.2	1.7	4.8	3.5	3.0	6.8	2.5	6.3	6.1	..	282
Scotland	1.0	3.3	4.7	5.7	9.1	13.6	22.6	19.5	21.6	27.2	30.0	24.5	13.4	11.4	9.1	8.9	9.1	11.3	10.7	4.9	8.2	..	1,372
Northern Ireland	0.9	0.0	1.7	1.7	6.0	7.6	4.2	4.1	3.3	5.7	6.5	7.2	2.4	1.6	1.6	0.8	0.8	3.8	0.0	0.0	0.6	..	74

Numbers of HIV diagnoses refer to diagnosis rates and not incidence rates.

1   Individuals with laboratory reports of infection plus those with AIDS or death reports for whom no matching laboratory report has been received. Reports to the end of June 2007.

2   Numbers, particularly for recent years, will rise as further reports are received. Table will include some records of (a) the same individuals which were unmatchable because of differences in the information supplied, and (b) of individuals who left the country at some point after diagnosis.

3   Excludes individuals diagnosed in the Channel Islands or the Isle of Man (new diagnoses) and deaths in the Channel Islands or the Isle of Man.

4   Includes all deaths among HIV infected individuals, regardless of whether the death was HIV or AIDS-related or not.

5   UK total includes deaths among HIV infected individuals where the place of death is not known.

Source: Health Protection Agency; Office for National Statistics

3

Table 3.12

Trends in diagnosed HIV-infected patients: by probable route of infection,[1] 1997-2006

United Kingdom

Percentages, numbers

Country of residence	Year	Probable route of infection						Total number of individuals
		Homosexual contact	Injecting drug use	Heterosexual contact	Blood/ Blood products	Mother to infant transmission	Not known	
United Kingdom	1997	57.8	7.6	23.4	3.3	1.5	6.4	15,925
	1998	55.5	7.3	25.9	3.0	1.8	6.5	17,658
	1999	54.7	6.7	28.8	2.6	2.0	5.3	19,807
	2000	52.1	5.7	31.2	2.2	2.3	6.5	22,299
	2001	49.6	4.9	36.2	1.9	2.3	5.1	25,801
	2002	46.0	4.1	41.2	1.6	2.3	4.8	30,942
	2003	43.8	3.7	45.3	1.3	2.2	3.7	36,151
	2004	43.0	3.2	47.8	1.2	2.2	2.5	41,096
	2005	42.1	2.9	49.3	1.1	2.2	2.3	46,558
	2006	41.7	2.7	49.5	1.0	2.2	2.9	51,713
England [2]	1997	59.6	5.4	23.3	3.1	1.6	7.0	14,531
	1998	56.9	5.3	26.0	2.8	1.9	7.0	16,151
	1999	55.9	4.9	29.0	2.5	2.1	5.7	18,178
	2000	53.1	4.1	31.4	2.0	2.4	7.0	20,549
	2001	50.3	3.5	36.7	1.7	2.3	5.5	23,880
	2002	46.4	3.0	41.7	1.4	2.4	5.1	28,807
	2003	44.0	2.8	45.9	1.2	2.3	3.9	33,723
	2004	43.2	2.4	48.4	1.1	2.3	2.6	38,277
	2005	42.1	2.2	50.0	1.0	2.3	2.4	43,347
	2006	41.6	2.1	50.2	0.9	2.2	3.0	48,061
Wales [2]	1997	53.7	5.0	26.0	13.2	0.4	1.7	242
	1998	55.3	5.1	25.1	10.9	0.7	2.9	275
	1999	57.1	5.8	24.7	10.3	0.6	1.6	312
	2000	54.8	4.8	26.3	8.7	2.4	3.0	334
	2001	51.8	5.1	29.3	7.8	3.8	2.3	396
	2002	53.9	3.4	32.8	6.5	1.7	1.7	464
	2003	48.7	3.2	38.4	5.3	2.3	2.1	563
	2004	50.1	2.8	38.7	4.6	2.1	1.6	672
	2005	51.9	2.6	38.0	3.4	2.1	2.1	757
	2006	51.4	2.9	37.9	3.2	2.7	1.9	884
Scotland	1997	33.5	39.1	24.0	2.9	0.5	0.1	1,060
	1998	34.8	37.5	24.1	2.9	0.5	0.2	1,138
	1999	35.4	34.6	25.9	2.9	0.6	0.6	1222
	2000	35.7	31.8	28.1	2.9	0.7	0.8	1311
	2001	36.5	29.0	30.2	2.8	0.8	0.8	1398
	2002	36.3	25.8	33.6	2.8	0.9	0.7	1528
	2003	37.0	22.4	36.3	2.9	1.0	0.5	1674
	2004	36.8	19.2	39.4	3.1	0.9	0.5	1912
	2005	37.7	17.1	39.7	4.0	0.8	0.6	2,173
	2006	39.5	15.2	40.8	2.0	1.9	0.6	2,446
Northern Ireland	1997	60.5	3.5	25.6	9.3	0.0	1.2	86
	1998	57.4	2.1	33.0	6.4	0.0	1.1	94
	1999	61.1	6.3	30.5	2.1	0.0	0.0	95
	2000	58.1	4.8	33.3	1.0	1.0	1.9	105
	2001	58.3	3.1	35.4	1.6	0.8	0.8	127
	2002	54.5	3.5	38.5	0.7	0.7	2.1	143
	2003	50.8	2.6	41.9	0.5	1.6	2.6	191
	2004	52.8	2.1	41.7	0.4	2.1	0.9	235
	2005	48.4	2.5	45.9	0.4	1.8	1.1	281
	2006	48.8	1.9	46.9	0.0	1.6	0.9	322

1   Total excludes HIV diagnosed individuals with country of residence not known, resident abroad or resident in the British Isles outside of the UK.
2   Total includes HIV diagnosed individuals whose SHA/HB of residence was not known.

Source: Health Protection Agency; Institute of Child Health (London); Health Protection Scotland (formerly SCIEH)

Additional notes

Table 3.2 – General Practice Consultations

Data on GP consultations presented in this report relate to consultations with both NHS and private sector general medical practitioners in the two weeks before interview. Visits to the surgery, home visits and telephone contacts are included, but contacts with a receptionist are excluded.

Table 3.3 – Road accident statistics

The Department for Transport road accident statistics include all road accidents in the UK which involve personal injury and which become known to the police within 30 days.

Table 3.4 – Age standardised rates

Age standardised rates: The incidence of cancer varies greatly with age. Differences in the age structure of populations between geographical areas over time therefore need to be controlled to give unbiased comparisons of incidence. This can be achieved through either direct or indirect standardisation. Direct standardisation is used in this table.

Table 3.6 – Reportable injuries

Reportable injuries to workers, under the Reporting of Injuries, Diseases and Dangerous Occurrences Regulations (RIDDOR) 1985 and 1995, are divided into:

- Fatalities

- Major injuries which include fractures (except to fingers, thumbs or toes), amputations, dislocations (of shoulder, hip, knee, spine) and other injuries leading to resuscitation or at least 24 hours admission to hospital

- Over-three-day injuries which include other injuries to workers which lead to their absence from work, or inability to do their usual job, for over three days

Table 3.7 – Communicable diseases

Communicable diseases are notifiable to Local Authority Proper Officers under the Public Health (Infectious Diseases) Regulations 1998. Not all diseases requiring notification by law are included in the table. Some diseases have been omitted due to low incidence producing near zero rates, for example Rabies.

Table 3.9 – HIV – infected individuals

An HIV infected individual is defined as an individual for whom HIV diagnosis and/or AIDS, and/or death with HIV infection has been reported. The European AIDS case definition is used for AIDS surveillance in the UK.

3

3

Health-related behaviour

This chapter contains key statistics about health-related behaviour (smoking, drinking, diet and physical activity) in the four countries of the UK. It also contains figures on the misuse of drugs and deaths related to drug use.

Where figures are based on survey data, it is important to be aware of differences in sampling and survey methodology and the implications of smaller sample sizes. The differences identified between the countries are for the purpose of drawing a general picture of health trends in the UK, and should not be taken as statistically significant without further investigation. Comparisons between the countries should therefore be made with caution.

Smoking

In 2006, Scotland had the highest proportion of men who were current smokers, at 27 per cent compared with the UK proportion of 25 per cent. However, Scotland also had the highest proportion of men who had never smoked. Northern Ireland had the highest proportion of female smokers, at 26 per cent, compared with 23 per cent in the UK as a whole. Northern Ireland had the highest proportion of current smokers who smoked 20 or more cigarettes a day, 45 per cent of male smokers and 36 per cent of female smokers, but not the highest average weekly number of cigarettes consumed (Table 4.1).

Smoking among children in Great Britain in 2006 was at its lowest level in over ten years. 'Regular smokers' were those children who reported smoking at least one cigarette per

week. In England, the proportion of children in all age groups who smoked regularly decreased between 1998 and 2006. In Scotland and Wales, smoking rates tended to rise between 1990 and 1998 then fell in 2006. Girls aged 15-16 had the highest smoking rates among children in all countries (Table 4.2).

Figure 4.1

Cigarette smoking among people aged 16 and over: by sex, 2006

United Kingdom

Percentages

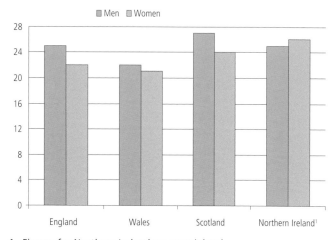

1   Figures for Northern Ireland are unweighted.

Source: Office for National Statistics; Northern Ireland Statistics and Reasearch Agency; Scottish Government

Table 4.1

Cigarette smoking among adults aged 16 and over: by sex, 2006

United Kingdom

Percentages

	Men					Women				
	Proportion of males who:			Of current smokers:		Proportion of females who:			Of current smokers:	
	Have never smoked [1]	Are ex-regular smokers	Smoke	Proportion who smoke 20 or more daily	Average weekly con-sumption (number)	Have never smoked [1]	Are ex-regular smokers	Smoke	Proportion who smoke 20 or more daily	Average weekly con-sumption (number)
United Kingdom	48	27	25	9	..	57	20	23	7	..
Great Britain	48	27	25	8	104	57	20	22	6	90
England	48	28	25	8	102	58	20	22	5	88
Wales	47	31	22	9	118	58	21	21	6	89
Scotland	50	23	27	12	118	56	20	24	8	106
Northern Ireland	41	34	25	45	117	50	24	26	36	102

..   *Data not available.*

1   *Have never smoked regularly.*

Source: Office for National Statistics; Northern Ireland Statistics and Research Agency; Scottish Government

Table 4.2

Trends in cigarette smoking among 11 to 16-years-old: by age and sex, 1990-2006

Great Britain

Percentages

	Regular smokers				
	1990	1994	1998	2002[1]	2006
England					
Males					
11-12 year olds	..	..	3	3	2
13-14 year olds	..	..	10	10	6
15-16 year olds	..	..	26	21	13
Females					
11-12 year olds	..	..	1	2	1
13-14 year olds	..	..	15	14	8
15-16 year olds	..	..	34	28	18
Wales					
Males					
11-12 year olds	3	1	2	2	1
13-14 year olds	8	8	8	8	6
15-16 year olds	14	18	21	15	12
Females					
11-12 year olds	2	1	3	2	1
13-14 year olds	11	13	19	15	12
15-16 year olds	22	26	29	27	23
Scotland					
Males					
11-12 year olds	2	2	2	1	2
13-14 year olds	7	7	9	6	4
15-16 year olds	15	21	22	16	15
Females					
11-12 year olds	3	2	3	1	1
13-14 year olds	9	12	13	11	8
15-16 year olds	18	26	28	23	23

Regular smokers are those children that smoke at least one cigarette a week.
.. Data not available.

Source: Health Behaviour in School-aged Children (HBSC) study; Department of Public Health and Health Professionals, Welsh Assembly Government; Child & Adolescent Health Research Unit, University of Edinburgh; Department of Health

In 2005, around a fifth of women in Wales and Scotland continued to smoke during their pregnancy; 21 per cent in each country, compared with 18 per cent in Northern Ireland and 17 per cent in England. This figure includes those who continued smoking but reduced the number of cigarettes consumed (Table 4.3).

Alcohol consumption

Data on alcohol consumption in Great Britain comes from the General Household Survey (GHS). Owing to recent changes to the type of alcoholic drinks available, the alcohol content of drinks and variable quantities, it has become necessary to reconsider the methodology made in obtaining estimates of alcohol consumption. A paper detailing the changes in conversion factors can be found on the National Statistics website. As the method of data collection has changed, comparisons with previous years should be made with caution.

Adults aged 16 and over were asked how many units of alcohol they had drunk on their heaviest drinking day in the last week.

Table 4.3

Changes to smoking habits during pregnancy, 2005

United Kingdom   Percentages

	United Kingdom	England	Wales	Scotland	Northern Ireland
Non-smokers	67	68	63	65	68
Smoked before pregnancy, of which:					
Gave up during pregnancy	16	16	15	16	14
Reduced smoking during pregnancy[1]	11	11	14	14	12
No change or increase in amount	6	6	7	7	6
Base[2]	11933	5896	2076	2137	1830

Figures may not add exactly due to rounding.

1 *Average number smoked per day during pregnancy was at least 5 cigarettes less than the average number smoked before pregnancy.*
2 *Excluding mothers for whom smoking status could not be classified.*

Source: Infant Feeding Survey, British Market Research Beareau (BMRB)

Table 4.4

Maximum daily alcohol consumption last week among adults aged 16 and over: by sex, 2006

Great Britain   Percentages

	Men					Women				
	Drank nothing	Drank less than 4 units	Drank 4-7 units	Drank 8 or more units	Base[1]	Drank nothing	Drank less than 3 units	Drank 3-6 units	Drank 7 or more units	Base[1]
Great Britain	29	31	11	29	7674	44	33	10	14	9013
England	28	32	11	29	6596	43	33	9	14	7698
Wales	32	27	12	30	411	47	31	10	11	477
Scotland	33	27	12	28	667	48	29	10	13	838

1 *Unweighted base.*

Source: Office for National Statistics

In England the highest proportion of men (32 per cent) had drunk less than four units of alcohol on their heaviest drinking day; this is within current Department of Health guidelines in 2006. In Scotland (33 per cent) and Wales (32 per cent) the highest proportion of men drank nothing in the last week (Table 4.4). In all countries the proportion of women reported not drinking any alcohol in the previous week was higher than the proportion that reported drinking any amount of alcohol.

In Great Britain, in all years, the proportion of young people who reported drinking in the last week increased with age up to age 16. This pattern was found for both boys and girls. (Table 4.5). In England the proportion of 15-16 year old boys who drank in the week preceding the interview was at its highest in 2002, with 52 per cent having had an alcoholic drink in the last week. This proportion has dropped since 2002

to 41 per cent in 2006. For girls the proportion of 15-16 year old girls who drank alcohol in the last week was at its highest in 2002 at 48 per cent, and this had dropped to 38 per cent in 2006.

In Wales there was a decline between 1994 and 2006 in the proportion of boys and girls drinking alcohol every week in all ages.

Physical activity

The questions used in surveys to measure physical activity differ between the countries of the UK. Surveys covering Northern Ireland and Wales ask respondents about physical activity over the last seven days, whereas surveys in England and Scotland ask about physical activity undertaken in the last four weeks. The data cover different time periods, and for these reasons are not directly comparable. In all countries and all age groups,

Table 4.5

Trends in alcohol consumption among 11- to 16-year-olds: by age and sex

Great Britain   Percentages

		Percentage who drank alcohol in the last week				
		1990	1994	1998	2002	2006
England						
Males						
	11-12 year olds	..	..	4	18	12
	13-14 year olds	..	..	16	32	20
	15-16 year olds [1]	..	..	48	52	41
Females						
	11-12 year olds	..	..	4	10	4
	13-14 year olds	..	..	21	28	17
	15-16 year olds [1]	..	..	40	48	38
Wales						
Males						
	11-12 year olds	21	19	16	10	7
	13-14 year olds	24	30	30	31	23
	15-16 year olds	52	51	59	57	42
Females						
	11-12 year olds	9	11	10	7	4
	13-14 year olds	19	22	24	24	20
	15-16 year olds	41	46	46	52	38
Scotland						
Males						
	11-12 year olds	11	11	11	8	8
	13-14 year olds	16	22	25	20	18
	15-16 year olds	30	41	44	42	39
Females						
	11-12 year olds	5	5	6	4	3
	13-14 year olds	16	16	18	19	16
	15-16 year olds	26	33	45	44	36

The figures presented are the percentage of children who reported drinking weekly.

1   Data are for 15 year olds only.

Source: Health Behaviour in School-aged Children (HBSC) study; Department of Public Health and Health Professionals, Welsh Assembly Government; Child & Adolescent Health Research Unit, University of Edinburgh; Department of Health

apart from Northern Ireland for the age group 45-54 years, the percentage of men meeting the physical activity level recommended was greater than that of women (Table 4.6). There was decreased physical activity with increasing age in all countries.

Food and nutrition

Consumption of, and expenditure on, selected foods is shown here in two tables. The first (Table 4.7) provides information on the food types purchased (and expenditure on these) by households in the four countries. The second table (Table 4.8) presents data on the energy and nutrient intakes of these households. All data are for 2004 to 2006.

The types of food purchased in the four countries showed marked differences. People in England purchased the most cheese (an average of 117g per week), the most vegetables excluding potatoes (1,165g), and the most fruit (1,286g).

Table 4.6

Proportion of people meeting physical activity recommendations,[1,2] by age and sex, 2005-06

United Kingdom

Percentage within age group

	16–24	25–34	35–44	45–54	55–64	65–74	75+	All ages
Male								
United Kingdom								
England[3]	56	46	41	37	32	18	8	37
Wales	53	43	45	40	30	25	16	38
Scotland	51	54	44	39	34	23	11	40
Northern Ireland	33	40	39	29	28	26	17	33
Female								
United Kingdom								
England[3]	32	30	32	30	20	14	4	25
Wales	32	26	29	28	25	19	11	25
Scotland	33	38	37	33	26	16	5	29
Northern Ireland	26	35	35	33	26	20	11	28

1 *Guidelines for England, Wales and Northern Ireland currently recommend that 'adults should do at least 30 minutes of moderate intensity physical activity on five or more days of the week'. The recommendation for Scotland is for adults to 'accumulate at least 30 minutes moderate activity on most days of the week'. For these reasons caution should be added when comparing directly, due to the difference in survey methodology.*

2 *For England, Wales and Scotland, those meeting the recommended levels of physical activity fall in the category 'High' = 30 minutes on at least five days a week. For Northern Ireland 'Above' = 30 minutes of moderate activity on at least five days a week.*

3 *Figures for 2004.*

Source: The Information Centre for health and social care; Welsh Assembly Government; NHS in Scotland; Northern Ireland Statistics and Research Agency

People in Wales purchased the most fats and oils (186g), the most sugar and preserves (144g) and the most alcohol (875ml).

People in Northern Ireland purchased the most milk and cream (2,136ml), the most cereals (1,733g), and the most potatoes (1,180g). Inhabitants of households in Scotland purchased the largest quantity of soft drinks (2,178ml), but the least amount of fats and oils (169g) and milk and cream (1,968ml).

Overall, households in Scotland spent the most money on food and drink (including alcohol), an average of £23.93 per person per week. Households in Wales spent the least on food and drink (including alcohol) with a mean weekly expenditure of £22.88.

Eating-out expenditure (including alcohol) was highest in England at an average of £11.62 per person per week and lowest in Scotland at £10.91 per person.

In 2004-06 households in Northern Ireland had the highest energy intake at 2,387 kcal per person per day, while Wales was only slightly lower at 2,381 kcal per person per day (Table 4.8). The intakes for England and Scotland were lower, with England at 2,352 kcal per person per day, and Scotland was the lowest at 2,326 per person per day.

Table 4.7

Purchases of and expenditure on selected foods, 2004-06

United Kingdom

		England	Wales	Scotland	Northern Ireland
Number of households in sample		14,450	912	1,589	1,462
Average age of household reference person		52	53	53	50
Average number of adults per household		1.9	1.9	1.8	1.9
Average number of children per household		0.5	0.5	0.5	0.6
Average gross weekly household income	(£)	627	507	554	508
		Grams per person per week unless otherwise stated			
Household Purchases					
Milk and cream	(ml)	1,997	2,102	1,968	2,136
Cheese		117	108	107	79
Carcase meat		232	245	191	252
Other meat and meat products		811	912	843	840
Fish		169	145	149	114
Eggs	(no.)	2	1	2	2
Fats and oils		183	186	169	184
Sugar and preserves		130	144	120	117
Potatoes		811	963	775	1,180
Vegetables		1,165	1,077	926	873
Fruit		1,286	1,137	1,137	1,024
Total cereals		1,596	1,582	1,609	1,733
Beverages		57	58	51	47
Soft drinks[2]	(ml)	1,741	2,111	2,178	1,815
Alcoholic drinks	(ml)	766	875	786	547
Confectionery		124	142	141	133
Eating out purchases					
Indian, Chinese and Thai meals		32	22	29	27
Meat and meat products		86	106	79	94
Fish and fish products		14	15	14	9
Cheese and egg dishes and pizza		24	20	20	16
Potatoes		75	94	69	85
Vegetables		33	33	21	25
Sandwiches		80	72	91	65
Ice creams, desserts and cakes		29	24	29	30
Beverages	(ml)	137	120	125	99
Soft drinks including milk	(ml)	346	376	416	415
Alcoholic drinks	(ml)	609	672	506	457
Confectionery		16	18	20	22

4

Table 4.7 – continued

Purchases of and expenditure on selected foods, 2004-06

United Kingdom

	England	Wales	Scotland	Northern Ireland
	Pence per person per week			
Household Expenditure				
Milk and cream	162	157	154	163
Cheese	64	53	59	44
Carcase meat	116	116	102	138
Other meat and meat products	377	401	415	439
Fish	108	83	96	74
Eggs	19	17	19	17
Fats and oils	38	37	38	37
Sugar and preserves	17	18	16	16
Potatoes	100	113	107	140
Vegetables	198	164	158	149
Fruit	190	158	166	149
Total cereals	385	370	403	438
Beverages	42	41	40	34
All other foods	126	117	127	123
Soft drinks	77	84	103	94
Alcoholic drinks	272	272	300	207
Confectionery	80	87	91	80
Total all food & drink excluding alcohol	2,100	2,016	2,093	2,136
Total all food & drink	2,373	2,288	2,393	2,343
Eating out expenditure				
Total all food & drink excluding alcohol	797	729	752	799
Total all food & drink	1,162	1,106	1,091	1,122

1 Based on average consumption April 2004-December 2006. From 2006 the Expenditure and Food Survey has moved onto a calendar year basis rather than the previous financial year basis.
2 Converted to unconcentrated equivalent by applying a factor of five to concentrated and low calorie concentrated soft drinks.

Source: Department for Environment, Food and Rural Affairs

Table 4.8

Energy and nutrient intakes, 2004-06[7]

United Kingdom

		England	Wales	Scotland	Northern Ireland
Number of households in sample		14,450	912	1,589	1,462
Average age of household reference person		52	53	53	50
Average number of adults per household		1.9	1.9	1.8	1.9
Average number of children per household		0.5	0.5	0.5	0.6
Average gross weekly household income	(£)	627	507	554	508
		intake per person			
Total energy and nutrient intakes[2]					
Energy	kcal	2,352	2,381	2,326	2,387
	MJ	9.9	10	9.8	10
Energy intake excluding alcohol	kcal	2,276	2,299	2,247	2,330
Total protein	g	81.3	82.9	79.3	82.3
Fat	g	97	97	95	98
Fatty acids:					
Saturates	g	37.1	37.6	37.4	38.1
Mono-unsaturates	g	35.7	35.8	34.6	36.2
Poly-unsaturates	g	17.5	17.2	16.4	17.3
Cholesterol	mg	274	277	267	273
Carbohydrate[3]	g	288	291	287	298
Total sugars	g	134	138	134	132
Non-milk extrinsic sugars	g	88	93	90	88
Starch	g	153	152	152	165
Fibre[4]	g	15.4	15.2	14.5	15.4
Alcohol	g	11	12	11	8
Calcium	mg	994	1,013	993	1,005
Iron	mg	12.5	12.5	12.1	12.6
Zinc	mg	9.6	9.8	9.3	9.7
Magnesium	mg	296	297	285	288
Sodium[5]	g	3.01	3.13	3.13	3.13
Potassium	g	3.33	3.39	3.17	3.34
Thiamin	mg	1.78	1.81	1.72	1.86
Riboflavin	mg	1.98	2.06	1.91	1.98
Niacin equivalent	mg	36.0	37.03	34.91	36
Vitamin B6	mg	2.55	2.69	2.45	2.73
Vitamin B12	µg	6.53	7.11	6.31	6.18
Folate	µg	309	311	286	306
Vitamin C	mg	78	74	73	72
Vitamin A					
Retinol	µg	528	589	502	446
β-carotene	µg	2,272	2,320	2,049	2,092
Retinol equivalent	µg	911	981	848	802
Vitamin D	µg	3.26	3.29	3.00	3.11
Vitamin E	mg	12.84	12.70	11.88	12.70

Table 4.8 – continued

Energy and nutrient intakes, 2004-06[7]

United Kingdom

		England	Wales	Scotland	Northern Ireland
		percentage contributions to energy intake (excluding alcohol)			
Fat	%	38.3	38.1	38.0	38.0
Fatty acids:					
Saturates	%	14.7	14.7	15.0	14.7
Mono-unsaturates	%	14.1	14.0	13.9	14.0
Poly-unsaturates	%	6.9	6.7	6.6	6.7
Carbohydrate	%	47.4	47.5	47.8	47.9
Total protein	%	14.3	14.4	14.1	14.1
		as a percentage of weighted reference nutrient intake[7]			
Energy[6]	%	102	103	102	105
Energy excluding alcohol[6]	%	99	100	98	102
Protein	%	162	165	161	169
Calcium	%	131	133	131	133
Iron	%	110	111	105	110
Zinc	%	110	111	107	112
Magnesium	%	101	101	99	101
Sodium[5]	%	191	190	193	210
Potassium	%	98	97	92	104
Thiamin	%	193	196	123	204
Riboflavin	%	157	164	153	160
Niacin equivalent	%	236	243	230	239
Vitamin B6	%	190	200	184	206
Vitamin B12	%	428	465	419	414
Folate	%	150	151	140	151
Vitamin C	%	186	176	175	174
Vitamin A (retinol equivalent)	%	134	144	125	119

1   Based on average consumption April 2004-December 2006. From 2006 the Expenditure and Food Survey has moved onto a calendar year basis rather than the previous financial year basis.
2   Contributions from pharmaceutical sources are not recorded by the survey.
3   Available carbohydrate, calculated as monosaccharide.
4   As non-starch polysaccharides.
5   (i) Excludes sodium from table salt (ii) The RNI does not take account of the SACN Report of Salt & Health 15th May 2003 which recommended that an adult's average daily intake should not exceed six grams of salt, equivalent to 2.4 grams of sodium.
6   As a percentage of Estimated Average Requirement.
7   Department of Health, 'Dietary Reference Values for Food Energy and Nutrients for the United Kingdom', HMSO 1991.

Source: Department for Environment, Food and Rural Affairs

Drug misuse

In the UK, the largest number (70,179) of drug treatment presentations in 2003/04 involved opiates as the primary drug, 60 per cent of the total presentations (Table 4.9). The largest proportion of drug presentations involved opiates in England (61 per cent), Scotland (57 per cent) and Wales (53 per cent). In Northern Ireland the largest proportion of drug treatment presentations involved cannabis as the primary drug.

Table 4.9

Number and percentage of drug treatment presentations[1] in 2003/04 in the United Kingdom: by primary drug and country

United Kingdom

Drug	United Kingdom		England		Wales		Scotland		Northern Ireland	
	number	%	number	%	number	%	number	%	number	%
Amphetamines	3,731	3	3,045	3	398	13	269	2	19	1
Benzodiazepines	2,503	2	1,395	1	135	4	791	6	182	10
Cannabis	14,801	13	12,021	12	377	12	1,593	11	810	46
Cocaine	5,093	4	4,637	5	52	2	278	2	126	7
Crack	5,842	5	5,715	6	76	2	48	0	3	0
Opiates	70,179	60	60,030	61	1,627	53	8,162	57	360	21
Other/NK	15,632	13	11,841	12	402	13	3,143	22	246	14
Total	117,781	100	98,684	100	3,067	100	14,284	100	1,746	100

1 Based on Treatment Demand Indicator (TDI) data for 2004/05.

Source: European Monitoring Centre on Drugs and Drug Addiction (EMCDDA)

A drug-related death is defined by the UK Drug Strategy as having an underlying cause of poisoning, drug abuse or drug dependence where any of the substances included in the Misuse of Drugs Act 1971 were involved. In 1996, 1,531 drug-related deaths were registered in the UK (Figure 4.2). The number of drug-related deaths increased to 2011 in 2000, after which the number fell to 1,592 in 2003. In 2004 the number rose to 1,786 drug-related deaths.

4

Figure 4.2

Trends in the total number of drug-related deaths[1,2] 1996-2004

United Kingdom

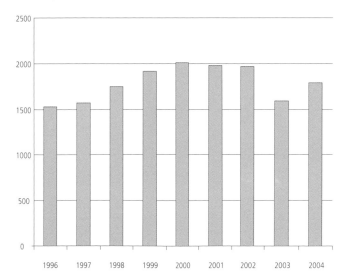

1 Based on General Mortality Registers (GMR) DRDs in the UK.
2 Drug related deaths (DRD), according to the United Kingdom Drug Strategy are where the underlying cause is poisoning, drug abuse or drug dependence and where any of the substances included in the Misuse of Drugs Act 1971 were involved. This definition has been adopted by the General Mortality Registers (GMRs) across the UK.

Source: European Monitoring Centre on Drugs and Drug Addiction (EMCDDA)

Additional notes

Table 4.1 – Weighted sample

The General Household Survey (GHS) (Longitudinal) is weighted using a two-step approach. In the first step, the data is weighted to compensate for non-response (sample based weighting). The second step weights the sample distribution so that it matches the population distribution in terms of region, age-group and sex (population-based weighting).

Table 4.4 – Alcohol consumption

Estimates of alcohol consumption in surveys are given in standard units derived from assumptions about the alcohol content of different types of drink, combined with information from the respondent about the volume drunk. Following recent changes to the type of alcoholic drinks available, the alcohol content of drinks, and variable quantities, it became necessary to reconsider the assumptions made in obtaining estimates of alcohol consumption.

The changes in conversion factor are discussed in detail in a paper in the National Statistics Methodology series, which also includes a table giving the original and updated factors for converting alcohol volume to units. See Goddard E, *Estimating alcohol consumption from survey data: updated method of converting volumes to units*, National Statistics Methodology Series NSM 37 (Office for National Statistics 2007), also available at: www.statistics.gov.uk/downloads/theme_compendia/drinkingmethodologyfinal.pdf

It was clear from the research undertaken that all surveys, including the General Household Survey (GHS) (Longitudinal), have been undercounting the number of units in some types of drink – predominantly wine, but also to a lesser degree beer, lager and cider. For example, using the latest method one-half pint of strong beer, larger or cider has two units, the number of units in a glass of wine depends on the size of glass and is counted as two units if the glass size is unspecified and bottle of alcopops has 1.5 units.

Table 4.6 – Physical activity levels

In Great Britain, health department guidelines currently recommend that adults should do at least 30 minutes of moderate intensity physical activity on five or more days a week. Examples of different types of activity are:

- Light activity = light housework or golf

- Moderate activity = heavy gardening or brisk walking

- Vigorous activity = aerobics or running

In Northern Ireland the recommendation for adults is to 'accumulate at least 30 minutes moderate activity on most days of the week'.

Those with a 'high' level of physical activity in Great Britain and those with 'above recommended level' in Northern Ireland are achieving or exceeding the recommended level of physical activity.

Preventive Healthcare

This chapter contains data about preventive healthcare, such as immunisations and cancer screening. Two important areas of health-related behaviour, breast-feeding and contraception, are also covered here because of their significance for the prevention of later ill-health.

Breastfeeding

The figures presented here are for new mothers whose initial method of feeding their child was breastfeeding. Overall, mothers in England and Wales had the highest incidence of breastfeeding, but the proportion of women who started breastfeeding increased between 1995 and 2005 in all four countries (Figure 5.1, Table 5.1). The largest increase was among mothers in Northern Ireland aged 30 years and over.

Despite this increase, Northern Ireland had the lowest incidence of breastfeeding among mothers in all age groups in 2005; the lowest incidence was seen in mothers aged under 20 years, at 35 per cent.

Women aged 20 years and under were least likely to begin breastfeeding, with the proportion increasing with the mother's age. In the UK in 2005, 82 per cent of mothers aged 30 and over began by breastfeeding compared to about half (51 per cent) of mothers aged 20 years and under.

Immunisation

All countries of the UK had high levels of immunisation in childhood throughout the period 1998-99 to 2006-07, with some variations. Uptake of diphtheria, tetanus and polio (DTP) immunisation declined by 1 percentage point in 2001-02, from 95 to 94 per cent, and has since remained constant. Whooping

cough immunisation remained at 94 per cent with a temporary dip of 1 percentage point in the middle of the period. Measles, mumps and rubella (MMR) immunisation fell to a low of 81 per cent in 2003-2004 but has since risen to 86 per cent in 2006-07 (Table 5.2). The decrease in the uptake of the MMR vaccination is well recognised and attributed to health concerns surrounding this vaccine.

For most of the period, immunisation uptake was highest in Scotland and Northern Ireland, and lowest in England.

Figure 5.1

Proportion of mothers breastfeeding,[1] 1995, 2000 and 2005

United Kingdom

Percentages

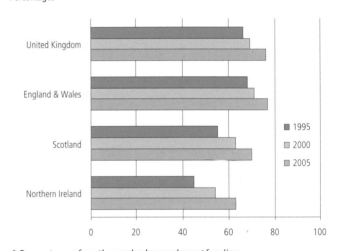

1 Percentage of mothers who began breastfeeding.

Source: Infant Feeding Survey, British Market Research Bureau (BMRB)

Table 5.1

Breastfeeding: by mother's age,[1] 1995, 2000 and 2005

United Kingdom   Percentages

Mother's age	United Kingdom			England & Wales			Scotland			Northern Ireland		
	1995	2000	2005	1995	2000	2005	1995	2000	2005	1995	2000	2005
Under 20	43	46	51	46	49	53	24	31	40	24	24	35
20-24	55	58	67	57	60	68	43	53	59	34	41	49
25-29	66	67	76	68	69	77	55	63	70	46	54	63
30 or over	74	78	82	76	79	85	65	70	78	50	62	70
All ages[2]	66	69	76	68	71	77	55	63	70	45	54	63
Base (100%) all ages	5,181	9,492	12,290	4,598	5,441	8,210	1,867	2,274	2,194	1,476	1,778	1,886

1 Percentage of mothers who began breastfeeding.
2 Includes mother's age not known.

Source: Infant Feeding Survey, British Market Research Bureau (BMRB)

Table 5.2

Completed primary courses: percentage of children immunised by 2nd birthday, 1998-99 to 2006-07[1]

United Kingdom   Percentages

	1998-99	1999-2000	2000-01	2001-02	2002-03	2003-04	2004-05	2005-06	2006-07
United Kingdom[2]									
Diphtheria, Tetanus, Polio	95	95	95	94	94	94	94	94	94
Whooping cough	94	94	94	93	93	93	94	94	94
MMR	88	88	88	84	83	81	82	85	86
England									
Diphtheria, Tetanus, Polio	95	95	94	94	94	94	94	94	93
Whooping cough	94	94	94	93	93	93	93	94	93
MMR	88	88	87	84	82	80	81	84	85
Wales									
Diphtheria, Tetanus, Polio	96	96	97	95	95	96	96	96	97
Whooping cough	93	94	95	94	94	95	95	96	96
MMR	86	85	88	84	81	80	82	85	88
Scotland									
Diphtheria, Tetanus, Polio	97	98	98	97	98	98	98	98	98
Whooping cough	96	97	97	98	97	97	97	98	98
MMR	92	93	93	88	88	87	88	91	92
Northern Ireland									
Diphtheria, Tetanus, Polio	97	97	97	97	96	97	98	98	98
Whooping cough	96	96	97	96	96	97	97	97	98
MMR	90	91	92	90	88	88	88	91	91

1 Data for England, Wales and Scotland are for the year ending 31 March. Data for Northern Ireland are per calendar year (January to December).
2 Data for the UK are based on actual numbers of immunisations for England, Wales and Scotland but on populations by calendar year for Northern Ireland.

Source: Department of Health; Welsh Assembly Government; Information Services Division, NHS in Scotland; Northern Ireland Statistics and Research Agency

However, differences in the way immunisation uptake is calculated in the four countries make direct comparison difficult. The dip in MMR uptake was seen most in England and Wales, with a low point of 80 per cent in 2003-04 in both countries (Table 5.2).

In the UK, 75.1 per cent of the population aged 65 years and over had been immunised against influenza in the last 12 months in 2005-06 (Table 5.3). The highest uptake of this immunisation was in Scotland where 77.8 per cent of the population aged 65 and over had been immunised against influenza. The lowest uptake was 68.0 per cent in Wales.

Contraception

In Great Britain around three quarters of women aged 16-49 use at least one method of contraception. The most popular single method is the contraceptive pill which is used by over a quarter of all women aged 16-49.

Table 5.3

Immunisation against influenza among the elderly population (65+), 2005-06[1]

United Kingdom   Thousands, percentages

	Pop. 65+ (000s)	Immunised (000s)	Immunised (% of pop.)
United Kingdom	9,649	7,243	75.1
England	8,058	6,123	75.3
Wales	521	328	68.0
Scotland	833	597	77.8
Northern Ireland	236	172	73.0

1 The proportion of people aged 65+ who have been immunised against influenza during the past 12 months.

Source: Health Protection Agency; National Public Health Service Wales; Health Protection Scotland; Communicable Diseases Surveillance Centre, Northern Ireland

Women in Wales were the most likely to use at least one method of contraception with a proportion of 78 per cent (Table 5.4). The most popular method of contraception in Wales was the pill which 23 per cent of women reported using, followed by the condom at 21 per cent. Scotland had the highest proportion of use of the pill, at 34 per cent.

Northern Ireland had the lowest proportion of women using contraception at 69 per cent, followed by Scotland and England both at 76 per cent.

Cancer screening

Data for cervical cancer screening are based on screening of the target population in the last five years (five and a half for Scotland) and include figures on the percentage of women screened as well as the percentage of screens with a positive result. The target population for cervical screening differs by country; in England it includes women aged 25-64 years, in Wales 20-64 years, in Scotland 20-60 years and in Northern Ireland 20-65 years. The comparisons presented here do not take these age differences into account (Table 5.5, Figure 5.2).

In 2005-06, 79.4 per cent of women of target age in the UK had a cervical cancer screen or smear test. Of the countries in the UK, Scotland had the highest proportion of screens, with 83.8 per cent of target age having been screened in the previous five and a half years. Northern Ireland had the lowest proportion of screens at 71.5 per cent. Cervical screens were

least common among women aged 25-34 years in England, Wales and Scotland and in women aged 55-64 years in Northern Ireland.

In England, 5.0 per cent of all adequate smear tests had a positive result; in Wales it was 5.6 per cent.

Data for breast screening are based on screening of the target population in the last three years and include figures on the percentage of women screened by age group. The target population for breast cancer screening is 50-64 in all four countries.

In the UK, in 2005-06 70.7 per cent of women in the target population had been screened for breast cancer in the last three years. Scotland had the highest proportion of women screened with 76.4 per cent of 50-64 year-olds screened; England had the lowest proportion with 69.9 per cent of 50-64 year-olds being screened.

The proportion of women screened in the last three years was lowest aged 50-54 years old in England, and in women aged 60-64 years old in Wales, Scotland and Northern Ireland.

However, while England and Wales coverage is calculated from population-based systems (see additional notes), calculations in Scotland and Northern Ireland use different methods and may not be comparable.

Figure 5.2

Cervical and breast cancer screening, 2005-06

United Kingdom

Percentages

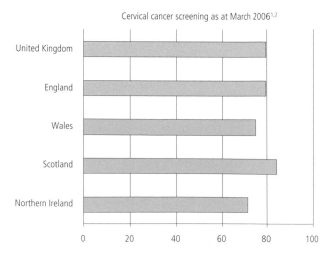

Cervical cancer screening as at March 2006[1,2]

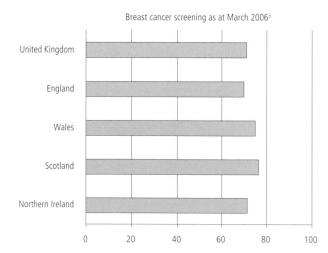

Breast cancer screening as at March 2006[3]

1 For England coverage is based on 10 August 2006 rather than 31 March 2006.
2 For England and Northern Ireland the target population relates to women aged 25-64, for Wales to women 20-64 and for Scotland to women 20-60 years screened in the previous five years(five and a half years in Scotland). Medically ineligible women (women who for example, as a result of surgery, do not require screening) in the target population are excluded from the figures.
3 Percentage of the target population – women aged 50-64 years – screened in the previous three years. Medically ineligible women in the target population are excluded from the figures, except in Scotland.

Source: Department of Health; Information Services Division, NHS in Scotland; Breast Test Wales; Cervical Screening Wales; QARC (Northern Ireland)

Table 5.4

Current use of contraception:[1] by country, 2006-07

United Kingdom   Percentages

		Great Britain[2]	England	Wales[3]	Scotland	Northern Ireland
Current usual method of contraception						
Non-surgical	Pill	27	26	23	34	29
	IUD	4	5	2	1	5
	Condom	22	22	21	25	20
	Cap	1	1	..	..	1
	Withdrawal	3	4	2	3	5
	Safe period	3	3	2	2	4
	Other	8	8	14	6	4
	At least one	**56**	**56**	**51**	**62**	**52**
Surgical	Female sterilisation	9	9	13	8	17
	Male sterilisation	11	11	15	6	6
	Total using at least one	**76**	**76**	**78**	**76**	**69**
Not using a method	Sterile after another operation	2	2	7	3	2
	Pregnant/wanting to get pregnant	4	4	8	9	6
	Abstinence/no partner	13	14	8	11	14
	Other	4	5	..	3	9
	Total not using a method	**24**	**24**	**22**	**24**	**31**
Base = 100%		1,252	1,086	63	103	1,128

1   Current use of contraception among 16-49 year olds.
2   UK data not available for 2006-07 due as latest Northern Ireland data is for 2003-04.
3   Figures indicate the estimates are unreliable and any analysis using these figures may be invalid.

Source: Office for National Statistics; Northern Ireland Statistics and Research Agency

5

Table 5.5

Cervical and breast cancer screening: by age, 2005-06[1]

United Kingdom

Percentages

	Cervical cancer screening					Percentage of all adequate smear tests with positive result: women aged 25-64 [5]	Breast cancer screening			
	Percentage of target population screened in last 5 years: women aged [2]						Percentage of target population screened in last 3 years: women aged [6]			
	25-34 [3,4]	35-44	45-54	55-64	All 25-64 [3,4]		50-54	55-59	60-64	All 50-64 [6]
United Kingdom	73.2	82.7	83.1	79.2	79.4	..	60.5	75.9	75.5	70.7
England	73.7	82.4	82.8	79.6	79.5	5.0	57.9	76.0	75.9	69.9
Wales	66.3	81.3	81.2	77.4	75.4	5.6	75.8	75.1	74.4	74.9
Scotland	75.0	89.0	89.5	86.8	83.8	..	77.5	76.7	74.9	76.4
Northern Ireland	67.0	78.9	77.5	60.6	71.5	..	73.3	71.8	68.1	71.2

1 For England coverage is based on 10 August 2006 rather than 31 March 2006.
2 For England and Northern Ireland the target population relates to women aged 25-64, for Wales to women 20-64 and for Scotland to women 20-60 years screened in the previous five years (five and a half years in Scotland). Medically ineligible women (women who for example, as a result of surgery, do not require screening) in the target population are excluded from the figures.
3 For Wales the age groups are 20-34 and 20-64 respectively.
4 For Scotland the age groups are 20-34, 55-59 and 20-60 respectively.
5 Women whose screening test results are borderline or show mild dyskaryosis are recalled for a repeat smear in approximately six months instead of the routine five years; if the condition persists they are referred to a gynaecologist.
6 Percentage of the target population – women aged 50-64 years – screened in the previous three years. Medically ineligible women (women who for example, as a result of surgery, do not require screening) in the target population are excluded from the figures, except in Scotland. For Wales, target population is 53-64 years.

Source: Department of Health; Information Services Division, NHS in Scotland; Breast Test Wales; Cervical Screening Wales; QARC (Northern Ireland)

Additional notes

Table 5.1 – Incidence of breastfeeding

Incidence of breast feeding is defined by the proportion of mothers who breastfed their babies initially. This includes all babies who were put to the breast at all, even if this was on one occasion only.

Table 5.2 – Childhood immunisations

The primary immunisations that children routinely get in the first two years of life are one vaccine (DTaP/IP/Hib) for diphtheria, tetanus, polio, hib (Haemophilus influenza type b) and pertussis (whooping cough) at two, three and four months of age and one vaccine (MMR) for measles, mumps and rubella at around 13 months of age. The meningitis C vaccine is optional and normally given at the same time as DTaP/IPV/Hib.

Table 5.5 – Breast and cervical cancer screening

Figures for the two cancer screening programmes are snapshots of the coverage of the target population for each programme at 31 March in each year presented. The target population for breast screening services is 50 to 64 years of age, but the target population for cervical screening is different in each country. In England the target population for cervical screening is 25-64 years, in Wales it is 20-64, in Scotland it is 20-60 and in Northern Ireland it is 20-64.

Data for women who do not require screening, for example as a result of surgery, are not included. Northern Ireland data refer to the percentage of women aged between 20 and 64 years who received at least one adequate cervical smear test in the five years up to 31st March 2006. As such they may include a small number of women who have been counted more than once due to early recall for screening. England data refer to percentage of women screened for cervical breast cancer up to 10 August 2006.

Figures for breast screening are provided for the target population of 50- to 64-year-olds. Figures for England and Wales are based on software that provides the eligibility and screening status of the current registered population, woman by woman. Breast screening figures for Northern Ireland are based on the percentage of invited women screened, while those for Scotland are estimates based on numbers screened and mid-year population estimates. Figures for England and Wales are therefore not directly comparable with those for Scotland and Northern Ireland, and this may be visible in the figures.

Use of services

This chapter contains figures about use of health and social services, including hospital in-patient activity, waiting times, prescriptions dispensed, and children on child protection registers. The information included has been substantially expanded since the second edition of UK Health Statistics, following collaborative efforts by the health departments of the four countries to produce comparable figures on hospital admissions, waiting times and lengths of stay.

A number of important differences between the countries remain in the way that data for the measures presented here are collected and classified, and these issues are referred to in the text or footnotes where appropriate. For this reason, all cross-UK comparisons should be treated with caution, and because of differences between countries in the organisation of health and social services.

Hospital activity: overview

In 2005-06, Scotland had the highest rate of daily available beds at 5.4 beds per 1,000 population (Table 6.1). Wales and Northern Ireland both had 4.7 daily available beds per 1,000 population, while England had the lowest rate at 3.8 per 1,000 population. Northern Ireland had the most in-patient admissions per head, with 205 admissions per 1,000 population, while Scotland had the lowest admission rate at 135 per 1,000 population. The average length of an in-patient stay ranged from 7.4 days in Scotland to 5.6 days in Northern Ireland.

These figures are not directly comparable because of different inclusions and exclusions in each of the countries. Bed numbers and throughput in Scotland may be affected by the inclusion in the Scottish figures of specialties providing longer-term care.

In England, there were 52,695,400 out-patient attendances in 2006-07, of which 88.8 per cent were in acute specialties (Table 6.2). Non-attendance was 10.3 per cent of appointments. Northern Ireland had the highest proportion of non-attendances at 11.4 per cent of appointments, and Wales had the lowest proportion at 7.3 per cent of appointments. In all countries, non-attendance was highest for mental illness appointments, ranging from 26.1 per cent in England to 17.3 per cent in Scotland.

Hospital activity: by diagnosis

Table 6.3a gives numbers of in-patient discharges (completed stays, including deaths in hospital) and rates per 100,000 population in 2005, broken down by chapter of the International Classification of Diseases (ICD-10). Table 6.3b gives a more detailed breakdown of the same data into specific diagnostic categories.

In the UK as a whole, the highest rate of hospital discharges was for patients classified as having 'symptoms, signs and abnormal clinical and laboratory findings' at 1,660.1 per 100,000 population. This category includes patients discharged without a specific medical diagnosis, for example those with unexplained abnormal test results, or non-specific symptoms such as pain or fever of unknown origin. Scotland had the highest discharge rate for neoplasms (cancers) at 1,327.9 per

Table 6.1

Hospital inpatient and day case activity, 2005/06[1]

United Kingdom

Rates, days, thousands

	Inpatients (all specialities)					
	Average daily available beds [2] per 1,000 population	Admissions [3] per available bed	Admissions [3] per 1,000 population	Hospital stays [4] (000's)	Average length of stay [3] (days)	Day cases [5] (000's)
England	3.8	43	160	9,887	6.8	4,113
Wales [6]	4.7	36	170	502	6.9	111
Scotland	5.4	25	135	688	7.4	379
Northern Ireland	4.7	44	205	354	5.6	159

1 Data for Northern Ireland is 2006 calendar period.
2 Excludes cots for healthy newborn babies except in Northern Ireland.
3 Admissions and length of stay excludes day cases. In Wales length of stay relates to acute specialities only. In Northern Ireland length of stay excludes mental illness/psychiatry specialities.
4 Finished consultant episodes in England; discharges and deaths in Wales; discharges, deaths and transfers in Scotland and Northern Ireland. Healthy newborn babies are included in Northern Ireland only.
5 Numbers of day cases are not directly comparable because of differences in recording for statistical purposes.
6 Patients treated in Wales, wherever resident.

Source: NHS Information Centre for Health and Social Care; Welsh Assembly Government; Information Services Division, NHS in Scotland; Department of Health, Social Services and Public Safety, Northern Ireland.

Table 6.2

Hospital outpatient activity, outpatient attendances: by sector, 2006-07

United Kingdom   Thousands, percentages

	England			Wales [1]			Scotland			Northern Ireland [1]		
	Total (000's)	Percentage within each speciality	Percentage did not attend	Total (000's)	Percentage within each speciality	Percentage did not attend	Total (000's)	Percentage within each speciality	Percentage did not attend	Total (000's)	Percentage within each speciality	Percentage did not attend
All specialties	52,695.4	100.0	10.3	2,932.8	100.0	7.3	4,484.7	100.0	10.1	1,523.7	100.0	11.4
Acute	46,794.9	88.8	10.0	2,570.5	87.6	9.6	3,881.5	86.5	10.1	1,273.2	83.6	11.5
Maternity	4,144.4	7.9	10.6	127.4	4.3	7.5	180.7	4.0	5.1	111.9	7.3	3.7
Mental illness	898.8	1.7	26.1	115.9	4.0	18.6	368.6	8.2	17.3	98.2	6.4	19.0
Learning disability	65.0	0.1	12.4	4.5	0.2	7.8	17.7	0.4	11.0	5.1	0.3	12.0
Geriatric	440.1	0.8	12.2	30.9	1.1	9.6	36.26	0.8	7.3	21.7	1.4	9.2
Other [2]	351.9	0.7	6.9	83.5	2.8	4.3				13.5	0.9	8.8

1   Patients treated in Wales and Northern Ireland, wherever resident.
2   Other for England, Wales and Northern Ireland is 'old age psychiatry'. Wales also includes 'community medicine' and 'pathology'.

Source: Department of Health; Welsh Assembly Government; Information Services Division, NHS in Scotland; Department of Health, Social Services and Public Safety, Northern Ireland

100,000 population, including the highest rate for lung cancer at 178.7 per 100,000. Northern Ireland had the highest discharge rate for diseases of the circulatory system at 1,556.6 per 100,000, while England had the lowest rate.

Wales had the highest rate of discharges for mental and behavioural disorders and diseases of the nervous system, possibly reflecting differences in the inclusion in the figures of services for people with dementia. Differences in the rates discharges relating to pregnancy and childbirth are also likely to relate to different service patterns and inclusions in the reported figures.

Table 6.4a gives the average length of completed in-patient stay in 2005, broken down by chapter of the International Classification of Diseases (ICD-10). Table 6.4b gives a more detailed breakdown of the same data into specific diagnostic categories.

The broad diagnostic category leading to the highest average length of hospital stay in England, Wales and Scotland was mental and behavioural disorders. Within this category, the average length of stay for individuals being treated for schizophrenia, schizotypal and delusional disorders was 110.2 days in England and 79.7 days in Wales. However, in Scotland and Northern Ireland, schizophrenia, schizotypal and delusional disorders accounted for an average hospital stay of only 5.4 and 5.8 days respectively. This large difference is likely to reflect different patterns of service provision and the inclusion/exclusion of certain specialties from the available figures.

In Scotland, individuals being treated for dementia had the highest average length of stay with 47.1 days. In Northern Ireland, individuals treated for Alzheimer's disease had the highest average length of stay in hospital at 54.0 days.

6

Table 6.3 (a)

Discharge numbers and rates: by ICD-10 chapter, 2005[1]

United Kingdom

Numbers

ICD-10		United Kingdom	England	Wales	Scotland	Northern Ireland
A00-B99	Certain infectious and parasitic diseases	125,760	100,807	7,478	13,071	4,404
C00-D48	Neoplasms	589,909	476,335	29,711	67,652	16,211
D50-D89	Diseases of the blood and bloodforming organs and certain disorders involving the immune mechanism	71,224	58,447	3,578	7,054	2,145
E00-E99	Endocrine, nutritional and metabolic diseases	108,681	88,143	6,414	10,256	3,868
F00-F99	Mental and behavioural disorders	189,234	166,728	12,453	7,732	2,321
G00-G99	Diseases of the nervous system	168,201	136,642	10,134	17,011	4,414
H00-H59	Diseases of the eye and adnexa	62,623	50,446	2,616	7,491	2,070
H60-H95	Diseases of the ear and mastoid process	36,290	29,109	2,591	3,547	1,043
I00-I99	Diseases of the circulatory system	802,637	658,396	43,677	73,722	26,842
J00-J99	Diseases of the respiratory system	699,563	564,803	41,854	67,594	25,312
K00-K93	Diseases of the digestive system	695,685	554,263	40,049	77,465	23,908
L00-L99	Diseases of the skin and subcutanous tissue	148,479	119,461	8,565	16,455	3,998
M00-M99	Diseases of the musculoskeletal system and connective tissue	450,780	376,193	24,266	41,439	8,882
N00-N99	Diseases of the genitourinary system	478,702	379,343	25,450	44,285	29,624
O00-O99	Pregnancy, childbirth and the puerperium	812,868	736,071	41,235	6,401	29,161
P00-P96	Certain conditions originating in the perinatal period	154,481	145,810	3,599	713	4,359
Q00-Q99	Congenital malformations, deformations and chromosomal abnormalities	67,128	58,453	2,267	4,452	1,956
R00-R99	Symptoms, signs and abnormal clinical and laboratory findings, not elsewhere classified	999,522	812,464	48,367	112,263	26,428
S00-T98	Injury, poisoning and certain other consequences of external causes	734,501	585,863	41,469	84,178	22,991
Z00-Z99	Factors influencing health status and contract with health services [2]	546,618	509,872	8,911	22,722	5,113
A00-Z99	All causes	7,942,886	6,607,649	404,684	685,503	245,050

1 Discharges following admission for an overnight hospital stay. For Wales and Northern Ireland these figures do not include any patients who were admitted and discharged on the same day.
2 In Wales data on well babies are not held, therefore this does not include liveborn infants.

Source: *The Information Centre for Health and Social Care; Information Services Division, NHS in Scotland; Health Solutions Wales; Department of Health, Social Services and Public Safety, Northern Ireland.*

Rates per 100,000 population

United Kingdom	England	Wales	Scotland	Northern Ireland		ICD-10
208.9	199.9	252.8	256.6	255.4	Certain infectious and parasitic diseases	A00-B99
979.8	944.5	1004.2	1327.9	940.1	Neoplasms	C00-D48
118.3	115.9	120.9	138.5	124.4	Diseases of the blood and bloodforming organs and certain disorders involving the immune mechanism	D50-D89
180.5	174.8	216.8	201.3	224.3	Endocrine, nutritional and metabolic diseases	E00-E99
314.3	330.6	420.9	151.8	134.6	Mental and behavioural disorders	F00-F99
279.4	270.9	342.5	333.9	256.0	Diseases of the nervous system	G00-G99
104.0	100.0	88.4	147.0	120.0	Diseases of the eye and adnexa	H00-H59
60.3	57.7	87.6	69.6	60.5	Diseases of the ear and mastoid process	H60-H95
1333.1	1305.5	1476.3	1447.0	1556.6	Diseases of the circulatory system	I00-I99
1161.9	1119.9	1414.7	1326.7	1467.9	Diseases of the respiratory system	J00-J99
1155.4	1099.0	1353.6	1520.5	1386.5	Diseases of the digestive system	K00-K93
246.6	236.9	289.5	323.0	231.8	Diseases of the skin and subcutanous tissue	L00-L99
748.7	745.9	820.2	813.4	515.1	Diseases of the musculoskeletal system and connective tissue	M00-M99
795.1	752.2	860.2	869.2	1717.9	Diseases of the genitourinary system	N00-N99
1350.1	1459.5	1393.7	125.6	1691.1	Pregnancy, childbirth and the puerperium	O00-O99
256.6	289.1	121.6	14.0	252.8	Certain conditions originating in the perinatal period	P00-P96
111.5	115.9	76.6	87.4	113.4	Congenital malformations, deformations and chromosomal abnormalities	Q00-Q99
1660.1	1611.0	1634.8	2203.5	1532.6	Symptoms, signs and abnormal clinical and laboratory findings, not elsewhere classified	R00-R99
1219.9	1161.7	1401.6	1652.2	1333.3	Injury, poisoning and certain other consequences of external causes	S00-T98
907.9	1011.0	301.2	446.0	296.5	Factors influencing health status and contract with health services [2]	Z00-Z99
13192.1	13102.2	13678.2	13455.0	14210.7	All causes	A00-Z99

6

Table 6.3 (b)

Discharge numbers and rates: by diagnostic categories,[1] 2005

United Kingdom

Numbers

ICD-10		United Kingdom	England	Wales	Scotland	Northern Ireland
A00-B99	**Certain infectious and parasitic diseases**	**125,760**	**100,807**	**7,478**	**13,071**	**4,404**
A00-A08	Intestinal infectious diseases except diarrhoea	31,027	24,109	2,094	3,610	1,214
A09	Diarrhoea, gastroenteritis of preseumed infectious origin	6,664	5,323	274	886	181
A15-A19, B90	Tuberculosis	4,423	3,952	124	291	56
A40-A41	Septicaemia	22,592	18,836	1,258	1,929	569
B20-B24	Human immunodeficiency virus (HIV) disease	3,167	2,832	:	329	6
Remainder of A00-B99	Other infectious parasitic diseases	57,860	45,755	3,701	6,026	2,378
C00-D48	**Neoplasms**	**589,909**	**476,335**	**29,711**	**67,652**	**16,211**
C18-C21	Malignant neoplasm of colon, rectum and anus	55,113	43,491	2,873	7,311	1,438
C33-C34	Malignant neoplasm of trachea, bronchus and lung	49,006	35,867	2,390	9,105	1,644
C43-C44	Malignant neoplasm of skin	15,306	11,709	1,037	2,146	414
C50	Malignant neoplasm of breast	52,983	43,193	2,604	5,699	1,487
C53-C55	Malignant neoplasm of uterus	15,920	12,623	851	1,779	667
C56	Malignant neoplasm of ovary	13,358	10,479	584	1,914	381
C61	Malignant neoplasm of prostate	24,291	20,097	1,389	2,232	573
C67	Malignant neoplasm of bladder	40,141	34,205	2,079	2,960	897
Remainder of C00-C97	Other malignant neoplasms	234,114	190,727	11,429	25,373	6,585
D00-D09	Carcinoma in situ	10,069	8,279	608	934	248
D12	Bening neoplasm of colon, rectum and anus	6,085	4,812	303	815	155
D25	Leiomyoma of uterus	19,550	16,986	990	1,150	424
Remainder of D00-D48	Other benign neoplasms and neoplasms of uncertain or unknown behaviour	53,973	43,867	2,574	6,234	1,298
D50-D89	**Diseases of the blood and bloodforming organs and certain disorders involving the immune mechanism**	**71,224**	**58,447**	**3,578**	**7,054**	**2,145**
D50-D64	Anaemias	195,914	41,464	2,461	5,010	1,561
D65-D89	Other diseases of the blood and bloodforming organs and certain disorders involving the immune mechanism	20,728	16,983	1,117	2,044	584
E00-E90	Endocrine, nutritional and metabolic diseases	108,681	88,143	6,414	10,256	3,868
E10-E14	Diabetes mellitus	44,427	35,389	2,942	4,449	1,647
Remainder of E00-E90	Other endocrine, nutritional and metabolic diseases	64,254	52,754	3,472	5,807	2,221
F00-F99	**Mental and behavioural disorders**	**189,234**	**166,728**	**12,453**	**7,732**	**2,321**
F00-F03	Dementia	24,366	20,525	2,400	1,156	285
F10	Mental and behavioural disorders due to alcohol	37,337	29,259	1,971	4,602	1,505
F11-F19	Mental and behavioural disorders due to use of other psychoactive subst.	8,042	7,420	418	161	43
F20-F29	Schizophrenia, schizotypal and delusional disorders	33,183	30,561	2,470	110	42
F30-F39	Mood [affective] disorders	40,455	36,980	3,004	355	116
Remainder of F00-F99	Other mental and behavioural disorders	45,851	41,983	2,190	1,348	330
G00-G99	**Diseases of the nervous system**	**168,201**	**136,642**	**10,134**	**17,011**	**4,414**

Rates per 100,000 population

United Kingdom	England	Wales	Scotland	Northern Ireland		ICD-10
208.9	**199.9**	**252.8**	**256.6**	**255.4**	**Certain infectious and parasitic diseases**	**A00-B99**
51.5	47.8	70.8	70.9	70.4	Intestinal infectious diseases except diarrhoea	A00-A08
11.1	10.6	9.3	17.4	10.5	Diarrhoea, gastroenteritis of preseumed infectious origin	A09
7.3	7.8	4.2	5.7	3.2	Tuberculosis	A15-A19, B90
37.5	37.3	42.5	37.9	33.0	Septicaemia	A40-A41
5.3	5.6	:	6.5	0.3	Human immunodeficiency virus (HIV) disease	B20-B24
96.1	90.7	125.1	118.3	137.9	Other infectious parasitic diseases	Remainder of A00-B99
979.8	**944.5**	**1004.2**	**1327.9**	**940.1**	**Neoplasms**	**C00-D48**
91.5	86.2	97.1	143.5	83.4	Malignant neoplasm of colon, rectum and anus	C18-C21
81.4	71.1	80.8	178.7	95.3	Malignant neoplasm of trachea, bronchus and lung	C33-C34
25.4	23.2	35.1	42.1	24.0	Malignant neoplasm of skin	C43-C44
88.0	85.6	88.0	111.9	86.2	Malignant neoplasm of breast	C50
26.4	25.0	28.8	34.9	38.7	Malignant neoplasm of uterus	C53-C55
22.2	20.8	19.7	37.6	22.1	Malignant neoplasm of ovary	C56
40.3	39.8	46.9	43.8	33.2	Malignant neoplasm of prostate	C61
66.7	67.8	70.3	58.1	52.0	Malignant neoplasm of bladder	C67
388.8	378.2	386.3	498.0	381.9	Other malignant neoplasms	Remainder of C00-C97
16.7	16.4	20.6	18.3	14.4	Carcinoma in situ	D00-D09
10.1	9.5	10.2	16.0	9.0	Bening neoplasm of colon, rectum and anus	D12
32.5	33.7	33.5	22.6	24.6	Leiomyoma of uterus	D25
89.6	87.0	87.0	122.4	75.3	Other benign neoplasms and neoplasms of uncertain or unknown behaviour	Remainder of D00-D48
118.3	**115.9**	**120.9**	**138.5**	**124.4**	**Diseases of the blood and bloodforming organs and certain disorders involving the immune mechanism**	**D50-D89**
325.4	82.2	83.2	98.3	90.5	Anaemias	D50-D64
34.4	33.7	37.8	40.1	33.9	Other diseases of the blood and bloodforming organs and certain disorders involving the immune mechanism	D65-D89
180.5	174.8	216.8	201.3	224.3	Endocrine, nutritional and metabolic diseases	E00-E90
73.8	70.2	99.4	87.3	95.5	Diabetes mellitus	E10-E14
106.7	104.6	117.4	114.0	128.8	Other endocrine, nutritional and metabolic diseases	Remainder of E00-E90
314.3	**330.6**	**420.9**	**151.8**	**134.6**	**Mental and behavioural disorders**	**F00-F99**
40.5	40.7	81.1	22.7	16.5	Dementia	F00-F03
62.0	58.0	66.6	90.3	87.3	Mental and behavioural disorders due to alcohol	F10
13.4	14.7	14.1	3.2	2.5	Mental and behavioural disorders due to use of other psychoactive subst.	F11-F19
55.1	60.6	83.5	2.2	2.4	Schizophrenia, schizotypal and delusional disorders	F20-F29
67.2	73.3	101.5	7.0	6.7	Mood [affective] disorders	F30-F39
76.2	83.2	74.0	26.5	19.1	Other mental and behavioural disorders	Remainder of F00-F99
279.4	**270.9**	**342.5**	**333.9**	**256.0**	**Diseases of the nervous system**	**G00-G99**

Table 6.3 (b) – continued

Discharge numbers and rates: by diagnostic categories,[1] 2005

United Kingdom

Numbers

ICD-10		United Kingdom	England	Wales	Scotland	Northern Ireland
G30	Alzheimer's disease	8,066	6,482	1,236	243	105
G35	Multiple sclerosis	9,317	7,266	379	1,522	150
G40-G41	Epilepsy	39,778	32,247	2,231	4,069	1,231
G45	Transient cerebral ischaemic attacks and related syndromes	19,624	15,392	1,455	2,010	767
Remainder of G00-G99	Others diseases of the nervous system	91,416	75,255	4,833	9,167	2,161
H00-H59	**Diseases of the eye and adnexa**	**62,623**	**50,446**	**2,616**	**7,491**	**2,070**
H25-H26. H28	Cataract	17,042	12,446	749	2,917	930
Remainder of H00-H59	Other diseases of the eye and adnexa	45,581	38,000	1,867	4,574	1,140
H60-H95	**Diseases of the ear and mastoid process**	**36,290**	**29,109**	**2,591**	**3,547**	**1,043**
I00-I99	**Diseases of the circulatory system**	**802,637**	**658,396**	**43,677**	**73,722**	**26,842**
I10-I15	Hypertensive diseases	16,249	13,737	940	1,196	376
I20	Angina pectoris	92,114	75,527	4,915	8,452	3,220
I21-I22	Acute myocardial infarction	98,791	81,100	5,381	8,454	3,856
I23-I25	Other ischaemic heart disease	98,197	81,562	4,098	8,739	3,798
I26-I28	Other ischaemic heart disease & diseases of pulmonary circulation	22,276	18,749	1,088	1,991	448
I44-I49	Conduction disorders and cardiac arrythmias	109,571	90,358	5,780	9,778	3,655
I50	Heart failures	78,427	63,896	4,917	6,612	3,002
I60-I69	Cerebrovascular diseases	124,540	103,155	7,248	10,862	3,275
I70	Atherosclerosis	7,637	6,448	545	615	29
I83	Varicose veins of lower extremities	19,741	14,685	1,474	2,657	925
Remainder of I00-I99	Other diseases of the circulatory system	135,094	109,179	7,291	14,366	4,258
J00-J99	**Diseases of the respiratory system**	**699,563**	**564,803**	**41,854**	**67,594**	**25,312**
J00-J11	Acute upper respiratory infections and influenza	69,890	51,788	4,799	10,955	2,348
J12-J18	Pneumonia	134,411	112,310	7,634	11,077	3,390
J20-J22	Other acute lower respiratory infections	117,742	94,079	6,961	11,568	5,134
J35	Chronic diseases of tonsils and adenoids	44,428	36,961	2,772	1,377	3,318
J30-J34, J36-J39	Other diseases of upper respiratory tract	60,246	48,339	3,625	6,092	2,190
J40-J44, J47	Chronic obstructive pulmonary disease and bronchiectasis	143,648	115,143	9,349	14,157	4,999
J45-J46	Asthma	64,475	52,830	3,425	6,319	1,901
J60-J99	Other diseases of the respiratory system	64,723	53,353	3,289	6,049	2,032
K00-K93	**Diseases of the digestive system**	**695,685**	**554,263**	**40,049**	**77,465**	**23,908**
K00-K08	Disorders of teeth and supporting structures	20,865	14,799	1,191	4,255	620
K09-K14	Other diseases of oral cavity, salivary glands and jaws	10,889	8,803	625	1,160	301
K20-K23	Diseases of oesophagus	34,087	26,603	1,835	4,429	1,220
K25-K28	Peptic ulcer	20,810	16,989	1,102	2,067	652

Rates per 100,000 population

United Kingdom	England	Wales	Scotland	Northern Ireland		ICD-10
13.4	12.9	41.8	4.8	6.1	Alzheimer's disease	G30
15.5	14.4	12.8	29.9	8.7	Multiple sclerosis	G35
66.1	63.9	75.4	79.9	71.4	Epilepsy	G40-G41
32.6	30.5	49.2	39.5	44.5	Transient cerebral ischaemic attacks and related syndromes	G45
151.8	149.2	163.4	179.9	125.3	Others diseases of the nervous system	Remainder of G00-G99
104.0	**100.0**	**88.4**	**147.0**	**120.0**	**Diseases of the eye and adnexa**	**H00-H59**
28.3	24.7	25.3	57.3	53.9	Cataract	H25-H26. H28
75.7	75.3	63.1	89.8	66.1	Other diseases of the eye and adnexa	Remainder of H00-H59
60.3	**57.7**	**87.6**	**69.6**	**60.5**	**Diseases of the ear and mastoid process**	**H60-H95**
1333.1	**1305.5**	**1476.3**	**1447.0**	**1556.6**	**Diseases of the circulatory system**	**I00-I99**
27.0	27.2	31.8	23.5	21.8	Hypertensive diseases	I10-I15
153.0	149.8	166.1	165.9	186.7	Angina pectoris	I20
164.1	160.8	181.9	165.9	223.6	Acute myocardial infarction	I21-I22
163.1	161.7	138.5	171.5	220.3	Other ischaemic heart disease	I23-I25
37.0	37.2	36.8	39.1	26.0	Other ischaemic heart disease & diseases of pulmonary circulation	I26-I28
182.0	179.2	195.4	191.9	212.0	Conduction disorders and cardiac arrythmias	I44-I49
130.3	126.7	166.2	129.8	174.1	Heart failures	I50
206.8	204.5	245.0	213.2	189.9	Cerebrovascular diseases	I60-I69
12.7	12.8	18.4	12.1	1.7	Atherosclerosis	I70
32.8	29.1	49.8	52.2	53.6	Varicose veins of lower extremities	I83
224.4	216.5	246.4	282.0	246.9	Other diseases of the circulatory system	Remainder of I00-I99
1161.9	**1119.9**	**1414.7**	**1326.7**	**1467.9**	**Diseases of the respiratory system**	**J00-J99**
116.1	102.7	162.2	215.0	136.2	Acute upper respiratory infections and influenza	J00-J11
223.2	222.7	258.0	217.4	196.6	Pneumonia	J12-J18
195.6	186.5	235.3	227.1	297.7	Other acute lower respiratory infections	J20-J22
73.8	73.3	93.7	27.0	192.4	Chronic diseases of tonsils and adenoids	J35
100.1	95.9	122.5	119.6	127.0	Other diseases of upper respiratory tract	J30-J34, J36-J39
238.6	228.3	316.0	277.9	289.9	Chronic obstructive pulmonary disease and bronchiectasis	J40-J44, J47
107.1	104.8	115.8	124.0	110.2	Asthma	J45-J46
107.5	105.8	111.2	118.7	117.8	Other diseases of the respiratory system	J60-J99
1155.4	**1099.0**	**1353.6**	**1520.5**	**1386.5**	**Diseases of the digestive system**	**K00-K93**
34.7	29.3	40.3	83.5	36.0	Disorders of teeth and supporting structures	K00-K08
18.1	17.5	21.1	22.8	17.5	Other diseases of oral cavity, salivary glands and jaws	K09-K14
56.6	52.8	62.0	86.9	70.7	Diseases of oesophagus	K20-K23
34.6	33.7	37.2	40.6	37.8	Peptic ulcer	K25-K28

6

Table 6.3 (b) – continued

Discharge numbers and rates: by diagnostic categories,[1] 2005

United Kingdom

Numbers

ICD-10		United Kingdom	England	Wales	Scotland	Northern Ireland
K29-K31	Dyspepsia and other diseases of stomach and duodenum	26,300	19,352	1,568	3,951	1,429
K35-K38	Diseases of appendix	45,960	38,585	2,294	3,373	1,708
K40	Inguinal hernia	47,282	37,923	2,796	5,229	1,334
K41-K46	Other adbominal hernia	34,404	28,114	2,046	3,248	996
K50-K51	Crohn's disease and ulcerative colitis	22,976	18,322	1,093	2,699	862
K52	Othe noninfective gastroentiritis and colitis	58,118	47,096	3,520	5,593	1,909
K56	Paralytic ileus and intestinal obstruction without hernia	23,183	19,261	1,207	1,949	766
K57	Divertcular disease of intestine	29,422	22,861	1,959	3,474	1,128
K60-K62	Diseases of anus and rectum	48,975	39,811	2,213	5,433	1,518
K55,K58-K59, K63	Other diseases of intestine	49,809	38,859	3,259	6,001	1,690
K70	Alcoholic liver disease	16,439	12,754	913	2,239	533
K71-K77	Other disease of liver	11,104	8,993	525	1,227	359
K80	Cholelithiasis	91,484	72,878	5,449	9,714	3,443
K81-K83	Other diseases of gall bladder and biliary tract	26,767	20,643	2,133	2,913	1,078
K85-K87	Disease of pancreas	28,442	22,792	1,454	3,162	1,034
Remainder of K00-K93	Other diseases of the digestive system	48,369	38,825	2,867	5,349	1,328
L00-L99	**Diseases of the skin and subcutanous tissue**	**148,479**	**119,461**	**8,565**	**16,455**	**3,998**
L00-L08	Infections of the skin and subcutaneous tissue	98,776	80,899	5,219	10,351	2,307
L20-L45	Dermatitis, eczema and papulosquamous disorders	12,200	8,555	926	1,857	862
Remainder of L00-L99	Other dieases of the skin and subcutaneous tissue	37,503	30,007	2,420	4,247	829
M00-M99	**Diseases of the musculoskeletal system and connective tissue**	**450,780**	**376,193**	**24,266**	**41,439**	**8,882**
M16	Coxarthrosis [arthrosis of hip]	56,935	47,407	3,219	5,074	1,235
M17	Gonathrosis [arthrosis of knee]	74,289	63,567	4,439	5,415	868
M23	Internal derangement of knee	19,001	16,263	993	1,408	337
M00-M15, M18-M22, M24-M25	Other arthropathies	111,958	93,225	5,944	10,198	2,591
M30-M36	Systemic connective tissue disorders	8,416	6,718	380	998	320
M40-M49	Deforming dorsopathies and spondylopathies	18,864	16,455	846	1,300	263
M50-M51	Intervertrebal disc disorders	22,510	19,132	1,193	1,817	368
M54	Dorsalgia	34,678	28,321	2,032	3,484	841
M60-M79	Soft tissue disorders	70,608	57,483	3,435	8,586	1,104
M53, M80-M99	Other disorders of the musculoskeletal system and connective tissue	33,521	27,622	1,785	3,159	955
N00-N99	**Diseases of the genitourinary system**	**478,702**	**379,343**	**25,450**	**44,285**	**29,624**
N00-N16	Glomerular and renal tubulo-interstitial diseases	29,130	24,800	1,306	2,347	677
N17-N19	Renal failure [2]	57,086	33,445	1,841	4,967	16,833
N20-N23	Urolithiasis	43,623	35,498	2,208	4,433	1,484
N25-N39	Other dieases of the urinary system	144,100	118,847	7,993	13,062	4,198

Rates per 100,000 population

United Kingdom	England	Wales	Scotland	Northern Ireland		ICD-10
43.7	38.4	53.0	77.5	82.9	Dyspepsia and other diseases of stomach and duodenum	K29-K31
76.3	76.5	77.5	66.2	99.0	Diseases of appendix	K35-K38
78.5	75.2	94.5	102.6	77.4	Inguinal hernia	K40
57.1	55.7	69.2	63.8	57.8	Other adbominal hernia	K41-K46
38.2	36.3	36.9	53.0	50.0	Crohn's disease and ulcerative colitis	K50-K51
96.5	93.4	119.0	109.8	110.7	Othe noninfective gastroentiritis and colitis	K52
38.5	38.2	40.8	38.3	44.4	Paralytic ileus and intestinal obstruction without hernia	K56
48.9	45.3	66.2	68.2	65.4	Divertcular disease of intestine	K57
81.3	78.9	74.8	106.6	88.0	Diseases of anus and rectum	K60-K62
82.7	77.1	110.2	117.8	98.0	Other diseases of intestine	K55,K58-K59, K63
27.3	25.3	30.9	43.9	30.9	Alcoholic liver disease	K70
18.4	17.8	17.7	24.1	20.8	Other disease of liver	K71-K77
151.9	144.5	184.2	190.7	199.7	Cholelithiasis	K80
44.5	40.9	72.1	57.2	62.5	Other diseases of gall bladder and biliary tract	K81-K83
47.2	45.2	49.1	62.1	60.0	Disease of pancreas	K85-K87
80.3	77.0	96.9	105.0	77.0	Other diseases of the digestive system	Remainder of K00-K93
246.6	**236.9**	**289.5**	**323.0**	**231.8**	**Diseases of the skin and subcutanous tissue**	**L00-L99**
164.1	160.4	176.4	203.2	133.8	Infections of the skin and subcutaneous tissue	L00-L08
20.3	17.0	31.3	36.4	50.0	Dermatitis, eczema and papulosquamous disorders	L20-L45
62.3	59.5	81.8	83.4	48.1	Other dieases of the skin and subcutaneous tissue	Remainder of L00-L99
748.7	**745.9**	**820.2**	**813.4**	**515.1**	**Diseases of the musculoskeletal system and connective tissue**	**M00-M99**
94.6	94.0	108.8	99.6	71.6	Coxarthrosis [arthrosis of hip]	M16
123.4	126.0	150.0	106.3	50.3	Gonathrosis [arthrosis of knee]	M17
31.6	32.2	33.6	27.6	19.5	Internal derangement of knee	M23
185.9	184.9	200.9	200.2	150.3	Other arthropathies	M00-M15, M18-M22, M24-M25
14.0	13.3	12.8	19.6	18.6	Systemic connective tissue disorders	M30-M36
31.3	32.6	28.6	25.5	15.3	Deforming dorsopathies and spondylopathies	M40-M49
37.4	37.9	40.3	35.7	21.3	Intervertrebal disc disorders	M50-M51
57.6	56.2	68.7	68.4	48.8	Dorsalgia	M54
117.3	114.0	116.1	168.5	64.0	Soft tissue disorders	M60-M79
55.7	54.8	60.3	62.0	55.4	Other disorders of the musculoskeletal system and connective tissue	M53, M80-M99
795.1	**752.2**	**860.2**	**869.2**	**1717.9**	**Diseases of the genitourinary system**	**N00-N99**
48.4	49.2	44.1	46.1	39.3	Glomerular and renal tubulo-interstitial diseases	N00-N16
94.8	66.3	62.2	97.5	976.2	Renal failure [2]	N17-N19
72.5	70.4	74.6	87.0	86.1	Urolithiasis	N20-N23
239.3	235.7	270.2	256.4	243.4	Other dieases of the urinary system	N25-N39

Table 6.3 (b) – continued

Discharge numbers and rates: by diagnostic categories,[1] 2005

United Kingdom

Numbers

ICD-10		United Kingdom	England	Wales	Scotland	Northern Ireland
N40	Hyperplasia of prostate	24,888	20,897	1,615	1,835	541
N41-N51	Other diseases of male genital organs	30,862	24,269	1,947	3,784	862
N60-N64	Disorders of breast	14,100	11,763	693	1,358	286
N70-N77	Inflammatory diseases of female pelvic organs	16,423	13,584	977	1,460	402
N91-N95	Menstrual, menopausal and other female genital conditions	39,634	31,244	2,441	4,362	1,587
Remainder of N00-N99	Other disorders of the genitourinary system	78,856	64,996	4,429	6,677	2,754
O00-O99	**Pregnancy, childbirth and the puerperium** [2]	**812,868**	**736,071**	**41,235**	**6,401**	**29,161**
O04	Medical abortion [3]	12,139	8,708	973	2,395	63
O00-O03, O05-O08	Other pregnancy with abortive outcome [3]	46,373	39,246	2,711	2,846	1,570
O10-O48	Complications of pregnancy predominantly in the antenatal period [3]	306,890	278,769	16,572	1,049	10,500
O60-O75	Complications of pregnancy predominantly during labour and delivery [3]	322,896	296,193	15,388	59	11,256
O80	Single spontaneous delivery [3]	77,913	70,337	3,815	0	3,761
O81-O84	Other delivery [3]	16,559	14,830	653	0	1,076
O85-O92	Complications predominantly related to the puerperium [3]	6,392	5,768	335	40	249
O95-O99	Other obstetric conditions [3]	23,706	22,220	788	12	686
P00-P96	**Certain conditions originating in the perinatal period**	**154,481**	**145,810**	**3,599**	**713**	**4,359**
P07	Disorders relating to short gestation and low birth weight	37,140	35,128	982	8	1,022
Remainder of P00-P96	Other conditions originating in the perinatal period	117,341	110,682	2,617	705	3,337
Q00-Q99	**Congenital malformations, deformations and chromosomal abnormalities**	**67,128**	**58,453**	**2,267**	**4,452**	**1,956**
R00-R99	**Symptoms, signs and abnormal clinical and laboratory findings, not elsewhere classified**	**999,522**	**812,464**	**48,367**	**112,263**	**26,428**
R07	Pain in throat and chest	183,599	141,403	10,051	26,391	5,754
R10	Abdominal and pelvic pain	181,493	143,226	10,653	21,843	5,771
R69	Unknown and unspecified causes of morbidity (incl. those without diagnoses)	129,059	128,955	4	100	0
Remainder of R00-R99	Other symptoms, signs and abnormal clinical and laboratory findings	505,371	398,880	27,659	63,929	14,903
S00-T98	**Injury, poisoning and certain other consequences of external causes**	**734,501**	**585,863**	**41,469**	**84,178**	**22,991**
S06	Intracranial injury	12,136	10,304	534	903	395
S00-S05, S07-S09	Other injuries to the head	96,041	71,345	4,690	16,477	3,529
S52	Fracture of forearm	57,051	46,391	3,349	5,893	1,418
S72	Fracture of femur	88,027	72,222	5,527	6,820	3,458
S82	Fracture of lower leg, including ankle	54,461	44,564	3,341	4,980	1,576

Rates per 100,000 population

United Kingdom	England	Wales	Scotland	Northern Ireland		ICD-10
41.3	41.4	54.6	36.0	31.4	Hyperplasia of prostate	N40
51.3	48.1	65.8	74.3	50.0	Other diseases of male genital organs	N41-N51
23.4	23.3	23.4	26.7	16.6	Disorders of breast	N60-N64
27.3	26.9	33.0	28.7	23.3	Inflammatory diseases of female pelvic organs	N70-N77
65.8	62.0	82.5	85.6	92.0	Menstrual, menopausal and other female genital conditions	N91-N95
131.0	128.9	149.7	131.1	159.7	Other disorders of the genitourinary system	Remainder of N00-N99
1350.1	**1459.5**	**1393.7**	**125.6**	**1691.1**	**Pregnancy, childbirth and the puerperium** [2]	**O00-O99**
20.2	17.3	32.9	47.0	3.7	Medical abortion [3]	O04
77.0	77.8	91.6	55.9	91.0	Other pregnancy with abortive outcome [3]	O00-O03, O05-O08
509.7	552.8	560.1	20.6	608.9	Complications of pregnancy predominantly in the antenatal period [3]	O10-O48
536.3	587.3	520.1	1.2	652.7	Complications of pregnancy predominantly during labour and delivery [3]	O60-O75
129.4	139.5	128.9	0.0	218.1	Single spontaneous delivery [3]	O80
27.5	29.4	22.1	0.0	62.4	Other delivery [3]	O81-O84
10.6	11.4	11.3	0.8	14.4	Complications predominantly related to the puerperium [3]	O85-O92
39.4	44.1	26.6	0.2	39.8	Other obstetric conditions [3]	O95-O99
256.6	**289.1**	**121.6**	**14.0**	**252.8**	**Certain conditions originating in the perinatal period**	**P00-P96**
61.7	69.7	33.2	0.2	59.3	Disorders relating to short gestation and low birth weight	P07
194.9	219.5	88.5	13.8	193.5	Other conditions originating in the perinatal period	Remainder of P00-P96
111.5	**115.9**	**76.6**	**87.4**	**113.4**	**Congenital malformations, deformations and chromosomal abnormalities**	**Q00-Q99**
1660.1	**1611.0**	**1634.8**	**2203.5**	**1532.6**	**Symptoms, signs and abnormal clinical and laboratory findings, not elsewhere classified**	**R00-R99**
304.9	280.4	339.7	518.0	333.7	Pain in throat and chest	R07
301.4	284.0	360.1	428.7	334.7	Abdominal and pelvic pain	R10
214.3	255.7	0.1	2.0	0.0	Unknown and unspecified causes of morbidity (incl. those without diagnoses)	R69
839.4	790.9	934.9	1254.8	864.2	Other symptoms, signs and abnormal clinical and laboratory findings	Remainder of R00-R99
1219.9	**1161.7**	**1401.6**	**1652.2**	**1333.3**	**Injury, poisoning and certain other consequences of external causes**	**S00-T98**
20.2	20.4	18.0	17.7	22.9	Intracranial injury	S06
159.5	141.5	158.5	323.4	204.7	Other injuries to the head	S00-S05, S07-S09
94.8	92.0	113.2	115.7	82.2	Fracture of forearm	S52
146.2	143.2	186.8	133.9	200.5	Fracture of femur	S72
90.5	88.4	112.9	97.7	91.4	Fracture of lower leg, including ankle	S82

6

Table 6.3 (b) – continued

Discharge numbers and rates: by diagnostic categories,[1] 2005

United Kingdom

Numbers

ICD-10		United Kingdom	England	Wales	Scotland	Northern Ireland
S10-S51, S53-S71, S73-S81, S83-T14, T79	Other injuries	195,786	156,664	11,526	21,919	5,677
T20-T32	Burns and corrosions	8,021	6,441	483	854	243
T36-T65	Poisoning by drugs, medicaments and biological substances and toxic effects of substances chiefly nonmedicinal as to source	87,787	66,080	4,924	13,486	3,297
T80-T88	Complications of surgical and medical care, not elsewhere classified	120,509	100,722	6,268	10,623	2,896
T90-T98	Sequelae of injuries, of poisoning and other consequences of external causes	234	216	16	0	2
Remainder of S00-T98	Other and unspecified effects of external causes	14,448	10,914	811	2,223	500
Z00-Z99	**Factors influencing health status and contract with health services** [3]	**546,618**	**509,872**	**8,911**	**22,722**	**5,113**
Z03	Medical observation and evaluation for suspected diseases and conditions [3]	9,959	8,199	289	1,339	132
Z30	Contraceptive management [3]	5,510	4,228	413	636	233
Z38	Liveborn infants according to place of birth ("healthy newborn babies") [3,4]	343,223	343,223	:	0	0
Z51	Other medical care (including radiotherapy and chemotherapy sessions) [3]	1,730	1,474	35	180	41
Remainder of Z00-Z99	Other factors influencing health status and contact with health services [3]	186,196	152,748	8,174	20,567	4,707
A00-Z99	**All causes**	**7,942,886**	**6,607,649**	**404,684**	**685,503**	**245,050+**

: Data not available

1 Discharges following admission for an overnight hospital stay. For Wales and Northern Ireland these figures do not include any patients who were admitted and discharged on the same day.
2 'Renal failure' does not include regular day patients for dialysis in Wales and Northern Ireland.
3 Scotland missing some variables for: 'Pregnancy, childbirth' and sub-groups ('Medical abortions' to 'Other obstetric conditions') and 'Factors and contacts' and sub-groups ('Medical observation' to 'Other factors'). For these variables the data provided in 2004 has been used and a 2005 figure estimated except 'Single delivery', 'Other delivery' and 'Healthy new born babies', where no data is provided.
4 In Wales data on well babies are not held, therefore this does not include liveborn infants.

Source: The Information Centre for Health and Social Care; Information Services Division, NHS in Scotland; Health Solutions Wales; Department of Health, Social Services and Public Safety, Northern Ireland.

Rates per 100,000 population

United Kingdom	England	Wales	Scotland	Northern Ireland		ICD-10
325.2	310.6	389.6	430.2	329.2	Other injuries	S10-S51, S53-S71, S73-S81, S83-T14, T79
13.3	12.8	16.3	16.8	14.1	Burns and corrosions	T20-T32
145.8	131.0	166.4	264.7	191.2	Poisoning by drugs, medicaments and biological substances and toxic effects of substances chiefly nonmedicinal as to source	T36-T65
200.1	199.7	211.9	208.5	167.9	Complications of surgical and medical care, not elsewhere classified	T80-T88
0.4	0.4	0.5	0.0	0.1	Sequelae of injuries, of poisoning and other consequences of external causes	T90-T98
24.0	21.6	27.4	43.6	29.0	Other and unspecified effects of external causes	Remainder of S00-T98
907.9	**1011.0**	**301.2**	**446.0**	**296.5**	**Factors influencing health status and contract with health services** [3]	**Z00-Z99**
16.5	16.3	9.8	26.3	7.7	Medical observation and evaluation for suspected diseases and conditions [3]	Z03
9.2	8.4	14.0	12.5	13.5	Contraceptive management [3]	Z30
570.0	680.6	:	0.0	0.0	Liveborn infants according to place of birth ("healthy newborn babies") [3,4]	Z38
2.9	2.9	1.2	3.5	2.4	Other medical care (including radiotherapy and chemotherapy sessions) [3]	Z51
309.2	302.9	276.3	403.7	273.0	Other factors influencing health status and contact with health services [3]	Remainder of Z00-Z99
13192.1	**13102.2**	**13678.2**	**13455.0**	**14210.7**	**All causes**	**A00-Z99**

6

Table 6.4 (a)

Average length of stay:[1] by ICD-10 chapter, 2005

United Kingdom

Days

ICD-10		United Kingdom	England	Wales	Scotland	Northern Ireland
A00-B99	Certain infectious and parasitic diseases	8.5	8.8	7.4	6.7	6.7
C00-D48	Neoplasms	9.4	9.3	10.8	8.9	10.9
D50-D89	Diseases of the blood and bloodforming organs and certain disorders involving the immune mechanism	7.5	7.3	9.3	7.9	7.8
E00-E99	Endocrine, nutritional and metabolic diseases	9.3	9.3	10.7	8.4	9.0
F00-F99	Mental and behavioural disorders	55.0	61.1	48.6	13.6	9.7
G00-G99	Diseases of the nervous system	14.3	14.3	23.3	10.4	10.8
H00-H59	Diseases of the eye and adnexa	2.7	2.6	3.2	3.0	2.2
H60-H95	Diseases of the ear and mastoid process	2.3	2.3	2.3	1.8	2.2
I00-I99	Diseases of the circulatory system	11.4	11.3	12.7	12.0	11.1
J00-J99	Diseases of the respiratory system	8.0	7.9	9.3	7.8	7.8
K00-K93	Diseases of the digestive system	6.7	6.7	6.9	6.3	6.7
L00-L99	Diseases of the skin and subcutanous tissue	8.7	8.8	9.8	7.0	8.3
M00-M99	Diseases of the musculoskeletal system and connective tissue	6.8	6.7	7.6	6.7	7.5
N00-N99	Diseases of the genitourinary system	6.4	6.5	6.5	6.2	3.6
O00-O99	Pregnancy, childbirth and the puerperium	2.6	2.7	2.7	0.9	3.4
P00-P96	Certain conditions originating in the perinatal period	7.2	7.4	9.9	4.0	7.6
Q00-Q99	Congenital malformations, deformations and chromosomal abnormalities	5.3	5.2	5.0	6.3	5.8
R00-R99	Symptoms, signs and abnormal clinical and laboratory findings, not elsewhere classified	7.6	8.0	6.1	5.7	5.0
S00-T98	Injury, poisoning and certain other consequences of external causes	8.9	9.0	9.9	7.1	9.0
Z00-Z99	Factors influencing health status and contract with health services [2]	4.4	3.5	9.8	5.4	16.9
A00-Z99	All causes	8.6	8.7	9.7	7.5	7.2

1 Discharges following admission for an overnight hospital stay. For Wales and Northern Ireland these figures do not include any patients who were admitted and discharged on the same day.
2 In Wales data on well babies are not held, therefore this does not include liveborn infants.

Source: The Information Centre for Health and Social Care; Information Services Division, Scotland; Health Solutions Wales; Department of Health, Social Services and Public Safety, Northern Ireland.

Table 6.4 (b)

Average length of stay:[1] by diagnostic categories, 2005

United Kingdom   Days

ICD-10		United Kingdom	England	Wales	Scotland	Northern Ireland
A00-B99	**Certain infectious and parasitic diseases**	**8.5**	**8.8**	**7.4**	**6.7**	**6.7**
A00-A08	Intestinal infectious diseases except diarrhoea	8.2	8.7	6.4	5.0	5.5
A09	Diarrhoea, gastroenteritis of preseumed infectious origin	5.4	5.4	5.0	5.6	6.1
A15-A19, B90	Tuberculosis	19.3	18.8	24.2	20.4	20.8
A40-A41	Septicaemia	16.2	16.1	17.3	16.4	18.3
B20-B24	Human immunodeficiency virus (HIV) disease	14.6	15.8	..	13.3	9.0
Remainder of A00-B99	Other infectious parasitic diseases	4.7	4.8	4.1	3.8	4.1
C00-D48	**Neoplasms**	**9.4**	**9.3**	**10.8**	**8.9**	**10.9**
C18-C21	Malignant neoplasm of colon, rectum and anus	13.6	13.6	16.4	11.3	16.0
C33-C34	Malignant neoplasm of trachea, bronchus and lung	11.5	11.6	13.8	9.5	11.1
C43-C44	Malignant neoplasm of skin	5.3	5.2	5.8	4.4	8.6
C50	Malignant neoplasm of breast	6.2	6.0	7.6	6.8	8.4
C53-C55	Malignant neoplasm of uterus	7.2	7.1	8.6	7.5	7.6
C56	Malignant neoplasm of ovary	9.9	9.7	14.5	7.9	12.4
C61	Malignant neoplasm of prostate	9.7	9.3	12.8	10.2	14.2
C67	Malignant neoplasm of bladder	6.1	5.9	7.2	7.1	6.6
Remainder of C00-C97	Other malignant neoplasms	10.9	10.8	12.2	10.4	12.2
D00-D09	Carcinoma in situ	4.2	4.2	4.2	4.3	4.1
D12	Bening neoplasm of colon, rectum and anus	6.9	6.8	8.6	6.1	7.9
D25	Leiomyoma of uterus	4.4	4.3	4.8	4.3	5.5
Remainder of D00-D48	Other benign neoplasms and neoplasms of uncertain or unknown behaviour	6.7	6.8	7.0	5.3	7.7
D50-D89	**Diseases of the blood and bloodforming organs and certain disorders involving the immune mechanism**	**7.5**	**7.3**	**9.3**	**7.9**	**7.8**
D50-D64	Anaemias	7.6	7.3	10.4	8.6	7.9
D65-D89	Other diseases of the blood and bloodforming organs and certain disorders involving the immune mechanism	7.2	7.3	6.9	6.1	7.4
E00-E90	**Endocrine, nutritional and metabolic diseases**	**9.3**	**9.3**	**10.7**	**8.4**	**9.0**
E10-E14	Diabetes mellitus	10.0	10.0	12.2	9.1	9.3
Remainder of E00-E90	Other endocrine, nutritional and metabolic diseases	8.7	8.8	9.5	7.8	8.8
F00-F99	**Mental and behavioural disorders**	**55.0**	**61.1**	**48.6**	**13.6**	**9.7**
F00-F03	Dementia	68.2	71.4	71.1	47.1	34.1
F10	Mental and behavioural disorders due to alcohol	9.7	10.0	14.8	5.8	5.1
F11-F19	Mental and behavioural disorders due to use of other psychoactive subst.	17.7	19.9	16.8	1.7	3.7
F20-F29	Schizophrenia, schizotypal and delusional disorders	96.8	110.2	79.7	5.4	5.8
F30-F39	Mood [affective] disorders	45.1	49.4	39.8	17.0	10.7
Remainder of F00-F99	Other mental and behavioural disorders	64.8	73.6	37.7	12.7	10.7
G00-G99	**Diseases of the nervous system**	**14.3**	**14.3**	**23.3**	**10.4**	**10.8**

6

Table 6.4 (b) – continued

Average length of stay:[1] by diagnostic categories, 2005

United Kingdom

Days

ICD-10		United Kingdom	England	Wales	Scotland	Northern Ireland
G30	Alzheimer's disease	70.6	73.5	78.3	43.7	54.0
G35	Multiple sclerosis	17.2	16.6	19.1	22.1	17.7
G40-G41	Epilepsy	6.8	7.1	6.7	4.5	6.0
G45	Transient cerebral ischaemic attacks and related syndromes	6.6	6.5	8.8	6.2	8.3
Remainder of G00-G99	Others diseases of the nervous system	13.8	13.7	21.5	11.1	11.9
H00-H59	**Diseases of the eye and adnexa**	**2.7**	**2.6**	**3.2**	**3.0**	**2.2**
H25-H26. H28	Cataract	1.9	1.8	2.4	2.9	1.6
Remainder of H00-H59	Other diseases of the eye and adnexa	2.9	2.9	3.4	3.1	2.7
H60-H95	**Diseases of the ear and mastoid process**	**2.3**	**2.3**	**2.3**	**1.8**	**2.2**
I00-I99	**Diseases of the circulatory system**	**11.4**	**11.3**	**12.7**	**12.0**	**11.1**
I10-I15	Hypertensive diseases	8.8	8.8	10.0	9.3	5.9
I20	Angina pectoris	5.3	5.4	6.8	3.9	4.3
I21-I22	Acute myocardial infarction	9.9	9.8	11.0	10.2	9.9
I23-I25	Other ischaemic heart disease	7.0	6.8	10.9	7.3	5.5
I26-I28	Other ischaemic heart disease & diseases of pulmonary circulation	11.3	11.1	13.0	11.0	13.8
I44-I49	Conduction disorders and cardiac arrythmias	6.5	6.5	7.7	6.3	5.6
I50	Heart failures	14.0	13.8	14.9	15.4	14.0
I60-I69	Cerebrovascular diseases	26.4	25.7	25.3	31.7	31.6
I70	Atherosclerosis	12.3	12.3	11.6	12.4	13.8
I83	Varicose veins of lower extremities	3.4	3.4	3.4	3.6	2.5
Remainder of I00-I99	Other diseases of the circulatory system	10.2	10.1	11.1	10.0	11.1
J00-J99	**Diseases of the respiratory system**	**8.0**	**7.9**	**9.3**	**7.8**	**7.8**
J00-J11	Acute upper respiratory infections and influenza	2.0	2.1	1.9	1.3	2.1
J12-J18	Pneumonia	13.0	12.5	17.0	14.9	14.0
J20-J22	Other acute lower respiratory infections	8.9	8.8	10.5	8.5	9.6
J35	Chronic diseases of tonsils and adenoids	1.2	1.2	1.5	1.3	1.3
J30-J34, J36-J39	Other diseases of upper respiratory tract	1.9	1.9	1.9	1.7	1.9
J40-J44, J47	Chronic obstructive pulmonary disease and bronchiectasis	9.8	9.7	11.2	9.5	10.1
J45-J46	Asthma	3.9	4.0	4.6	3.0	3.9
J60-J99	Other diseases of the respiratory system	12.7	12.4	14.0	14.1	14.1
K00-K93	**Diseases of the digestive system**	**6.7**	**6.7**	**6.9**	**6.3**	**6.7**
K00-K08	Disorders of teeth and supporting structures	2.0	2.1	2.2	0.8	2.9
K09-K14	Other diseases of oral cavity, salivary glands and jaws	3.1	3.1	3.2	3.3	3.3
K20-K23	Diseases of oesophagus	6.5	6.6	6.3	6.4	5.1
K25-K28	Peptic ulcer	11.4	11.4	12.1	11.4	10.8
K29-K31	Dyspepsia and other diseases of stomach and duodenum	6.7	6.8	6.6	5.7	5.5
K35-K38	Diseases of appendix	4.1	4.1	4.0	4.3	4.0

Table 6.4 (b) – continued

Average length of stay:[1] by diagnostic categories, 2005

United Kingdom

Days

ICD-10		United Kingdom	England	Wales	Scotland	Northern Ireland
K40	Inguinal hernia	2.4	2.4	3.0	2.1	2.6
K41-K46	Other adbominal hernia	5.4	5.3	5.8	5.8	6.0
K50-K51	Crohn's disease and ulcerative colitis	10.3	10.4	9.7	9.1	11.0
K52	Othe noninfective gastroentiritis and colitis	6.3	6.3	6.4	5.8	6.0
K56	Paralytic ileus and intestinal obstruction without hernia	11.8	11.8	12.3	11.6	12.0
K57	Divertcular disease of intestine	9.8	9.9	10.0	8.9	10.0
K60-K62	Diseases of anus and rectum	4.3	4.3	4.2	3.9	4.1
K55,K58-K59, K63	Other diseases of intestine	8.0	8.1	7.5	7.1	7.5
K70	Alcoholic liver disease	14.3	14.1	15.6	15.0	15.8
K71-K77	Other disease of liver	12.2	12.3	12.4	11.6	12.0
K80	Cholelithiasis	5.0	4.9	5.8	4.9	5.4
K81-K83	Other diseases of gall bladder and biliary tract	7.3	7.3	7.0	7.0	7.4
K85-K87	Disease of pancreas	9.3	9.3	10.0	8.9	8.1
Remainder of K00-K93	Other diseases of the digestive system	8.4	8.4	8.6	8.1	8.7
L00-L99	**Diseases of the skin and subcutanous tissue**	**8.7**	**8.8**	**9.8**	**7.0**	**8.3**
L00-L08	Infections of the skin and subcutaneous tissue	6.8	6.9	7.7	5.5	6.2
L20-L45	Dermatitis, eczema and papulosquamous disorders	9.5	9.2	9.4	11.9	9.6
Remainder of L00-L99	Other dieases of the skin and subcutaneous tissue	13.1	13.5	14.5	8.5	12.7
M00-M99	**Diseases of the musculoskeletal system and connective tissue**	**6.8**	**6.7**	**7.6**	**6.7**	**7.5**
M16	Coxarthrosis [arthrosis of hip]	8.5	8.4	10.1	9.0	6.9
M17	Gonathrosis [arthrosis of knee]	7.7	7.6	8.0	7.9	7.8
M23	Internal derangement of knee	1.8	1.8	2.0	1.4	1.5
M00-M15, M18-M22, M24-M25	Other arthropathies	6.2	6.1	6.6	6.9	7.4
M30-M36	Systemic connective tissue disorders	10.7	10.9	11.7	7.8	10.3
M40-M49	Deforming dorsopathies and spondylopathies	11.8	11.5	12.7	12.7	16.5
M50-M51	Intervertrebal disc disorders	6.8	6.7	8.7	6.2	8.0
M54	Dorsalgia	6.3	6.2	7.9	6.7	6.3
M60-M79	Soft tissue disorders	3.9	3.9	4.7	3.3	5.5
M53, M80-M99	Other disorders of the musculoskeletal system and connective tissue	9.7	9.7	9.9	9.2	10.1
N00-N99	**Diseases of the genitourinary system**	**6.4**	**6.5**	**6.5**	**6.2**	**3.6**
N00-N16	Glomerular and renal tubulo-interstitial diseases	6.2	6.2	6.9	5.8	6.8
N17-N19	Renal failure	12.6	12.8	13.9	14.0	2.1
N20-N23	Urolithiasis	3.3	3.3	3.4	3.1	3.7
N25-N39	Other dieases of the urinary system	9.8	9.9	9.5	8.9	8.5
N40	Hyperplasia of prostate	4.8	4.8	5.8	4.6	5.1
N41-N51	Other diseases of male genital organs	2.7	2.8	3.0	2.0	2.8
N60-N64	Disorders of breast	2.5	2.5	2.8	2.1	2.7

6

Table 6.4 (b) – continued

Average length of stay:[1] by diagnostic categories, 2005

United Kingdom

Days

ICD-10		United Kingdom	England	Wales	Scotland	Northern Ireland
N70-N77	Inflammatory diseases of female pelvic organs	3.3	3.3	3.5	3.0	3.7
N91-N95	Menstrual, menopausal and other female genital conditions	2.8	2.8	2.7	2.4	2.9
Remainder of N00-N99	Other disorders of the genitourinary system	4.0	4.0	4.3	3.9	4.7
O00-O99	**Pregnancy, childbirth and the puerperium**	**2.6**	**2.7**	**2.7**	**0.9**	**3.4**
O04	Medical abortion	2.2	2.4	1.6	0.6	1.6
O00-O03, O05-O08	Other pregnancy with abortive outcome	1.9	2.0	2.0	1.0	1.7
O10-O48	Complications of pregnancy predominantly in the antenatal period	2.8	2.9	2.8	1.1	3.7
O60-O75	Complications of pregnancy predominantly during labour and delivery	2.7	2.8	2.9	1.1	3.5
O80	Single spontaneous delivery	1.7	1.8	1.7	0.0	2.6
O81-O84	Other delivery	3.4	3.7	3.0	0.0	4.3
O85-O92	Complications predominantly related to the puerperium	3.3	3.2	2.9	4.4	3.7
O95-O99	Other obstetric conditions	2.8	2.8	3.2	2.1	3.5
P00-P96	**Certain conditions originating in the perinatal period**	**7.2**	**7.4**	**9.9**	**4.0**	**7.6**
P07	Disorders relating to short gestation and low birth weight	15.9	16.5	19.9	7.4	16.1
Remainder of P00-P96	Other conditions originating in the perinatal period	4.6	4.5	6.2	4.0	4.9
Q00-Q99	**Congenital malformations, deformations and chromosomal abnormalities**	**5.3**	**5.2**	**5.0**	**6.3**	**5.8**
R00-R99	**Symptoms, signs and abnormal clinical and laboratory findings, not elsewhere classified**	**7.6**	**8.0**	**6.1**	**5.7**	**5.0**
R07	Pain in throat and chest	2.9	2.9	3.4	2.1	2.8
R10	Abdominal and pelvic pain	3.3	3.3	3.6	2.9	3.8
R69	Unknown and unspecified causes of morbidity (incl. those without diagnoses)	21.3	23.3	11.0	14.9	
Remainder of R00-R99	Other symptoms, signs and abnormal clinical and laboratory findings	6.8	6.6	8.1	8.2	6.2
S00-T98	**Injury, poisoning and certain other consequences of external causes**	**8.9**	**9.0**	**9.9**	**7.1**	**9.0**
S06	Intracranial injury	18.1	17.6	17.7	21.5	22.4
S00-S05, S07-S09	Other injuries to the head	3.4	3.5	3.9	2.4	3.2
S52	Fracture of forearm	4.1	4.1	5.1	3.8	4.7
S72	Fracture of femur	25.8	25.4	28.2	30.1	22.0
S82	Fracture of lower leg, including ankle	10.0	10.0	10.9	9.3	11.1
S10-S51, S53-S71, S73-S81, S83-T14, T79	Other injuries	7.4	7.4	7.8	6.4	8.5
T20-T32	Burns and corrosions	8.3	8.2	7.4	8.5	10.5
T36-T65	Poisoning by drugs, medicaments and biological substances and toxic effects of substances chiefly nonmedicinal as to source	2.6	2.7	2.7	1.5	2.3

Table 6.4 (b) – continued

Average length of stay:[1] by diagnostic categories, 2005

United Kingdom

Days

ICD-10		United Kingdom	England	Wales	Scotland	Northern Ireland
T80-T88	Complications of surgical and medical care, not elsewhere classified	9.4	9.4	10.1	8.5	9.4
T90-T98	Sequelae of injuries, of poisoning and other consequences of external causes	13.7	15.6	12.6	0.0	1.5
Remainder of S00-T98	Other and unspecified effects of external causes	3.0	3.0	3.0	2.8	2.8
Z00-Z99	**Factors influencing health status and contract with health services**	**4.4**	**3.5**	**9.8**	**5.4**	**16.9**
Z03	Medical observation and evaluation for suspected diseases and conditions	5.1	5.5	2.9	2.2	5.0
Z30	Contraceptive management	1.6	1.6	1.6	1.2	1.4
Z38	Liveborn infants according to place of birth ("healthy newborn babies") [2]	1.7	2.0		0.0	0.0
Z51	Other medical care (including radiotherapy and chemotherapy sessions)	12.3	11.4	15.2	8.3	45.5
Remainder of Z00-Z99	Other factors influencing health status and contact with health services	7.0	6.5	10.4	5.7	17.8
A00-Z99	**All causes**	**8.6**	**8.7**	**9.7**	**7.5**	**7.2**

:   Data not available.

1   Discharges following admission for an overnight hospital stay. For Wales and Northern Ireland these figures do not include any patients who were admitted and discharged on the same day.
2   Data on 'Healthy newborn babies' not held in Wales.

Source:The Information Centre for Health and Social Care; Information Services Division, NHS in Scotland; Health Solutions Wales; Department of Health, Social Services and Public Safety, Northern Ireland.

Time waited for elective hospital admission

In 'Enhancing the Value of Health Statistics: User Perspectives' (Report Number 21), the Statistics Commission recommended that inconsistencies in definitions of waiting times for treatment between the four UK nations should be addressed. Following the creation of a UK Comparative Waiting Times Group (UKCWTG) in 2005, a review of waiting time criteria across the UK recommended that the four nations should consider 'publishing harmonised data for completed waits – (it is understood) that data already exists in most countries from the Hospital Episode Statistics and other sources which could be published in an agreed common format'.

The UKCWTG undertook a project to address this recommendation and identified a list of 11 inpatient procedures, selected on the basis of both volume and data quality within each country for analysis. It was agreed that an analysis of the length of time a patient had waited, from the initial decision to admit to the date of admission for the procedure, including periods of suspension for medical and social reasons, should be performed. This analysis adopted the

financial year 2005-06 as the base year and measured the median completed waiting time in days, together with an estimate of the value of the 90th percentile completed wait, for each of 11 common operative procedures. It should be noted that the measurement of a completed wait, including periods of suspension, is not comparable with the monitoring of waiting times targets as the latter typically excludes suspension periods from a patient's 'statistical' waiting time.

Table 6.5a shows the median (50th percentile) and 90th percentile waiting times in completed days for each of the operative procedures included, in 2005-06 and 2006-07. Table 6.5b helps to set this in context by giving the numbers of these procedures performed in each year.

The analysis identified increases in the number of elective hospital admissions in most of these common procedures in the UK between 2005-06 and 2006-07. There was nearly a 20% rise in the number of admissions to NHS hospitals in England for 'endoscope of upper gastro intestinal tract' from 208,621 in 2005-06 to 249,542 in 2006-07. More modest increases in admissions for this procedure were seen all UK countries.

6

Table 6.5 (a)

Time waited in days[1,2,6] for elective hospital admission:[3,4] selected procedures, 2005-06 and 2006-07

United Kingdom

Completed days

| Procedure[7,10] | Percentile[5] | 2005-06 | | | | 2006-07 | | | |
		England[8]	Scotland[9]	Wales[9]	Northern Ireland[9]	England[8]	Scotland[9]	Wales[9]	Northern Ireland[9]
Cataract Surgery	50th	69	97	70	148	70	69	70	101
	90th	112	190	125	308	116	146	125	172
Angiography	50th	65	35	71	41	56	35	67	27
	90th	163	57	138	279	132	56	119	176
Bypass Surgery	50th	65	47	117	91	68	56	107	117
	90th	110	124	254	203	112	122	203	191
Endoscope of Upper Gastro Intestinal Tract	50th	29	35	33	31	26	34	30	39
	90th	109	117	161	133	95	98	147	176
Hernia Repair	50th	99	92	108	79	99	79	118	102
	90th	219	204	335	340	187	179	315	241
Hip Replacement	50th	161	156	260	295	151	122	221	168
	90th	272	286	494	508	223	221	367	337
Knee Replacement	50th	169	165	299	318	157	126	243	196
	90th	287	310	549	565	238	247	388	432
Endoscope of Bladder	50th	36	48	54	73	31	39	50	66
	90th	140	183	249	335	129	140	239	213
Angioplasty	50th	56	41	107	8	51	38	90	14
	90th	91	105	216	105	88	85	182	153
Tonsillectomy	50th	102	93	176	165	113	93	195	161
	90th	211	198	363	417	188	168	343	267
Varicose Surgery	50th	133	141	175	127	127	103	217	150
	90th	266	332	392	484	217	219	371	307

1 Time waited calculated as difference between admission date and the date the decision to admit was made. This is not adjusted for self-deferrals or periods of medical /social suspension. Includes waits for all selected patients, including those whose reported wait was zero days.
2 For suspension policies for the four UK nations see Additional Notes at the end of the chapter.
3 Data relate solely to NHS activity in NHS hospitals.
4 Data are based on country of treatment rather than country of residence.
5 50th percentile relates to time in days within which 50 percent of patients were admitted. The 90th percentile relates to the time within which 90 percent of patients were admitted.
6 These data include only patients who have been treated electively and were classified as either waiting list or booked.
7 Operative procedure codes were revised for 2006/07. 2006/07 data use OPCS 4.3 codes, whereas earlier data use OPCS 4.2 codes.
8 England data are based on finished in-year admissions and so only include cases where the patient has been admitted and a finished consultant episode had been recorded within each financial year. For most of the listed procedures, over 99.5% of cases are admitted and have a FCE recorded in the same financial year. For hip, knees and CABGs this is in over 97% of cases.
9 Data for Scotland, Wales and Northern Ireland relates to those patients admitted during the financial year irrespective of the year in which they were discharged.
10 For a list of Office of Population Censuses and Surveys (OPCS) codes used to define procedures, see Additional Notes at the end of the chapter.

Source: Department of Health, Social Services and Public Safety, Northern Ireland; Health Solutions Wales; Welsh Assembly Government; Information Centre for Health and Social Care; Department of Health; Scottish Government

The other large volume procedure, cataract surgery, showed the biggest decrease in hospital admissions in England and Northern Ireland over the two-year period, from 238,050 to 231,859 in England, and from 8,159 to 7,785 in Northern Ireland. In Scotland and Wales, admissions for cataract surgery increased from 26,409 to 28,193 in Scotland and from 17,096 to 17,894 in Wales, over the two years.

The procedure with the longest median waiting time across all UK countries for both 2005-06 and 2006-07 was knee replacement, although the median waiting time fell by 12 days in England, 39 days in Scotland, 56 days in Wales and 122 days in Northern Ireland over the period.

Of the procedures analysed, patients awaiting an 'endoscope of the upper gastro intestinal tract' in England, Scotland and Wales experienced the shortest median waiting time in both 2005-06 and 2006-07, whereas patients awaiting an angioplasty procedure experienced the shortest median waiting time in Northern Ireland in both years.

Table 6.5 (b)

Number of elective hospital admissions:[1,2,3] selected procedures, 2005-06 and 2006-07

United Kingdom   Numbers

Procedure [4,7]	2005-06				2006-07			
	England[5]	Scotland[6]	Wales[6]	Northern Ireland[6]	England[5]	Scotland[6]	Wales[6]	Northern Ireland[6]
Cataract Surgery	238,050	26,409	17,096	8,159	231,859	28,193	17,894	7,785
Angiography	94,138	9,348	4,449	3,402	96,385	8,653	4,971	3,581
Bypass Surgery	13,450	1,644	601	459	13,117	1,359	597	454
Endoscope of Upper Gastro Intestinal Tract	208,621	30,460	19,563	17,052	249,542	31,772	20,852	17,760
Hernia Repair	70,670	7,172	3,972	2,073	69,438	7,137	3,950	1,985
Hip Replacement	46,150	5,798	2,857	1,464	48,192	6,143	3,200	1,756
Knee Replacement	52,652	5,436	3,509	1,043	54,695	6,138	3,998	1,324
Endoscope of Bladder	128,025	15,735	13,623	5,888	134,294	14,775	13,616	5,951
Angioplasty	24,095	2,589	681	1,259	25,382	2,481	842	1,695
Tonsillectomy	55,822	5,291	3,166	3,583	55,083	4,759	3,437	4,051
Varicose Surgery	34,062	4,068	1,930	1,483	32,606	4,200	2,088	1,400

1   Data relate solely to NHS activity in NHS hospitals.
2   Data are based on country of treatment rather than country of residence.
3   Data include only patients who have been treated electively and were classified as either waiting list or booked.
4   Operative procedure codes were revised for 2006/07. 2006/07 data use OPCS 4.3 codes, whereas earlier data use OPCS 4.2 codes.
5   England data based on finished in-year admissions and only include cases where patient has been admitted and a finished consultant episode had been recorded within each financial year. For most of the listed procedures, over 99.5% of cases are admitted and have a FCE recorded in the same financial year. For hip, knees and CABGs this is in over 97% of cases.
6   Data for Scotland, Wales and Northern Ireland relates to those patients admitted during the financial year irrespective of the year in which they were discharged.
7   For a list of Office of Population Censuses and Surveys (OPCS) codes used to define procedures, see Additional Notes at the end of the chapter.

Source: Department of Health, Social Services and Public Safety, Northern Ireland; Health Solutions Wales; Welsh Assembly Government; Information Centre for Health and Social Care; Department of Health; Information Services Division, NHS in Scotland.

Children on child protection registers

Children who are considered to be 'at risk' may be placed on a local authority child protection register. In England, registration is governed by the Children Act 1989 and takes place following a case conference in which decisions are made about the child's welfare, and subsequently the child's name may be placed on a register and a plan set out in order to protect the child. Similar procedures exist in each country, but because child protection in each country is carried out under different legal provisions and administrative systems, the data available differ slightly and comparisons should be made with caution.

In Northern Ireland in 2006, 38 in every 10,000 children aged 18 and under were on a child protection register, while the next highest rate was Wales at 33 in every 10,000 children (Table 6.6). The lowest rate was in Scotland at 22 per 10,000 children under age 18, although this relatively low figure at least partly reflects differences between the countries in the legal status of young people aged 16-17.

Of those children on a child protection register, Scotland had the highest proportion in the under-five age group; 46 per cent

compared with 42 per cent in Wales, 39 per cent in England and 35 per cent in Northern Ireland.

Neglect was the most common reason for a child being on the register in all four countries, with 49 per cent in Wales, 45 per cent in both England and Scotland and 36 per cent in Northern Ireland. Sexual abuse was the least common cause for being on the child protection register in all four countries.

Prescriptions dispensed.

In 2006, Wales had the most prescription items dispensed per person, an average of 19.9 items per person (Table 6.7). Northern Ireland was the next highest at 16.9 items, while Scotland and England had similar figures with 15.4 and 15.1 items dispensed respectively.

Data for prescriptions exempt from charge are not comparable between countries due to different data collection methods. Figures for England and Wales exclude prescriptions for which prepayment certificates have been purchased. For Scotland and Northern Ireland these have been included. Consequently, comparison between the countries of proportions exempt from charge and prescription costs are not considered reliable.

79

Table 6.6

Children and young people on child protection registers: by age and category, at 31 March 2006

United Kingdom

Numbers, percentages

	Percentage of children on register aged					Number of children on registers (=100%)[3]	Rate per 10,000 children under 18[4]	Percentage of children on register in each category of abuse				
	Under 1	1 to 4	5 to 9[1]	10 to 15[1]	16 and over[2]			Neglect	Physical injury	Sexual abuse	Emotional abuse	Multiple injuries
England	11	28	29	29	2	26,400	24	45	14	9	23	10
Wales	12	30	29	27	2	2,163	33	49	16	7	19	10
Scotland	-	46	34	19	1	2,288	22	45	27	12	16	-
Northern Ireland	9	26	38	21	6	1,639	38	36	20	14	16	15

1 Age bands for Northern Ireland are five to 11 and 12 to 15. For Scotland they are under five, five to ten, 11 to 15 and 16+.
2 For Wales data includes 16-18 year olds, Scotland data includes 16-17 year olds.
3 Includes a number of unborn children not included elsewhere in this table.
4 Calculated using mid-2005 population estimates.

Source: Department of Health; Department of Health, Social Services and Public Safety, Northern Ireland; Welsh Assembly Government; Information Services Division, NHS in Scotland.

6

Table 6.7

Prescriptions dispensed, numbers and cost, 2006

United Kingdom

Numbers, percentages

	Prescription items dispensed (millions) [2]	Percentage of prescription items exempt from charge [3,4]	Number of prescription items per person	Average net ingredient cost [1]	
				£ per person	£ per prescription item
England	752.0	90.0	15.1	164.40	10.90
Wales	58.9	92.6	19.9	193.52	9.70
Scotland	79.0	92.7	15.4	191.40	12.30
Northern Ireland	29.2	94.3	16.9	219.50	12.80

1 Net ingredient cost is the cost of medicines before any discounts and does not include any dispensing costs or fees. This is known as Gross Ingredient Cost in Scotland and Ingredient Cost in Northern Ireland.

2 Figures relate to NHS prescription items dispensed by community pharmacies, appliance contractors (appliance suppliers in Scotland and in Northern Ireland), and dispensing doctors, and prescriptions submitted by prescribing doctors for items personally administered, known as stock orders in Scotland and Northern Ireland.

3 For England figures relate to items dispensed by community pharmacists, dispensing doctors and appliance contractors. Personally administerd items are free of charge and are therefore excluded. For Scotland, figures relate to items dispensed by community pharmacists and appliance contractors only. For Northern Ireland population estimates are based on 2005 data.

4 Figures for England and Wales exclude prescriptions for which prepayment certificates have been purchased. For Scotland and Northern Ireland they are included. Due to this, comparisons across the four areas should not be made. For Northern Ireland population estimates are based on 2005 data.

Source: Department of Health; Welsh Assembly Government; Information Services Division, NHS in Scotland; Central Services Agency, Northern Ireland

Additional notes

Table 6.1 – Hospital inpatient and day case activity

Hospital stays

Data for England are based on Finished Consultant Episodes (FCEs) which are completed periods of care of a patient using an NHS hospital bed, under one consultant within one healthcare provider. If a patient is transferred from one consultant to another, even if this is within the same provider unit, the episode ends and another one begins. The transfer of one patient from one hospital to another with the same consultant and within the same NHS Trust does not end the episode.

Data for Wales are based on discharges and deaths. Data for Scotland and Northern Ireland are based on a system where transfers between consultants do not count as a discharge. Although in Scotland figures include patients transferred from one consultant to another within the same hospital – provided there is a change of speciality, or significant facilities, for example a change of ward – transfers from one hospital to another with the same consultant count as a discharge. Newborn babies are included in Northern Ireland but not in England, Scotland or Wales. Deaths in hospitals are included in all four countries.

For Scotland, figures include NHS beds/activity in joint-user and contractual hospitals; these hospitals account for a relatively small proportion of total NHS activity.

Average length of stay

Average length of stay is calculated as the total bed-days divided by the number of ordinary admissions (FCEs in England and Wales, in-patient discharges (including transfers) in Scotland, and deaths and discharges in Northern Ireland). An ordinary admission is one where the patient is expected to remain in hospital for at least one night. Scottish figures exclude patients with learning disabilities and those requiring non-psychiatric specialities. Figures for Wales relate only to acute specialities. Population figures are based on estimates for 1999 Health Authorities for people of all ages.

For Northern Ireland, mid-year population estimates for 2000 have been used. It should be noted that where figures are presented to the nearest whole number, this is to facilitate the calculation rates and the aggregation of age bands. Cases treated per available bed are for ordinary admissions (in-patient discharges including transfers in Scotland) and do not include day case admissions.

Day cases

A day case is a patient who comes for investigation, treatment or operation under clinical supervision on a planned non-resident basis, who occupies a bed for part or all of that day, and returns home the same day. Scottish figures also include day cases that have been transferred to or from in-patient care. Numbers of day cases in the different countries are not directly comparable because of differences in recording for statistical purposes.

Table 6.2 – Hospital outpatient activity

Outpatients

An outpatient is a non-resident of a hospital seen by a consultant for treatment or advice at a clinical outpatient department. A new outpatient is one whose first attendance (or only attendance) is part of a continuous series for the same course of treatment falling within the period in question.

Each outpatient attendance of a series is included in the year the attendance occurred. People attending more than one department are counted in each department. Data presented are for total outpatient attendance which includes follow-ups as well as new outpatients.

Data for Wales are for people treated in Wales, not necessarily residents of Wales.

Categorisation of specialities varies in each country, for example 'Other' in England and Northern Ireland, is comprised of geriatric medicine but this is included in 'General and Acute' in Wales and Scotland.

Did not attend

Did not attend refers to patients with an appointment who did not attend and failed to give advance warning to the hospital. These should not be confused with those who could not attend and who warn the hospital in advance.

Table 6.5 – Time waited in days for elective hospital admission

These data include only patients who have been treated electively and were classified as either waiting list or booked. The 50th percentile relates to the time in days within which 50 per cent of patients were admitted. Likewise, the 90th percentile relates to the time within which 90 per cent of patients were admitted.

Procedure codes

Operative procedure codes were revised for 2006/07. Consequently, 2006/07 data use Office of Population Censuses and Surveys (OPCS-4) version 4.3 codes, whereas earlier data use version 4.2 codes (see table below).

Data years

England data are based on finished in-year admissions and so only include cases where the patient has been admitted and a finished consultant episode had been recorded within each financial year. For most of the listed procedures, over 99.5 per cent of cases are admitted and have a FCE recorded in the same financial year. For hip, knees and CABGs this is in over 97 per cent of cases.

Data for Scotland, Wales and Northern Ireland relates to those patients admitted during the financial year irrespective of the year in which they were discharged.

Suspensions policies

Scotland – Availability status codes were applied to patients on a waiting list who were at some point unavailable for treatment, or if the procedure the patient was waiting for was judged to be of low clinical priority or to be of a high specialised nature, or if the patient had failed to attend a previous appointment. Once an availability status code was attached to a patient's record, it remained until they were removed from the waiting list. Patients with availability status codes were not covered by national waiting times guarantees. There was no maximum period that a patient with an availability status could be on the waiting list. The system of availability status codes was abolished from 1 January 2008.

Northern Ireland – Prior to the introduction of an Integrated Elective Access Protocol in August 2006, there was no policy on the management of patient suspensions in the

Name of procedure grouping	OPCS 4.2 Codes	OPCS 4.3 Codes
Cataract surgery	C71, C72, C74 and C75	C71, C72, C74 and C75
Hip replacement	W37, W38 and W39	W37, W38, W39, W93, W94 and W95
Knee replacement	W40, W41 and W42	W40, W41 and W42
Bypass surgery	K40, K41, K42, K43, K44, K45 and K46	K40, K41, K42, K43, K44, K45 and K46
Angioplasty	K49 and K50	K49, K50 and K75
Angiography	K63 and K65	K63, K65, U10.2 and U10.5
Hernia repair	T19, T20 and T21	T19, T20 and T21
Varicose surgery	L85, L86 and L87	L84, L85, L86, L87 and L88
Tonsillectomy	E20, F34 and F36	E20, F34 and F36
Endoscope of bladder	M45	M45
Endoscope of upper gastro intestinal tract	G45	G45

Health Service in Northern Ireland. This effectively meant that a patient awaiting inpatient treatment could have been suspended for an indefinite period due to social or medical reasons. Since August 2006, patients in Northern Ireland can only be suspended for a maximum period of three months within a single inpatient wait.

England – Patients can be suspended from the inpatient waiting list for the following reasons:

a) the patient is medically unfit for treatment

b) the patient is unavailable for admission because of 'social' reasons (e.g. family commitments, holidays)

Once the period of suspension has elapsed, the patient returns to the active waiting list with the same waiting time they had when entering the suspension period. There are no limits relating to the length of time a patient can be suspended for medical or social reasons.

Wales - Patients can be suspended from the inpatient waiting list for the following reasons:

a) the patient is medically unfit for treatment

b) the patient is unavailable for admission because of 'social' reasons (e.g. family commitments, holidays)

Once the period of suspension has elapsed, the patient returns to the active waiting list with the same waiting time they had when entering the suspension period. Patients can only be suspended for a maximum of six months, though this can be extended in the case of suspensions for pregnancy.

Mortality and life expectancy

Chapter 7

DATA

Download data by clicking the online pdf

www.statistics.gov.uk/
downloads/theme_health/
ukhs3/

This chapter contains key statistics on mortality and life expectancy in the four countries of the UK.

Mortality

In 2006, England had the lowest overall mortality rates in the UK, for all ages except the under two years age group. Scotland had the highest overall mortality rate for adults aged 16 and over (Table 7.1). The absolute variation in mortality rates between the countries increased from the age of 35 years and was greatest in the over-85 years group.

The Standardised Mortality Ratio (SMR) compares mortality experience in each constituent country with the UK as a whole, taking into account differences in the age and sex structure of each country's population. For both sexes, the highest SMR was in Scotland (118 for males, 115 for females) and the lowest was in England (98 for both sexes).

Table 7.1

Age specific death rates: by sex, 2006

United Kingdom

Rates and Standardised Mortality Ratios[1]

| | Deaths per 1,000 population for specific age groups[2] | | | | | | | | | | | SMR |
	Under 1[3]	1-4	5-15	16-24	25-34	35-44	45-54	55-64	65-74	75-84	85+	(UK = 100)
All Persons												
United Kingdom	5.0	0.2	0.1	0.5	0.7	1.3	3.0	7.4	19.2	54.3	150.9	100
England	5.0	0.2	0.1	0.4	0.6	1.2	2.9	7.1	18.6	53.4	149.7	98
Wales	4.1	0.2	0.1	0.5	0.8	1.4	3.3	7.8	19.7	55.1	150.0	101
England, Wales & Elsewhere	5.0	0.2	0.1	0.4	0.6	1.2	2.9	7.2	18.8	53.6	149.8	98
Scotland	4.5	0.2	0.1	0.6	1.0	1.8	3.9	9.5	23.5	61.5	159.7	117
Northern Ireland	5.2	0.3	0.2	0.6	0.7	1.4	3.4	7.9	19.6	55.5	163.2	106
Males												
United Kingdom	5.4	0.2	0.1	0.6	0.9	1.6	3.7	9.1	23.7	65.5	164.5	100
England	5.4	0.2	0.1	0.6	0.9	1.5	3.5	8.8	23.0	64.4	163.3	98
Wales	4.5	0.2	0.2	0.7	1.2	1.8	4.0	9.3	24.1	66.2	163.0	101
England, Wales & Elsewhere	5.4	0.2	0.1	0.6	0.9	1.5	3.6	8.8	23.2	64.7	163.4	98
Scotland	5.1	0.2	0.2	1.0	1.5	2.5	4.9	11.7	28.6	73.7	174.5	118
Northern Ireland	5.8	0.3	0.2	0.9	1.0	1.8	4.2	10.0	24.5	69.1	177.5	108
Females												
United Kingdom	4.5	0.2	0.1	0.3	0.4	0.9	2.4	5.7	15.2	46.4	144.9	100
England	4.6	0.2	0.1	0.2	0.4	0.9	2.3	5.5	14.7	45.5	143.7	98
Wales	3.7	0.2	0.1	0.2	0.4	1.0	2.5	6.3	15.6	47.2	144.3	101
England, Wales & Elsewhere	4.6	0.2	0.1	0.2	0.4	0.9	2.3	5.6	14.8	45.7	143.8	98
Scotland	3.8	0.2	0.1	0.3	0.5	1.2	3.0	7.3	19.1	53.6	153.7	115
Northern Ireland	4.5	0.2	0.2	0.3	0.5	1.0	2.6	5.9	15.4	46.7	157.1	105

1 Standardised Mortality Ratio is the ratio of observed deaths to those expected by applying a standard death ratio to the country-specific population.
2 All data based on year of registration. Previously England and Wales were based on occurences, Scotland and Northern Ireland on registrations.
3 Rates per thousand live births.

Source: Office for National Statistics; General Register Office for Scotland; Northern Ireland Statistics and Research Agency

Figure 7.1

Life expectancy at birth, 2005

United Kingdom

Years

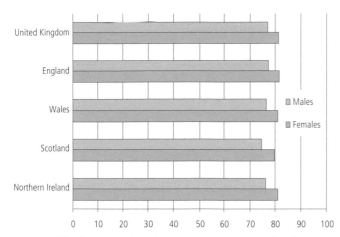

Source: Office for National Statistics; General Register Office for Scotland; Northern Ireland Statistics and Research Agency

Tables 7.2a and 7.2b show deaths by underlying cause for the four countries in the UK in 2006. The underlying cause of death is: (i) the disease which initiated the train of events leading directly to death; or (ii) the circumstances of the accident or violence which produced the fatal injury. Cause of death was defined using the Tenth Revision of the International Classification of Diseases (ICD-10).

Table 7.2a lists cause of death by ICD-10 chapter. Table 7.2b shows in addition selected specific causes of death.

Males in Northern Ireland and females in Wales had the highest death rates from malignant neoplasm of the colon (Table 7.2b); the lowest for both sexes was in England. Scotland had the highest death rates for males and females from malignant neoplasm of trachea, bronchus and lung. Death rates from breast cancer and prostrate cancer were highest in Wales and lowest in Northern Ireland.

Scotland had the highest death rates from ischaemic heart disease, mental and behavioural disorders, cerebrovascular diseases, diseases of the respiratory system, and diseases of the digestive system. England had the lowest death rates from most of these causes.

Northern Ireland had the highest death rate from pneumonia and accidents.

In 2006, death rates related to drug poisoning were highest in Scotland for both males and females (Table 7.3). Northern Ireland had the lowest death rate for males, and England had the lowest death rate related to drug poisoning for females. Males aged 15-44 in Scotland had the highest death rates from drug-related poisoning, with the death rate in that country being more than twice that of any other country. Females aged between 45-64 years had the highest death rates from drug-related poisoning, with the exception of females in Scotland where the death rate was highest in the 15-44 year age group.

Alcohol-related death rates in 2006 were highest in Scotland for both men and women, and lowest in England (Table 7.4). Alcohol-related death rates were highest among both males and females aged 45-64, with the exception of females in Northern Ireland, where the highest rate was among those aged 65-74.

Life expectancy

Life expectancy is the number of years a person would be expected to live if current age-specific mortality rates continued. Table 7.5 shows expectation of life at birth for selected years from 1981 to 2005, representing the average number of years a new-born baby would survive if he or she experienced the particular area's age-specific mortality rates for that time period throughout his or her life.

Scotland had the lowest life expectancy at birth, for both men and women, over the whole period considered. In 2005 the life expectancy in Scotland was 74.6 years for men and 79.6 years for women (Figure 7.1 and Table 7.5). England had the highest life expectancy throughout this period. In 2005, life expectancy at birth in England was 77.2 years for males and 81.5 years for females.

The largest increases in life expectancy since 1981 have been observed in Northern Ireland, by seven years for men and five years for women.

Table 7.6 shows the number of additional years a person would live at various stages throughout their life, if they experienced the relevant 2005 mortality rates for the remainder of their life.

In the UK, on average men could expect to live for a further 16.9 years when they reach 65 years. This figure was highest in England at 17.1 years and lowest in Scotland at 15.8 years. In the UK, life expectancy at 65 years for women was 19.7 years. This figure was highest in England at 19.9 years and lowest in Scotland at 18.6 years.

7

Table 7.2 (a)

Deaths by underlying cause, ICD-10 chapter, age and sex, 2006

United Kingdom   Death rates per 100,000 population

ICD-10			All Ages[3] (standardised)		1–14		15–44		45–64	
			M	F	M	F	M	F	M	F
A00-R99	All causes	UK	741.2	523.7	16.4	13.4	108.3	55.8	628.3	399.3
V01-Y89		E	722.2	511.2	16.1	12.8	100.3	53.5	601.2	383.0
		W	758.5	538.3	15.2	12.6	121.7	58.1	665.8	441.3
		E & W[4]	726.7	514.2	16.3	13.2	102.4	54.1	608.9	388.4
		S	878.8	612.9	14.6	13.8	166.7	72.5	806.8	502.2
		NI	792.4	543.4	23.6	18.6	125.4	59.3	678.4	411.0
A00-B99	I Infectious and	UK	10.0	8.3	0.8	0.8	1.8	1.4	7.5	4.4
	parasitic diseases	E	9.9	8.3	0.8	0.8	1.9	1.4	7.4	4.1
		W	7.6	5.9	..	0.4	1.4	0.3	4.2	3.6
		E & W[4]	9.9	8.2	0.8	0.8	1.8	1.4	7.3	4.2
		S	12.0	8.7	1.0	0.5	1.5	1.2	9.7	6.3
		NI	8.7	7.9	..	0.6	0.5	0.3	5.0	4.4
C00-D48	II Neoplasms	UK	224.3	160.7	3.6	2.5	14.9	18.3	232.8	207.9
		E	219.6	157.5	3.4	2.5	14.7	17.9	226.5	203.8
		W	234.1	168.8	3.6	1.3	15.9	21.4	258.0	224.5
		E & W[4]	220.9	158.5	3.5	2.5	14.9	18.2	229.1	205.8
		S	257.9	182.7	3.7	2.3	16.4	19.1	266.8	226.6
		NI	231.4	160.1	3.5	2.5	10.7	18.5	242.8	215.8
D50-D89	III Diseases of the blood	UK	1.4	1.2	0.2	0.2	0.4	0.3	1.6	0.9
	and blood forming organs	E	1.4	1.2	0.2	0.1	0.4	0.3	1.6	0.9
	and certain disorders	W	1.0	1.2	..	..	..	0.3	1.6	0.3
	involving the immune	E & W[4]	1.4	1.2	0.2	0.2	0.4	0.3	1.6	0.9
	mechanism	S	1.7	1.4	0.5	0.3	0.3	0.2	1.8	1.0
		NI	1.3	1.6	..	..	0.5	0.5	1.5	2.0
E00-E90	IV Endocrine, nutritional	UK	10.4	8.4	0.8	0.8	1.8	1.7	8.5	5.9
	and metabolic diseases	E	9.7	7.9	0.8	0.8	1.7	1.6	7.5	5.5
		W	9.8	9.4	1.2	0.8	2.3	1.6	7.4	6.9
		E & W[4]	9.7	8.0	0.8	0.8	1.7	1.6	7.5	5.6
		S	15.9	12.3	1.0	1.3	2.7	2.7	17.8	8.8
		NI	15.6	9.8	1.2	0.6	1.6	1.6	11.6	5.4
F00-F99	V Mental and behavioural	UK	16.4	16.6	0.0	0.1	7.7	1.8	7.6	3.6
	disorders	E	14.2	15.1	0.0	..	5.8	1.2	4.9	2.6
		W	16.3	16.0	..	0.4	9.1	1.9	5.0	2.8
		E & W[4]	14.3	15.2	0.0	0.0	6.1	1.3	5.0	2.7
		S	38.4	31.7	..	0.5	26.5	7.1	30.5	12.3
		NI	18.7	15.7	..	..	5.4	1.1	19.1	7.3
G00-H95	VI-VIII Diseases of the	UK	21.3	16.9	2.1	1.7	4.8	3.2	15.9	14.2
	nervous system and	E	21.4	16.6	2.3	1.6	4.7	3.0	15.9	13.6
	sense organs	W	22.0	18.0	1.6	1.7	6.3	2.9	14.3	18.2
		E & W[4]	21.4	16.7	2.2	1.7	4.8	3.0	15.8	14.0
		S	18.8	17.3	1.0	1.3	4.9	4.4	17.9	16.9
		NI	25.5	22.9	2.9	3.1	4.6	3.2	14.6	12.2

65–74		75–84		85 and over				ICD 10
M	F	M	F	M	F			
2,367.0	1,520.5	6,547.8	4,638.1	16,448.7	14,488.8	UK	All causes	A00-R99
2,302.0	1,468.3	6,444.8	4,551.2	16,330.3	14,371.2	E		V01-Y89
2,414.0	1,560.0	6,623.3	4,719.9	16,299.7	14,432.5	W		
2,315.7	1,478.8	6,465.0	4,567.1	16,339.3	14,382.6	E & W[4]		
2,863.4	1,908.7	7,367.1	5,357.7	17,454.3	15,370.8	S		
2,445.2	1,536.6	6,910.1	4,666.6	17,753.8	15,713.5	NI		
24.4	19.0	84.9	80.8	278.4	256.9	UK	I Infectious and	A00-B99
23.5	18.8	84.3	81.5	275.6	262.4	E	parasitic diseases	
20.8	19.6	67.4	57.2	247.9	163.1	W		
23.5	19.0	83.4	80.3	274.5	256.8	E & W[4]		
33.1	16.6	103.2	90.4	316.3	258.8	S		
23.3	27.4	79.3	65.1	317.3	255.0	NI		
952.6	653.6	2,005.6	1,230.9	3,221.3	1,784.5	UK	II Neoplasms	C00-D48
928.3	635.9	1,973.4	1,208.3	3,187.7	1,768.9	E		
985.5	686.0	2,037.0	1,268.5	3,213.3	1,735.9	W		
933.2	640.6	1,979.5	1,213.4	3,190.7	1,767.9	E & W[4]		
1,121.7	782.6	2,291.4	1,432.9	3,626.2	1,939.4	S		
1,044.9	631.4	2,024.0	1,152.8	3,159.9	1,909.9	NI		
3.4	3.3	9.5	8.5	28.2	31.2	UK	III Diseases of the blood	D50-D89
3.5	3.1	9.5	8.2	27.5	30.0	E	and blood forming organs	
0.8	4.9	9.1	9.2	29.8	38.6	W	and certain disorders	
3.3	3.2	9.6	8.3	27.6	30.5	E & W[4]	involving the immune	
3.8	4.4	11.5	12.1	36.8	33.8	S	mechanism	
6.6	2.9	..	3.9	25.4	54.3	NI		
34.9	25.2	88.9	74.1	213.2	205.5	UK	IV Endocrine, nutritional	E00-E90
32.6	22.6	83.4	69.4	208.2	200.2	E	and metabolic diseases	
24.6	30.2	93.4	75.6	218.2	238.2	W		
32.1	23.1	84.1	69.8	208.8	202.5	E & W[4]		
58.1	46.1	128.8	108.3	220.7	214.7	S		
53.2	20.2	137.2	108.6	380.7	298.4	NI		
17.9	16.4	131.4	149.2	609.9	931.1	UK	V Mental and behavioural	F00-F99
15.4	14.2	121.2	140.2	579.9	875.6	E	disorders	
15.4	13.3	140.0	136.4	590.1	942.0	W		
15.5	14.2	122.3	140.0	580.5	879.7	E & W[4]		
42.7	38.8	231.1	251.7	970.9	1523.3	S		
15.0	10.1	137.2	118.4	647.2	917.0	NI		
59.7	43.6	198.6	146.3	453.1	410.2	UK	VI-VIII Diseases of the	G00-H95
60.0	43.7	198.2	144.6	459.1	401.4	E	nervous system and	
63.1	37.9	213.9	141.0	456.2	497.8	W	sense organs	
60.2	43.3	199.2	144.4	458.9	407.2	E & W[4]		
51.8	42.0	166.7	142.8	342.0	370.5	S		
68.1	59.1	286.5	225.0	583.8	683.7	NI		

7

Table 7.2 (a)– continued

Deaths by underlying cause, ICD-10 chapter, age and sex, 2006

United Kingdom Death rates per 100,000 population

ICD-10			All Ages[3] (standardised)		1–14		15–44		45–64	
			M	F	M	F	M	F	M	F
I00-I99	IX Diseases of the circulatory system	UK	251.5	161.6	0.9	1.0	16.0	7.0	195.7	72.1
		E	245.5	157.0	0.9	1.0	15.0	6.7	187.1	67.6
		W	266.8	173.3	1.2	1.7	19.6	7.8	215.1	86.2
		E & W[4]	247.9	158.5	0.9	1.0	15.5	6.8	190.9	69.3
		S	288.9	190.7	0.7	0.3	22.8	9.1	243.2	97.3
		NI	256.7	171.5	0.6	1.2	14.0	5.4	198.9	79.1
J00-J99	X Diseases of the respiratory system	UK	91.2	66.3	1.4	1.2	3.0	2.0	42.2	29.9
		E	89.8	64.9	1.4	1.2	2.9	2.0	40.9	28.2
		W	89.6	65.1	0.8	0.4	3.0	2.1	42.3	30.4
		E & W[4]	89.9	65.0	1.4	1.2	2.9	2.0	41.1	28.5
		S	102.2	78.3	1.5	0.5	4.2	3.0	54.1	43.6
		NI	97.8	71.7	2.4	1.9	2.7	1.1	39.3	29.8
K00-K93	XI Diseases of the digestive system	UK	40.0	29.8	0.5	0.4	8.9	5.5	59.7	32.4
		E	38.6	28.8	0.6	0.4	8.5	5.2	55.9	29.6
		W	38.9	30.3	0.4	..	7.9	5.9	63.5	37.1
		E & W[4]	38.7	28.9	0.6	0.4	8.5	5.3	56.5	30.1
		S	54.7	40.0	..	0.5	14.8	8.3	93.0	56.3
		NI	35.2	25.5	1.2	..	6.2	3.8	56.9	26.4
L00-L99	XII Diseases of the skin and subcutaneous tissue	UK	1.6	2.1	..	..	0.1	0.1	0.9	0.8
		E	1.7	2.1	..	..	0.2	0.1	0.9	0.9
		W	1.2	2.1	..	..	0.2	..	0.3	0.5
		E & W[4]	1.7	2.1	..	..	0.2	0.1	0.9	0.9
		S	1.4	1.6	..	..	0.1	0.2	0.9	0.6
		NI	0.7	1.0	..	..	..	..	1.0	..
M00-M99	XIII Diseases of the musculoskeletal system and connective tissue	UK	3.7	5.3	0.0	0.1	0.3	0.5	2.3	3.1
		E	3.8	5.3	0.0	0.0	0.3	0.5	2.4	2.9
		W	3.6	4.9	0.4	0.4	0.5	0.3	1.6	4.3
		E & W[4]	3.8	5.3	0.0	0.1	0.3	0.5	2.4	3.0
		S	3.4	5.2	..	..	0.5	0.5	2.0	4.1
		NI	2.1	4.1	..	..	0.3	0.5	..	2.4
N00-N99	XIV Diseases of the genitourinary system	UK	12.7	10.8	0.1	0.0	0.5	0.6	4.3	3.9
		E	12.4	10.7	0.1	..	0.5	0.6	3.9	3.9
		W	11.7	10.4	..	0.4	1.0	0.3	6.1	5.6
		E & W[4]	12.4	10.7	0.1	0.0	0.5	0.6	4.1	4.0
		S	14.9	12.0	..	..	0.5	0.7	7.2	4.1
		NI	16.8	12.9	..	0.6	..	..	3.0	1.5
O00-O99	XV Pregnancy, childbirth and the puerperium	UK	..	0.2	..	..	..	0.4	..	0.0
		E	..	0.2	..	..	..	0.4	..	0.0
		W	..	..	..	..	..	..	..	..
		E & W[4]	..	0.2	..	..	..	0.4	..	0.0
		S	..	0.3	..	..	..	0.7	..	..
		NI	..	0.3	..	..	..	0.8	..	..
P00-P99	XVI Certain conditions originating in the perinatal period	UK	0.8	0.7	0.1	0.2	0.0	..	..	..
		E	0.4	0.4	0.2	0.2	0.0	..	..	..
		W	0.3	0.2	..	0.8	..	..	..	..
		E & W[4]	0.4	0.4	0.2	0.2	0.0	..	..	..
		S	4.9	3.0	..	..	..	..	..	..
		NI	4.5	2.8	..	..	..	..	..	..

65–74		75–84		85 and over					ICD-10
M	F	M	F	M	F				
813.3	427.7	2,490.0	1,721.8	6,392.4	5,870.1	UK	IX Diseases of the		I00-I99
790.5	410.8	2,456.9	1,684.1	6,309.6	5,768.9	E	circulatory system		
870.1	434.2	2,567.4	1,859.4	6,654.8	6,182.0	W			
799.1	414.6	2,468.5	1,697.5	6,336.8	5,797.5	E & W[4]			
959.9	542.1	2,713.0	1,963.3	6,976.6	6,554.7	S			
804.0	461.3	2,551.3	1,747.0	6,802.0	6,408.0	NI			
257.4	177.8	971.8	686.3	3,168.5	2,453.3	UK	X Diseases of the		J00-J99
250.2	170.2	958.7	674.6	3,163.6	2,439.6	E	respiratory system		
256.2	180.3	938.8	673.0	3,109.2	2,353.9	W			
251.2	171.1	958.3	675.0	3,161.6	2,435.7	E & W[4]			
330.2	242.1	1,086.6	792.4	3,078.2	2,517.2	S			
220.9	173.0	1,094.3	718.5	3,781.7	2,957.1	NI			
110.2	81.9	250.2	237.4	588.8	641.7	UK	XI Diseases of the		K00-K93
106.8	78.4	248.2	236.2	589.8	645.1	E	digestive system		
95.4	81.4	250.3	226.8	540.5	596.5	W			
106.5	78.7	248.6	235.7	587.5	642.6	E & W[4]			
152.6	116.0	272.5	266.6	639.9	620.5	S			
91.4	66.3	234.7	195.4	469.5	683.7	NI			
4.4	5.6	16.6	20.7	55.2	80.0	UK	XII Diseases of the skin		L00-L99
4.4	5.5	17.5	21.7	57.5	83.4	E	and subcutaneous tissue		
3.1	9.8	16.9	22.1	34.7	57.9	W			
4.4	5.7	17.4	21.7	56.1	81.9	E & W[4]			
4.3	4.0	11.5	16.1	51.5	63.2	S			
3.3	5.8	..	..	25.4	59.7	NI			
11.1	13.9	36.5	50.2	112.7	182.8	UK	XIII Diseases of the		M00-M99
11.4	13.7	35.5	51.6	119.6	190.5	E	musculoskeletal system		
11.5	11.2	44.1	42.4	74.4	152.4	W	and connective tissue		
11.5	13.5	36.1	51.1	116.9	188.2	E & W[4]			
9.6	19.0	42.3	44.3	73.6	133.8	S			
5.0	10.1	33.5	39.5	63.5	135.6	NI			
26.1	23.9	133.3	112.0	553.7	457.0	UK	XIV Diseases of the		N00-N99
25.4	23.4	131.1	108.9	547.8	454.2	E	genitourinary system		
21.5	20.3	121.9	97.7	461.2	444.2	W			
25.2	23.4	130.7	108.3	542.7	453.7	E & W[4]			
28.8	27.9	153.5	135.3	625.2	466.1	S			
46.5	27.4	164.6	161.9	786.8	564.3	NI			
..	..	..	..	..	..	UK	XV Pregnancy, childbirth		O00-O99
..	..	..	..	..	..	E	and the puerperium		
..	..	..	..	..	..	W			
..	..	..	..	..	..	E & W[4]			
..	..	..	..	..	..	S			
..	..	..	..	..	..	NI			
..	..	..	..	..	..	UK	XVI Certain conditions		P00-P99
..	..	..	..	..	..	E	originating in the		
..	..	..	..	..	..	W	perinatal period		
..	..	..	..	..	..	E & W[4]			
..	..	..	..	..	..	S			
..	..	..	..	..	..	NI			

7

Table 7.2 (a) – continued

Deaths by underlying cause, ICD-10 chapter, age and sex, 2006

United Kingdom

Death rates per 100,000 population

ICD-10			All Ages[3] (standardised)		1–14		15–44		45–64	
			M	F	M	F	M	F	M	F
Q00-Q99	XVII Congenital malformations, deformations and chromosomal abnormalities	UK	2.6	2.3	1.3	1.5	1.3	1.0	2.9	1.9
		E	2.4	2.1	1.2	1.4	1.2	0.9	2.9	1.9
		W	2.4	2.0	2.0	0.4	1.9	1.2	1.9	2.6
		E & W[4]	2.5	2.1	1.3	1.4	1.2	1.0	2.9	2.0
		S	3.6	3.3	1.2	2.6	1.7	1.4	2.8	1.6
		NI	5.6	5.0	0.6	1.9	1.1	1.3	5.5	2.0
R00-R99	XVIII Symptoms, signs and abnormal clinical and laboratory findings, not elsewhere classified	UK	8.0	11.2	0.3	0.3	2.3	0.9	5.0	1.9
		E	8.5	12.0	0.3	0.2	2.2	0.9	5.3	1.9
		W	6.1	10.1	0.4	1.7	2.6	1.2	2.6	2.0
		E & W[4]	8.4	11.9	0.3	0.3	2.2	1.0	5.1	1.9
		S	4.9	4.8	0.2	0.8	3.5	0.6	3.7	1.8
		NI	5.4	5.8	..	..	0.8	0.8	4.0	1.0
V01-Y89	XX External causes of mortality	UK	39.7	16.7	4.1	2.7	44.6	11.2	41.3	16.3
		E	36.8	16.0	3.8	2.5	40.4	10.6	38.3	15.5
		W	41.9	16.7	3.6	2.1	50.1	10.7	41.8	16.4
		E & W[4]	37.4	16.1	3.8	2.5	41.5	10.7	38.9	15.6
		S	55.2	19.7	3.9	3.1	66.5	13.4	55.3	20.9
		NI	66.4	24.8	11.2	6.2	77.1	20.4	75.0	22.0

Rates based on less than 20 cases are in italics as a warning to the user that their reliability as a measure may be affected by the small number of events.

1   *Cause of death was defined using International Classification of Diseases, Tenth Revision (ICD-10).*
2   *All data based on year of registration. Previously England and Wales were based on occurences, Scotland and Northern Ireland on registrations.*
3   *Rates for 'All Ages' are based on the European Standard Population and include the under ones.*
4   *'England, Wales and Elsewhere' covers both Residents and Non-Residents, comparable with Scotland and Northern Ireland data. Separate 'England' and 'Wales' categories cover Residents Only.*

Source: Office for National Statistics; General Register Office for Scotland; Northern Ireland Statistics and Research Agency

65–74		75–84		85 and over				ICD-10
M	F	M	F	M	F			
2.9	3.0	3.5	3.4	5.3	3.7	UK	XVII Congenital	Q00-Q99
3.1	3.0	3.4	3.7	5.9	3.8	E	malformations,	
1.5	1.4	7.8	0.9	-	6.4	W	deformations and	
3.0	2.9	3.7	3.5	5.5	4.0	E & W[4]	chromosomal abnormalities	
1.4	2.4	1.8	2.3	3.7	1.5	S		
3.3	8.6	3.0	3.9	..	..	NI		
5.1	3.3	21.2	34.9	420.9	856.1	UK	XVIII Symptoms, signs and	R00-R99
5.5	3.3	23.1	38.4	458.5	931.8	E	abnormal clinical and	
0.8	4.2	13.0	29.5	322.3	684.5	W	laboratory findings, not	
5.2	3.4	22.5	37.9	450.5	917.1	E & W[4]	elsewhere classified	
4.8	2.4	8.8	10.9	95.6	275.0	S		
5.0	1.4	15.2	9.9	253.8	428.6	NI		
43.6	22.3	105.6	81.8	347.0	324.7	UK	XX External causes of	V01-Y89
41.3	21.7	100.5	80.0	340.2	315.5	E	mortality	
43.8	25.3	102.4	80.2	347.1	339.0	W		
41.6	22.0	101.0	80.2	340.6	317.4	E & W[4]		
60.5	22.2	144.6	88.1	397.2	398.5	S		
54.8	31.7	149.4	116.5	456.9	358.1	NI		

Table 7.2 (b)

Deaths by underlying cause, ICD-10 chapter, selected causes by age and sex, 2006

United Kingdom

Death rates per 100,000 population

ICD-10			All Ages[3] (standardised)		1-14		15-44		45-64	
			M	F	M	F	M	F	M	F
A00-R99	All causes	UK	741.2	523.7	16.4	13.4	108.3	55.8	628.3	399.3
V01-Y89		E	722.2	511.2	16.1	12.8	100.3	53.5	601.2	383.0
		W	758.5	538.3	15.2	12.6	121.7	58.1	665.8	441.3
		E & W[6]	726.7	514.2	16.3	13.2	102.4	54.1	608.9	388.4
		S	878.8	612.9	14.6	13.8	166.7	72.5	806.8	502.2
		NI	792.4	543.4	23.6	18.6	125.4	59.3	678.4	411.0
A00-B99	I Infectious and	UK	10.0	8.3	0.8	0.8	1.8	1.4	7.5	4.4
	parasitic diseases	E	9.9	8.3	0.8	0.8	1.9	1.4	7.4	4.1
		W	7.6	5.9	..	0.4	1.4	0.3	4.2	3.6
		E & W[6]	9.9	8.2	0.8	0.8	1.8	1.4	7.3	4.2
		S	12.0	8.7	1.0	0.5	1.5	1.2	9.7	6.3
		NI	8.7	7.9	..	0.6	0.5	0.3	5.0	4.4
C00-D48	II Neoplasms	UK	224.3	160.7	3.6	2.5	14.9	18.3	232.8	207.9
		E	219.6	157.5	3.4	2.5	14.7	17.9	226.5	203.8
		W	234.1	168.8	3.6	1.3	15.9	21.4	258.0	224.5
		E & W[6]	220.9	158.5	3.5	2.5	14.9	18.2	229.1	205.8
		S	257.9	182.7	3.7	2.3	16.4	19.1	266.8	226.6
		NI	231.4	160.1	3.5	2.5	10.7	18.5	242.8	215.8
C00-C97	Malignant neoplasms	UK	219.7	157.5	3.3	2.3	14.5	17.8	229.6	205.6
		E	215.1	154.3	3.2	2.3	14.3	17.4	223.2	201.7
		W	229.4	165.5	3.2	1.3	15.2	20.9	254.3	220.9
		E & W[6]	216.4	155.3	3.3	2.3	14.4	17.7	225.8	203.5
		S	254.0	179.5	3.7	2.3	16.0	18.9	264.7	224.3
		NI	224.7	156.3	3.5	2.5	10.2	18.3	237.7	212.3
C00-C14	Malignant neoplasms of	UK	3.9	1.6	0.0	..	0.5	0.3	7.1	2.6
	lip, oral cavity and	E	3.6	1.5	0.0	..	0.5	0.3	6.7	2.4
	pharynx	W	4.8	1.7	..	..	0.2	0.2	10.3	3.3
		E & W[6]	3.7	1.5	0.0	..	0.4	0.3	6.9	2.4
		S	5.8	2.1	..	..	0.9	0.2	9.5	4.1
		NI	4.9	1.9	..	..	0.5	0.3	7.1	2.9
C15	Malignant neoplasm of	UK	13.6	5.0	..	..	0.6	0.2	18.5	5.8
	oesophagus	E	13.2	4.9	..	..	0.5	0.2	17.7	5.7
		W	14.6	5.4	..	..	0.3	0.3	21.4	6.4
		E & W[6]	13.3	5.0	..	..	0.5	0.2	17.9	5.8
		S	16.5	6.2	..	..	1.2	0.3	23.8	6.4
		NI	12.6	3.5	..	..	0.5	0.5	18.6	2.9
C16	Malignant neoplasm of	UK	8.7	3.8	..	..	0.5	0.5	7.5	3.0
	stomach	E	8.3	3.6	..	..	0.5	0.4	7.2	2.9
		W	10.5	4.4	..	..	0.5	0.7	9.0	2.8
		E & W[6]	8.5	3.6	..	..	0.5	0.4	7.4	2.9
		S	10.9	4.9	..	..	0.9	0.9	8.9	3.8
		NI	10.3	5.2	..	..	0.3	1.3	8.6	3.4
C18	Malignant neoplasm of	UK	13.6	9.7	..	..	0.6	0.7	12.6	9.7
	colon	E	13.3	9.5	..	..	0.7	0.7	11.9	9.4
		W	15.0	11.1	..	..	0.9	1.0	15.1	12.8
		E & W[6]	13.4	9.6	..	..	0.7	0.7	12.2	9.6
		S	15.1	10.2	..	..	0.6	0.6	15.5	10.1
		NI	16.1	10.8	..	..	..	0.5	16.1	10.3

65-74		75-84		85 and over				ICD-10
M	F	M	F	M	F			
2367.0	1520.5	6547.8	4638.1	16448.7	14488.8	UK	All causes	A00-R99
2302.0	1468.3	6444.8	4551.2	16330.3	14371.2	E		V01-Y89
2414.0	1560.0	6623.3	4719.9	16299.7	14432.5	W		
2315.7	1478.8	6465.0	4567.1	16339.3	14382.6	E & W[6]		
2863.4	1908.7	7367.1	5357.7	17454.3	15370.8	S		
2445.2	1536.6	6910.1	4666.6	17753.8	15713.5	NI		
24.4	19.0	84.9	80.8	278.4	256.9	UK	I Infectious and	A00-B99
23.5	18.8	84.3	81.5	275.6	262.4	E	parasitic diseases	
20.8	19.6	67.4	57.2	247.9	163.1	W		
23.5	19.0	83.4	80.3	274.5	256.8	E & W[6]		
33.1	16.6	103.2	90.4	316.3	258.8	S		
23.3	27.4	79.3	65.1	317.3	255.0	NI		
952.6	653.6	2005.6	1230.9	3221.3	1784.5	UK	II Neoplasms	C00-D48
928.3	635.9	1973.4	1208.3	3187.7	1768.9	E		
985.5	686.0	2037.0	1268.5	3213.3	1735.9	W		
933.2	640.6	1979.5	1213.4	3190.7	1767.9	E & W[6]		
1121.7	782.6	2291.4	1432.9	3626.2	1939.4	S		
1044.9	631.4	2024.0	1152.8	3159.9	1909.9	NI		
938.5	643.9	1958.5	1199.7	3110.7	1706.5	UK	Malignant neoplasms	C00-C97
914.3	625.8	1926.3	1177.2	3078.0	1692.3	E		
968.5	678.3	1998.1	1237.1	3104.2	1667.3	W		
919.0	630.6	1932.9	1182.3	3081.0	1691.8	E & W[6]		
1110.6	777.3	2251.7	1401.2	3504.8	1839.4	S		
1026.6	615.5	1932.5	1121.2	3045.7	1834.0	NI		
15.8	5.5	16.1	9.0	28.2	17.6	UK	Malignant neoplasms of	C00-C14
14.1	5.2	14.9	8.9	27.2	17.2	E	lip, oral cavity and	
20.0	5.6	11.7	7.4	39.7	17.2	W	pharynx	
14.5	5.2	14.8	8.8	27.9	17.2	E & W[6]		
27.8	6.9	25.6	10.9	29.4	22.1	S		
21.6	8.6	33.5	7.9	38.1	16.3	NI		
60.1	19.5	107.3	48.3	128.3	69.4	UK	Malignant neoplasm of	C15
58.5	19.1	106.5	46.5	127.6	69.5	E	oesophagus	
66.9	23.1	103.7	44.2	133.9	73.0	W		
59.1	19.3	106.4	46.4	128.0	69.7	E & W[6]		
72.0	24.7	116.4	70.8	150.8	64.7	S		
54.8	8.6	109.7	39.5	63.5	76.0	NI		
38.7	14.6	89.1	37.7	122.7	66.9	UK	Malignant neoplasm of	C16
36.3	13.1	85.7	36.1	118.9	66.1	E	stomach	
50.0	16.1	93.4	52.5	173.6	68.7	W		
37.1	13.5	86.3	37.1	122.1	66.2	E & W[6]		
53.3	21.8	110.2	42.0	128.7	76.5	S		
43.2	25.9	125.0	45.4	126.9	59.7	NI		
57.9	37.5	132.0	88.2	221.7	171.2	UK	Malignant neoplasm of	C18
56.7	36.2	129.8	87.0	220.0	170.4	E	colon	
68.5	41.4	140.0	96.8	183.5	169.5	W		
57.5	36.7	130.6	87.6	217.8	170.5	E & W[6]		
57.6	41.2	149.9	93.9	246.4	173.5	S		
74.8	49.0	125.0	88.8	304.6	195.3	NI		

7

Table 7.2 (b) – continued

Deaths by underlying cause, ICD-10 chapter, selected causes by age and sex, 2006

United Kingdom

Death rates per 100,000 population

ICD-10			All Ages[3] (standardised)		1-14		15-44		45-64	
			M	F	M	F	M	F	M	F
C19-C21	Malignant neoplasm of rectosigmoid junction, rectum and anus	UK	9.5	4.8	..	..	0.5	0.4	10.8	5.7
		E	9.1	4.7	..	..	0.5	0.3	10.5	5.5
		W	10.5	4.7	..	..	0.7	0.2	11.1	6.1
		E & W[6]	9.2	4.7	..	..	0.5	0.3	10.5	5.6
		S	12.3	6.4	..	..	0.7	0.9	13.2	7.6
		NI	9.5	3.6	..	..	..	0.3	12.6	3.4
C22	Malignant neoplasm of liver and intrahepatic bile ducts	UK	5.2	2.5	0.1	0.0	0.4	0.1	6.3	2.9
		E	5.1	2.4	0.1	..	0.4	0.2	6.2	2.7
		W	4.8	3.3	..	..	0.5	..	5.8	4.9
		E & W[6]	5.1	2.4	0.1	..	0.4	0.1	6.2	2.8
		S	7.1	3.1	..	0.3	0.2	0.1	7.2	3.4
		NI	5.5	2.9	0.6	0.6	..	0.3	8.6	4.4
C25	Malignant neoplasm of pancreas	UK	10.1	7.6	..	..	0.4	0.2	13.5	8.8
		E	10.2	7.7	..	..	0.4	0.2	13.4	8.9
		W	10.2	7.0	..	..	0.3	0.3	16.9	6.9
		E & W[6]	10.2	7.7	..	..	0.4	0.2	13.6	8.9
		S	8.9	7.1	..	..	0.4	0.6	12.0	7.9
		NI	10.6	8.1	..	..	0.5	..	13.1	10.3
C32	Malignant neoplasm of larynx	UK	1.8	0.4	..	..	0.1	0.0	2.7	0.6
		E	1.6	0.4	..	..	0.1	0.0	2.5	0.6
		W	2.4	0.3	..	..	0.2	..	3.4	0.3
		E & W[6]	1.7	0.4	..	..	0.1	0.0	2.6	0.6
		S	2.5	0.6	..	..	0.1	..	3.8	0.7
		NI	2.9	0.4	..	..	0.3	..	2.5	0.5
C33-C34	Malignant neoplasm of trachea, bronchus and lung	UK	53.6	32.2	..	0.0	1.4	1.3	59.5	43.1
		E	51.5	30.5	..	0.0	1.3	1.2	56.7	40.6
		W	56.8	32.9	..	..	2.1	1.6	71.7	46.8
		E & W[6]	51.9	30.7	..	0.0	1.4	1.2	57.7	41.1
		S	70.6	47.6	..	..	1.7	2.0	75.4	62.5
		NI	58.4	29.0	..	..	1.3	1.9	65.0	43.0
C43	Malignant melanoma of skin	UK	3.1	1.9	..	..	1.0	0.6	4.8	2.8
		E	3.1	1.8	..	..	1.0	0.5	4.7	2.9
		W	3.6	2.3	..	..	1.6	1.0	5.6	3.3
		E & W[6]	3.1	1.9	..	..	1.1	0.6	4.8	2.9
		S	3.1	1.8	..	..	0.8	0.6	4.3	2.2
		NI	2.9	1.9	..	..	..	1.3	6.0	2.0
C50	Malignant neoplasm of breast	UK	0.2	28.4	..	..	0.0	5.6	0.3	48.9
		E	0.2	28.2	..	..	0.0	5.4	0.2	49.2
		W	0.5	29.5	..	..	0.2	6.9	0.5	46.3
		E & W[6]	0.2	28.3	..	..	0.0	5.6	0.3	49.2
		S	0.1	29.0	..	..	..	5.8	0.2	46.3
		NI	0.1	27.5	..	..	..	5.6	0.5	49.8
C53	Malignant neoplasm of cervix uteri	UK	..	2.5	..	..	..	1.4	..	4.2
		E	..	2.3	..	..	..	1.4	..	3.9
		W	..	3.3	..	..	..	2.8	..	5.4
		E & W[6]	..	2.4	..	..	..	1.4	..	4.0
		S	..	2.8	..	..	..	1.5	..	5.1
		NI	..	2.9	..	..	..	1.1	..	6.8

65-74		75-84		85 and over					ICD-10
M	F	M	F	M	F				
43.0	19.5	79.5	39.3	113.7	72.3	UK	Malignant neoplasm of		C19-C21
41.0	19.1	76.1	38.5	109.7	71.1	E	rectosigmoid junction,		
47.7	20.3	93.4	34.1	124.0	60.1	W	rectum and anus		
41.5	19.2	77.3	38.2	110.5	70.6	E & W[6]			
57.6	24.7	108.5	51.8	143.4	86.7	S			
43.2	11.5	61.0	31.6	152.3	92.2	NI			
24.8	11.4	41.6	21.6	50.7	26.4	UK	Malignant neoplasm of		C22
23.2	10.8	40.3	20.9	50.0	26.0	E	liver and intrahepatic		
20.8	18.2	44.1	20.3	39.7	21.5	W	bile ducts		
23.1	11.3	40.6	20.9	49.4	25.7	E & W[6]			
42.7	13.7	54.7	27.1	62.5	30.9	S			
23.3	5.8	33.5	25.7	63.5	38.0	NI			
46.1	35.7	77.5	65.5	103.2	88.1	UK	Malignant neoplasm of		C25
47.0	36.0	78.2	65.9	105.4	89.4	E	pancreas		
36.9	33.7	77.8	67.3	89.3	73.0	W			
46.4	36.0	78.2	66.1	104.4	88.5	E & W[6]			
37.9	35.2	72.3	56.4	95.6	77.9	S			
61.5	30.3	67.1	77.0	76.1	108.5	NI			
6.8	1.7	12.7	2.8	21.1	2.2	UK	Malignant neoplasm of		C32
5.9	1.4	11.6	2.6	20.7	2.3	E	larynx		
8.5	2.1	23.3	1.8	14.9	..	W			
6.1	1.5	12.3	2.6	20.6	2.2	E & W[6]			
12.0	3.6	11.5	5.2	29.4	2.9	S			
15.0	2.9	33.5	2.0	12.7	..	NI			
258.6	156.5	482.2	260.4	559.5	207.1	UK	Malignant neoplasm of		C33-C34
246.0	147.3	468.5	249.2	547.5	200.6	E	trachea, bronchus and		
259.3	152.9	470.7	264.6	570.3	193.1	W	lung		
247.2	148.0	469.0	250.6	548.8	200.3	E & W[6]			
354.7	243.7	635.0	370.3	713.5	301.4	S			
325.6	131.2	463.3	229.0	494.9	146.5	NI			
11.9	7.0	16.3	9.5	19.3	14.6	UK	Malignant melanoma of		C43
11.8	6.9	16.2	9.3	18.8	14.2	E	skin		
13.1	7.7	13.0	12.0	19.8	12.9	W			
11.9	7.0	16.0	9.5	18.9	14.1	E & W[6]			
13.4	8.1	15.9	9.8	29.4	14.7	S			
8.3	2.9	27.4	9.9	..	32.6	NI			
0.7	90.9	1.3	154.6	5.0	280.9	UK	Malignant neoplasm of		C50
0.8	88.3	1.2	151.8	4.6	286.4	E	breast		
..	107.3	3.9	168.7	14.9	248.9	W			
0.7	89.7	1.3	153.0	5.2	284.3	E & W[6]			
0.5	102.7	0.9	176.8	3.7	248.5	S			
..	87.9	..	132.3	..	260.4	NI			
..	5.5	..	9.6	..	13.2	UK	Malignant neoplasm of		C53
..	5.3	..	9.6	..	13.9	E	cervix uteri		
..	4.9	..	12.0	..	6.4	W			
..	5.3	..	9.7	..	13.5	E & W[6]			
..	8.9	..	7.5	..	8.8	S			
..	2.9	..	11.8	..	16.3	NI			

7

Table 7.2 (b) – continued

Deaths by underlying cause, ICD-10 chapter, selected causes by age and sex, 2006

United Kingdom

Death rates per 100,000 population

ICD-10			All Ages[3] (standardised)		1-14		15-44		45-64	
			M	F	M	F	M	F	M	F
C54-C55	Malignant neoplasm of other and unspecified parts of uterus	UK	..	3.5	..	..	..	0.1	..	4.6
		E	..	3.5	..	..	..	0.1	..	4.6
		W	..	4.1	..	..	..	0.2	..	6.9
		E & W[6]	..	3.6	..	..	..	0.1	..	4.7
		S	..	3.4	..	..	..	-	..	4.4
		NI	..	3.5	..	..	..	0.3	..	3.4
C56	Malignant neoplasm of ovary	UK	..	10.2	..	..	..	0.8	..	16.9
		E	..	10.1	..	..	..	0.8	..	17.0
		W	..	9.5	..	..	..	0.2	..	14.1
		E & W[6]	..	10.1	..	..	..	0.8	..	16.8
		S	..	10.6	..	..	..	0.9	..	16.1
		NI	..	12.0	..	..	..	0.8	..	22.9
C61	Malignant neoplasm of prostate	UK	25.5	..	..	..	0.1	..	9.5	..
		E	25.5	..	..	..	0.1	..	9.4	..
		W	25.6	..	..	..	..	..	7.9	..
		E & W[6]	25.6	..	..	..	0.1	..	9.3	..
		S	24.8	..	..	..	..	..	12.3	..
		NI	22.9	..	..	..	..	..	6.0	..
C64	Malignant neoplasm of kidney, except renal pelvis	UK	6.3	2.7	0.1	0.1	0.4	0.2	8.9	3.1
		E	6.1	2.7	0.0	0.1	0.4	0.2	8.7	3.1
		W	7.9	2.4	0.4	..	0.5	0.5	13.2	2.3
		E & W[6]	6.2	2.7	0.1	0.1	0.4	0.2	9.0	3.0
		S	6.9	3.1	..	..	0.6	0.3	9.2	3.5
		NI	6.3	2.9	..	..	..	0.3	6.5	3.4
C67	Malignant neoplasm of bladder	UK	8.3	3.0	0.0	..	0.1	0.1	5.2	2.1
		E	8.3	3.0	0.0	..	0.1	0.1	5.3	2.1
		W	7.8	2.8	..	..	0.3	0.2	3.4	1.8
		E & W[6]	8.3	2.9	0.0	..	0.1	0.1	5.2	2.1
		S	9.0	3.1	..	..	0.1	0.1	5.5	2.2
		NI	6.4	2.8	..	..	0.3	0.3	3.0	2.4
C81-C96	Malignant neoplasm of lymphoid, haematopoietic and related tisue	UK	17.9	11.0	1.1	0.6	2.5	1.8	19.0	10.6
		E	17.9	10.9	1.1	0.6	2.6	1.8	19.2	10.5
		W	16.9	11.2	1.6	0.4	1.6	1.4	17.7	11.8
		E & W[6]	17.9	11.0	1.1	0.6	2.6	1.8	19.3	10.7
		S	18.9	11.3	1.5	0.5	2.7	1.9	17.9	9.8
		NI	15.3	11.9	..	0.6	1.6	0.8	11.1	12.7
D50-D89	III Diseases of the blood and blood forming organs and certain disorders involving the immune mechanism	UK	1.4	1.2	0.2	0.2	0.4	0.3	1.6	0.9
		E	1.4	1.2	0.2	0.1	0.4	0.3	1.6	0.9
		W	1.0	1.2	..	..	..	0.3	1.6	0.3
		E & W[6]	1.4	1.2	0.2	0.2	0.4	0.3	1.6	0.9
		S	1.7	1.4	0.5	0.3	0.3	0.2	1.8	1.0
		NI	1.3	1.6	..	..	0.5	0.5	1.5	2.0
E00-E90	IV Endocrine, nutritional and metabolic diseases	UK	10.4	8.4	0.8	0.8	1.8	1.7	8.5	5.9
		E	9.7	7.9	0.8	0.8	1.7	1.6	7.5	5.5
		W	9.8	9.4	1.2	0.8	2.3	1.6	7.4	6.9
		E & W[6]	9.7	8.0	0.8	0.8	1.7	1.6	7.5	5.6
		S	15.9	12.3	1.0	1.3	2.7	2.7	17.8	8.8
		NI	15.6	9.8	1.2	0.6	1.6	1.6	11.6	5.4

65-74		75-84		85 and over					ICD-10
M	F	M	F	M	F				
..	16.9	..	25.8	..	37.0	UK	Malignant neoplasm of	C54-C55
..	17.2	..	25.6	..	36.1	E	other and unspecified	
..	15.4	..	21.7	..	38.6	W	parts of uterus	
..	17.1	..	25.8	..	36.3	E & W[6]		
..	15.4	..	25.9	..	41.2	S		
..	17.3	..	25.7	..	54.3	NI		
..	46.0	..	59.9	..	60.3	UK	Malignant neoplasm of	C56
..	44.7	..	60.1	..	59.5	E	ovary	
..	48.4	..	59.0	..	73.0	W		
..	44.9	..	60.1	..	60.3	E & W[6]		
..	53.0	..	61.6	..	63.2	S		
..	56.2	..	49.4	..	48.8	NI		
90.4	..	306.6	..	754.5	..	UK	Malignant neoplasm of	C61
90.6	..	308.1	..	759.7	..	E	prostate	
95.4	..	300.8	..	788.5	..	W		
91.1	..	308.0	..	761.4	..	E & W[6]		
83.5	..	294.6	..	702.4	..	S		
88.0	..	295.7	..	634.5	..	NI		
26.6	12.9	45.7	21.2	64.4	29.7	UK	Malignant neoplasm of	C64
26.2	13.2	44.5	20.1	61.2	29.5	E	kidney, except renal	
26.9	10.5	58.3	23.0	69.4	19.3	W	pelvis	
26.2	13.0	45.4	20.4	61.7	28.9	E & W[6]		
26.9	11.3	52.9	30.5	84.6	39.7	S		
36.5	15.9	33.5	19.7	114.2	27.1	NI		
31.3	11.9	90.1	32.3	200.8	58.5	UK	Malignant neoplasm of	C67
31.4	11.8	89.2	32.3	200.8	58.9	E	bladder	
27.7	10.5	101.1	32.3	178.5	55.8	W		
31.1	11.7	90.1	32.4	199.8	58.9	E & W[6]		
37.0	13.7	99.7	31.7	198.6	57.3	S		
16.6	10.1	61.0	29.6	253.8	48.8	NI		
73.5	46.3	150.1	94.1	219.6	144.1	UK	Malignant neoplasm of	C81-C96
72.8	45.7	149.8	93.2	215.0	141.8	E	lymphoid, haematopoietic	
74.6	47.7	145.2	91.3	188.4	154.5	W	and related tisue	
73.1	46.1	149.7	93.2	213.5	142.7	E & W[6]		
79.7	46.5	151.7	101.9	283.2	154.4	S		
63.1	51.9	158.5	98.7	266.5	162.8	NI		
3.4	3.3	9.5	8.5	28.2	31.2	UK	III Diseases of the blood	D50-D89
3.5	3.1	9.5	8.2	27.5	30.0	E	and blood forming organs	
0.8	4.9	9.1	9.2	29.8	38.6	W	and certain disorders	
3.3	3.2	9.6	8.3	27.6	30.5	E & W[6]	involving the immune	
3.8	4.4	11.5	12.1	36.8	33.8	S	mechanism	
6.6	2.9	..	3.9	25.4	54.3	NI		
34.9	25.2	88.9	74.1	213.2	205.5	UK	IV Endocrine, nutritional	E00-E90
32.6	22.6	83.4	69.4	208.2	200.2	E	and metabolic diseases	
24.6	30.2	93.4	75.6	218.2	238.2	W		
32.1	23.1	84.1	69.8	208.8	202.5	E & W[6]		
58.1	46.1	128.8	108.3	220.7	214.7	S		
53.2	20.2	137.2	108.6	380.7	298.4	NI		

7

Table 7.2 (b) – continued

Deaths by underlying cause, ICD-10 chapter, selected causes by age and sex, 2006

United Kingdom

Death rates per 100,000 population

ICD-10			All Ages[3] (standardised)		1-14		15-44		45-64	
			M	F	M	F	M	F	M	F
E14	Unspecified Diabetes mellitus	UK	5.6	4.0	..	0.0	0.7	0.5	4.2	2.6
		E	5.4	3.9	..	0.0	0.7	0.5	3.8	2.6
		W	5.9	5.3	..	..	0.2	1.0	5.3	2.8
		E & W[6]	5.5	4.0	..	0.0	0.7	0.5	3.9	2.6
		S	6.0	3.9	..	..	1.0	0.8	6.1	2.8
		NI	7.8	3.9	..	..	0.5	0.8	6.5	1.5
F00-F99	V Mental and behavioural disorders	UK	16.4	16.6	0.0	0.1	7.7	1.8	7.6	3.6
		E	14.2	15.1	0.0	..	5.8	1.2	4.9	2.6
		W	16.3	16.0	..	0.4	9.1	1.9	5.0	2.8
		E & W[6]	14.3	15.2	0.0	0.0	6.1	1.3	5.0	2.7
		S	38.4	31.7	..	0.5	26.5	7.1	30.5	12.3
		NI	18.7	15.7	..	..	5.4	1.1	19.1	7.3
G00-H95	VI-VIII Diseases of the nervous system and sense organs	UK	21.3	16.9	2.1	1.7	4.8	3.2	15.9	14.2
		E	21.4	16.6	2.3	1.6	4.7	3.0	15.9	13.6
		W	22.0	18.0	1.6	1.7	6.3	2.9	14.3	18.2
		E & W[6]	21.4	16.7	2.2	1.7	4.8	3.0	15.8	14.0
		S	18.8	17.3	1.0	1.3	4.9	4.4	17.9	16.9
		NI	25.5	22.9	2.9	3.1	4.6	3.2	14.6	12.2
I00-I99	IX Diseases of the circulatory system	UK	251.5	161.6	0.9	1.0	16.0	7.0	195.7	72.1
		E	245.5	157.0	0.9	1.0	15.0	6.7	187.1	67.6
		W	266.8	173.3	1.2	1.7	19.6	7.8	215.1	86.2
		E & W[6]	247.9	158.5	0.9	1.0	15.5	6.8	190.9	69.3
		S	288.9	190.7	0.7	0.3	22.8	9.1	243.2	97.3
		NI	256.7	171.5	0.6	1.2	14.0	5.4	198.9	79.1
I20-I25	Ischaemic heart diseases	UK	141.1	67.5	..	0.1	7.6	1.7	131.4	32.7
		E	136.6	64.5	..	0.1	6.8	1.6	124.8	29.9
		W	151.4	74.6	..	..	10.5	2.4	141.6	40.9
		E & W[6]	138.2	65.3	..	0.1	7.1	1.6	127.3	30.7
		S	168.1	87.3	..	..	12.4	3.2	168.4	49.2
		NI	155.4	79.5	..	..	8.3	1.1	147.6	43.9
I60-I69	Cerebrovascular diseases	UK	54.4	50.8	0.1	0.1	2.5	2.0	25.4	18.9
		E	52.8	49.4	0.1	0.1	2.4	2.0	23.8	17.7
		W	57.7	52.3	..	..	2.6	1.9	29.9	21.5
		E & W[6]	53.3	49.7	0.1	0.1	2.4	2.0	24.4	18.1
		S	66.8	61.8	..	0.3	4.1	2.0	35.1	26.1
		NI	56.4	52.1	..	..	1.3	1.9	26.2	19.5
J00-J99	X Diseases of the respiratory system	UK	91.2	66.3	1.4	1.2	3.0	2.0	42.2	29.9
		E	89.8	64.9	1.4	1.2	2.9	2.0	40.9	28.2
		W	89.6	65.1	0.8	0.4	3.0	2.1	42.3	30.4
		E & W[6]	89.9	65.0	1.4	1.2	2.9	2.0	41.1	28.5
		S	102.2	78.3	1.5	0.5	4.2	3.0	54.1	43.6
		NI	97.8	71.7	2.4	1.9	2.7	1.1	39.3	29.8
J10-J11	Influenza	UK	0.0	0.0	0.1	..	0.0	0.0	0.0	..
		E	0.0	0.0	0.1	..	0.0	0.0	..	..
		W	..	0.0	..	..	..	..	..	..
		E & W[6]	0.0	0.0	0.1	..	0.0	0.0	..	..
		S	0.1	..	0.2	..	..	..	0.2	..
		NI	..	0.1	..	..	..	..	..	..

65-74		75-84		85 and over				ICD-10
M	F	M	F	M	F			
19.6	13.4	51.9	38.6	132.0	99.3	UK	Unspecified Diabetes	E14
18.9	12.4	50.8	38.4	133.8	100.4	E	mellitus	
18.5	19.6	66.1	48.9	119.0	128.7	W		
19.0	12.9	51.9	39.0	132.9	102.1	E & W[6]		
22.1	19.8	53.8	30.5	91.9	63.2	S		
33.2	7.2	45.7	51.3	228.4	113.9	NI		
17.9	16.4	131.4	149.2	609.9	931.1	UK	V Mental and behavioural	F00-F99
15.4	14.2	121.2	140.2	579.9	875.6	E	disorders	
15.4	13.3	140.0	136.4	590.1	942.0	W		
15.5	14.2	122.3	140.0	580.5	879.7	E & W[6]		
42.7	38.8	231.1	251.7	970.9	1523.3	S		
15.0	10.1	137.2	118.4	647.2	917.0	NI		
59.7	43.6	198.6	146.3	453.1	410.2	UK	VI-VIII Diseases of the	G00-H95
60.0	43.7	198.2	144.6	459.1	401.4	E	nervous system and	
63.1	37.9	213.9	141.0	456.2	497.8	W	sense organs	
60.2	43.3	199.2	144.4	458.9	407.2	E & W[6]		
51.8	42.0	166.7	142.8	342.0	370.5	S		
68.1	59.1	286.5	225.0	583.8	683.7	NI		
813.3	427.7	2490.0	1721.8	6392.4	5870.1	UK	IX Diseases of the	I00-I99
790.5	410.8	2456.9	1684.1	6309.6	5768.9	E	circulatory system	
870.1	434.2	2567.4	1859.4	6654.8	6182.0	W		
799.1	414.6	2468.5	1697.5	6336.8	5797.5	E & W[6]		
959.9	542.1	2713.0	1963.3	6976.6	6554.7	S		
804.0	461.3	2551.3	1747.0	6802.0	6408.0	NI		
502.2	208.4	1340.5	741.4	2970.0	2177.2	UK	Ischaemic heart diseases	I20-I25
484.2	196.7	1314.6	715.5	2916.2	2108.2	E		
548.5	207.6	1415.9	805.7	3074.5	2465.5	W		
491.1	198.5	1323.3	722.5	2930.4	2130.6	E & W[6]		
606.7	293.9	1502.0	904.8	3328.3	2593.7	S		
528.2	237.8	1444.8	844.9	3464.5	2604.4	NI		
138.9	106.8	608.4	545.6	1899.9	2130.7	UK	Cerebrovascular diseases	I60-I69
133.7	103.4	597.7	534.3	1852.8	2081.9	E		
139.2	112.9	600.3	556.8	2127.3	2139.3	W		
134.5	104.4	599.0	536.1	1870.0	2086.4	E & W[6]		
179.5	129.3	705.6	644.4	2261.8	2595.1	S		
152.8	106.7	634.0	538.9	1954.3	2284.3	NI		
257.4	177.8	971.8	686.3	3168.5	2453.3	UK	X Diseases of the	J00-J99
250.2	170.2	958.7	674.6	3163.6	2439.6	E	respiratory system	
256.2	180.3	938.8	673.0	3109.2	2353.9	W		
251.2	171.1	958.3	675.0	3161.6	2435.7	E & W[6]		
330.2	242.1	1086.6	792.4	3078.2	2517.2	S		
220.9	173.0	1094.3	718.5	3781.7	2957.1	NI		
..	..	0.1	0.1	..	0.5	UK	Influenza	J10-J11
..	..	0.2	0.1	..	0.4	E		
..	..	..	..	..	2.1	W		
..	..	0.2	0.1	..	0.5	E & W[6]		
..	..	..	..	..	..	S		
..	..	..	2.0	..	..	NI		

Table 7.2 (b) – continued

Deaths by underlying cause, ICD-10 chapter, selected causes by age and sex, 2006

United Kingdom

Death rates per 100,000 population

ICD-10			All Ages[3] (standardised)		1-14		15-44		45-64	
			M	F	M	F	M	F	M	F
J12-J18	Pneumonia	UK	32.8	27.2	0.4	0.3	1.4	0.9	12.2	7.9
		E	32.7	27.0	0.4	0.3	1.4	0.9	12.0	7.7
		W	32.1	27.1	..	0.4	1.4	0.9	11.4	7.2
		E & W[6]	32.7	27.1	0.4	0.3	1.4	0.9	12.0	7.7
		S	31.6	27.1	0.2	..	1.9	1.2	14.4	9.5
		NI	38.3	33.9	..	..	1.3	0.8	12.6	7.8
J40-J47	Chronic lower respiratory disease	UK	37.9	25.7	0.6	0.3	0.7	0.5	21.2	16.4
		E	37.2	24.6	0.5	0.3	0.7	0.5	20.9	15.2
		W	38.5	26.7	0.8	..	0.7	0.7	22.0	17.6
		E & W[6]	37.3	24.7	0.6	0.3	0.7	0.5	21.0	15.4
		S	44.1	35.1	0.5	..	1.3	0.7	24.5	26.3
		NI	36.5	24.5	1.2	1.2	0.5	0.3	17.6	17.6
J40-J44	Bronchitis, emphysema and other chronic obstructive pulmonary disease	UK	35.8	23.0	0.0	..	0.3	0.1	19.4	14.1
		E	35.0	21.9	0.0	..	0.3	0.1	18.9	13.0
		W	37.2	23.8	0.4	..	..	..	20.4	14.6
		E & W[6]	35.2	22.0	0.0	..	0.3	0.1	19.0	13.1
		S	42.4	32.8	..	..	0.7	0.4	23.6	24.1
		NI	34.6	21.4	..	..	..	..	17.6	12.7
J45-J46	Asthma	UK	1.0	1.6	0.5	0.3	0.4	0.4	1.1	1.6
		E	1.0	1.6	0.5	0.3	0.4	0.4	1.2	1.6
		W	0.7	1.9	..	..	0.7	0.3	0.8	2.0
		E & W[6]	1.0	1.6	0.5	0.3	0.4	0.4	1.2	1.6
		S	1.0	1.3	0.5	..	0.5	0.3	0.5	1.3
		NI	1.3	2.0	1.2	1.2	0.5	0.3	..	2.9
K00-K93	XI Diseases of the digestive system	UK	40.0	29.8	0.5	0.4	8.9	5.5	59.7	32.4
		E	38.6	28.8	0.6	0.4	8.5	5.2	55.9	29.6
		W	38.9	30.3	0.4	..	7.9	5.9	63.5	37.1
		E & W[6]	38.7	28.9	0.6	0.4	8.5	5.3	56.5	30.1
		S	54.7	40.0	..	0.5	14.8	8.3	93.0	56.3
		NI	35.2	25.5	1.2	..	6.2	3.8	56.9	26.4
L00-L99	XII Diseases of the skin and subcutaneous tissue	UK	1.6	2.1	..	..	0.1	0.1	0.9	0.8
		E	1.7	2.1	..	..	0.2	0.1	0.9	0.9
		W	1.2	2.1	..	..	0.2	..	0.3	0.5
		E & W[6]	1.7	2.1	..	..	0.2	0.1	0.9	0.9
		S	1.4	1.6	..	..	0.1	0.2	0.9	0.6
		NI	0.7	1.0	..	..	..	..	1.0	..
M00-M99	XIII Diseases of the musculoskeletal system and connective tissue	UK	3.7	5.3	0.0	0.1	0.3	0.5	2.3	3.1
		E	3.8	5.3	0.0	0.0	0.3	0.5	2.4	2.9
		W	3.6	4.9	0.4	0.4	0.5	0.3	1.6	4.3
		E & W[6]	3.8	5.3	0.0	0.1	0.3	0.5	2.4	3.0
		S	3.4	5.2	..	..	0.5	0.5	2.0	4.1
		NI	2.1	4.1	..	..	0.3	0.5	..	2.4
N00-N99	XIV Diseases of the genitourinary system	UK	12.7	10.8	0.1	0.0	0.5	0.6	4.3	3.9
		E	12.4	10.7	0.1	..	0.5	0.6	3.9	3.9
		W	11.7	10.4	..	0.4	1.0	0.3	6.1	5.6
		E & W[6]	12.4	10.7	0.1	0.0	0.5	0.6	4.1	4.0
		S	14.9	12.0	..	..	0.5	0.7	7.2	4.1
		NI	16.8	12.9	..	0.6	..	..	3.0	1.5

65-74		75-84		85 and over				ICD-10
M	F	M	F	M	F			
60.7	40.6	306.4	246.1	1555.5	1452.1	UK	Pneumonia	J12-J18
60.4	39.6	302.0	246.0	1571.3	1443.0	E		
64.6	38.6	311.2	236.9	1467.8	1489.2	W		
60.8	39.6	303.2	245.8	1565.8	1446.8	E & W[6]		
64.3	46.5	324.6	244.2	1287.2	1365.9	S		
44.9	50.5	365.8	264.5	2030.5	1996.7	NI		
140.2	107.2	448.6	307.8	886.5	451.4	UK	Chronic lower respiratory	J40-J47
136.2	100.8	443.8	297.9	872.5	448.3	E	disease	
127.7	115.7	446.0	324.5	1026.5	414.1	W		
136.0	101.9	444.1	299.7	882.1	446.5	E & W[6]		
189.1	162.1	499.2	391.0	915.7	513.1	S		
121.3	89.4	445.0	307.9	977.2	428.6	NI		
134.2	98.4	432.3	284.8	845.3	394.2	UK	Bronchitis, emphysema and	J40-J44
130.0	92.0	426.8	274.4	829.2	389.2	E	other chronic obstructive	
124.6	106.6	439.6	299.6	1006.6	366.9	W	pulmonary disease	
130.0	93.1	427.7	276.1	840.2	388.0	E & W[6]		
183.3	153.2	485.1	372.6	879.0	472.0	S		
113.0	83.6	426.7	288.2	951.8	369.0	NI		
1.9	3.5	5.8	12.1	17.4	38.3	UK	Asthma	J45-J46
1.9	3.3	5.7	12.2	17.0	39.5	E		
..	4.9	2.6	17.5	14.9	38.6	W		
1.8	3.5	5.5	12.5	16.9	39.6	E & W[6]		
1.9	4.0	7.1	8.1	22.1	25.0	S		
3.3	2.9	12.2	11.8	25.4	32.6	NI		
110.2	81.9	250.2	237.4	588.8	641.7	UK	XI Diseases of the	K00-K93
106.8	78.4	248.2	236.2	589.8	645.1	E	digestive system	
95.4	81.4	250.3	226.8	540.5	596.5	W		
106.5	78.7	248.6	235.7	587.5	642.6	E & W[6]		
152.6	116.0	272.5	266.6	639.9	620.5	S		
91.4	66.3	234.7	195.4	469.5	683.7	NI		
4.4	5.6	16.6	20.7	55.2	80.0	UK	XII Diseases of the skin	L00-L99
4.4	5.5	17.5	21.7	57.5	83.4	E	and subcutaneous tissue	
3.1	9.8	16.9	22.1	34.7	57.9	W		
4.4	5.7	17.4	21.7	56.1	81.9	E & W[6]		
4.3	4.0	11.5	16.1	51.5	63.2	S		
3.3	5.8	..	..	25.4	59.7	NI		
11.1	13.9	36.5	50.2	112.7	182.8	UK	XIII Diseases of the	M00-M99
11.4	13.7	35.5	51.6	119.6	190.5	E	musculoskeletal system	
11.5	11.2	44.1	42.4	74.4	152.4	W	and connective tissue	
11.5	13.5	36.1	51.1	116.9	188.2	E & W[6]		
9.6	19.0	42.3	44.3	73.6	133.8	S		
5.0	10.1	33.5	39.5	63.5	135.6	NI		
26.1	23.9	133.3	112.0	553.7	457.0	UK	XIV Diseases of the	N00-N99
25.4	23.4	131.1	108.9	547.8	454.2	E	genitourinary system	
21.5	20.3	121.9	97.7	461.2	444.2	W		
25.2	23.4	130.7	108.3	542.7	453.7	E & W[6]		
28.8	27.9	153.5	135.3	625.2	466.1	S		
46.5	27.4	164.6	161.9	786.8	564.3	NI		

Table 7.2 (b) – continued

Deaths by underlying cause, ICD-10 chapter, selected causes by age and sex, 2006

United Kingdom

Death rates per 100,000 population

ICD-10			All Ages[3] (standardised)		1-14		15-44		45-64	
			M	F	M	F	M	F	M	F
O00-O99	XV Pregnancy, childbirth and the puerperium	UK	..	0.2	..	..	..	0.4	..	0.0
		E	..	0.2	..	..	..	0.4	..	0.0
		W	..	-	..	..	..	0.0	..	..
		E & W[6]	..	0.2	..	..	..	0.4	..	0.0
		S	..	0.3	..	..	..	0.7	..	..
		NI	..	0.3	..	..	..	0.8	..	..
P00-P99	XVI Certain conditions originating in the perinatal period	UK	0.8	0.7	0.1	0.2	0.0	..	..	..
		E	0.4	0.4	0.2	0.2	0.0	..	..	..
		W	0.3	0.2	..	0.8	..	..	..	..
		E & W[6]	0.4	0.4	0.2	0.2	0.0	..	..	..
		S	4.9	3.0	..	..	..	..	..	..
		NI	4.5	2.8	..	..	..	..	..	..
Q00-Q99	XVII Congenital malformations, deformations and chromosomal abnormalities	UK	2.6	2.3	1.3	1.5	1.3	1.0	2.9	1.9
		E	2.4	2.1	1.2	1.4	1.2	0.9	2.9	1.9
		W	2.4	2.0	2.0	0.4	1.9	1.2	1.9	2.6
		E & W[6]	2.5	2.1	1.3	1.4	1.2	1.0	2.9	2.0
		S	3.6	3.3	1.2	2.6	1.7	1.4	2.8	1.6
		NI	5.6	5.0	0.6	1.9	1.1	1.3	5.5	2.0
R00-R99	XVIII Symptoms, signs and abnormal clinical and laboratory findings, not elsewhere classified	UK	8.0	11.2	0.3	0.3	2.3	0.9	5.0	1.9
		E	8.5	12.0	0.3	0.2	2.2	0.9	5.3	1.9
		W	6.1	10.1	0.4	1.7	2.6	1.2	2.6	2.0
		E & W[6]	8.4	11.9	0.3	0.3	2.2	1.0	5.1	1.9
		S	4.9	4.8	0.2	0.8	3.5	0.6	3.7	1.8
		NI	5.4	5.8	..	..	0.8	0.8	4.0	1.0
V01-Y89	XX External causes of mortality	UK	39.7	16.7	4.1	2.7	44.6	11.2	41.3	16.3
		E	36.8	16.0	3.8	2.5	40.4	10.6	38.3	15.5
		W	41.9	16.7	3.6	2.1	50.1	10.7	41.8	16.4
		E & W[6]	37.4	16.1	3.8	2.5	41.5	10.7	38.9	15.6
		S	55.2	19.7	3.9	3.1	66.5	13.4	55.3	20.9
		NI	66.4	24.8	11.2	6.2	77.1	20.4	75.0	22.0
V01-X59	Accidents	UK	22.8	11.1	3.3	2.1	22.6	5.5	19.7	7.8
		E	21.7	10.9	3.0	1.9	21.4	5.5	18.7	7.7
		W	24.6	10.1	2.8	1.3	27.4	4.1	20.4	6.4
		E & W[6]	22.1	10.9	3.0	1.9	22.0	5.5	19.0	7.8
		S	26.2	11.5	3.4	2.8	24.5	5.0	21.9	7.6
		NI	36.8	16.2	10.6	5.0	33.6	9.4	35.8	9.8
V01-V89	Land transport accidents	UK	8.6	2.5	1.8	1.2	13.4	3.0	6.7	1.9
		E	8.1	2.4	1.6	1.0	12.5	2.9	6.3	1.9
		W	9.7	1.8	0.8	0.8	17.6	2.2	5.3	1.3
		E & W[6]	8.2	2.4	1.6	1.1	12.9	2.9	6.3	1.9
		S	10.0	2.5	2.2	1.5	15.0	3.2	8.6	1.9
		NI	15.3	5.2	5.9	5.0	21.5	5.4	13.1	2.4
W00-W19	Falls	UK	5.3	3.3	0.3	0.1	1.5	0.4	5.0	2.2
		E	4.8	3.0	0.2	0.1	1.3	0.4	4.6	2.0
		W	6.0	3.1	..	..	1.0	0.2	6.9	1.3
		E & W[6]	4.9	3.0	0.2	0.1	1.3	0.3	4.8	2.0
		S	8.7	6.8	0.7	0.3	1.9	0.7	5.4	3.2
		NI	8.2	3.6	..	..	4.0	1.6	12.1	3.9

65-74		75-84		85 and over				ICD-10
M	F	M	F	M	F			
..	..	..	..	..	..	UK	XV Pregnancy, childbirth	O00-O99
..	..	..	..	..	..	E	and the puerperium	
..	..	..	..	..	..	W		
..	..	..	..	..	..	E & W[6]		
..	..	..	..	..	..	S		
..	..	..	..	..	..	NI		
..	..	..	..	..	..	UK	XVI Certain conditions	P00-P99
..	..	..	..	..	..	E	originating in the	
..	..	..	..	..	..	W	perinatal period	
..	..	..	..	..	..	E & W[6]		
..	..	..	..	..	..	S		
..	..	..	..	..	..	NI		
2.9	3.0	3.5	3.4	5.3	3.7	UK	XVII Congenital	Q00-Q99
3.1	3.0	3.4	3.7	5.9	3.8	E	malformations,	
1.5	1.4	7.8	0.9	..	6.4	W	deformations and	
3.0	2.9	3.7	3.5	5.5	4.0	E & W[6]	chromosomal abnormalities	
1.4	2.4	1.8	2.3	3.7	1.5	S		
3.3	8.6	3.0	3.9	..	..	NI		
5.1	3.3	21.2	34.9	420.9	856.1	UK	XVIII Symptoms, signs and	R00-R99
5.5	3.3	23.1	38.4	458.5	931.8	E	abnormal clinical and	
0.8	4.2	13.0	29.5	322.3	684.5	W	laboratory findings, not	
5.2	3.4	22.5	37.9	450.5	917.1	E & W[6]	elsewhere classified	
4.8	2.4	8.8	10.9	95.6	275.0	S		
5.0	1.4	15.2	9.9	253.8	428.6	NI		
43.6	22.3	105.6	81.8	347.0	324.7	UK	XX External causes of	V01-Y89
41.3	21.7	100.5	80.0	340.2	315.5	E	mortality	
43.8	25.3	102.4	80.2	347.1	339.0	W		
41.6	22.0	101.0	80.2	340.6	317.4	E & W[6]		
60.5	22.2	144.6	88.1	397.2	398.5	S		
54.8	31.7	149.4	116.5	456.9	358.1	NI		
27.7	15.4	85.8	73.1	316.2	310.4	UK	Accidents	V01-X59
26.3	15.3	81.7	71.0	308.6	302.0	E		
25.4	14.0	80.4	77.4	327.3	324.0	W		
26.3	15.3	82.0	71.6	309.7	303.8	E & W[6]		
38.9	12.5	112.0	77.2	356.7	376.4	S		
39.9	27.4	140.2	110.5	456.9	347.3	NI		
5.4	2.6	11.7	6.8	19.8	7.4	UK	Land transport accidents	V01-V89
5.3	2.6	10.9	6.4	18.5	7.9	E		
3.8	1.4	11.7	7.4	19.8	..	W		
5.2	2.5	11.2	6.5	18.6	7.6	E & W[6]		
6.7	1.2	13.2	6.3	25.7	5.9	S		
6.6	10.1	27.4	19.7	50.8	5.4	NI		
11.4	6.0	40.3	32.8	132.7	119.2	UK	Falls	W00-W19
10.6	6.0	36.4	29.3	119.6	100.4	E		
17.7	6.3	37.6	36.9	148.8	115.9	W		
11.0	6.1	36.5	29.9	121.3	101.4	E & W[6]		
16.3	5.7	82.0	62.8	275.8	336.7	S		
10.0	4.3	45.7	33.6	139.6	65.1	NI		

7

Table 7.2 (b) – continued

Deaths by underlying cause, ICD-10 chapter, selected causes by age and sex, 2006

United Kingdom

Death rates per 100,000 population

ICD-10			All Ages[3] (standardised)		1-14		15-44		45-64	
			M	F	M	F	M	F	M	F
X40-X49	Accidental poisoning by and exposure to noxious substances	UK	2.7	1.1	0.1	0.0	4.6	1.4	2.5	1.5
		E	2.7	1.1	0.0	0.0	4.6	1.5	2.6	1.6
		W	3.4	0.8	0.4	..	5.6	0.7	2.9	1.3
		E & W[6]	2.8	1.1	0.0	0.0	4.7	1.5	2.7	1.6
		S	2.3	0.4	..	..	3.6	0.8	1.7	0.0
		NI	1.4	1.2	0.6	..	1.9	1.6	1.0	2.0
X59	Accidental exposure to unspecified factor	UK	3.1	3.0	0.0	..	0.6	0.2	1.4	0.6
		E	3.3	3.2	..	..	0.6	0.2	1.4	0.7
		W	2.5	3.0	..	..	0.5	-	0.8	0.5
		E & W[6]	3.2	3.2	..	..	0.6	0.2	1.4	0.7
		S	1.1	0.5	..	..	0.5	..	0.9	0.4
		NI	5.3	4.9	0.6	..	1.3	0.3	1.5	..
X60-X84, Y10-Y34,[4] with verdict 'open'	Intentional self-harm, and injury/poisoning of undetermined intent with inquest verdict 'open'	UK	13.0	4.0	0.2	0.1	17.0	4.2	17.8	6.9
		E	12.1	3.8	0.2	0.1	15.3	3.9	17.0	6.6
		W	14.8	4.9	..	..	18.9	5.9	20.6	7.9
		E & W[6]	12.4	3.9	0.2	0.1	15.6	4.1	17.3	6.7
		S	24.0	6.5	0.5	0.2	34.8	7.3	27.4	11.4
		NI	23.0	5.9	..	1.2	34.4	7.8	29.7	8.3
X85-Y09, Y33.9[5] with verdict 'pending'	Assault and other specified events of undetermined intent with inquest verdict 'pending'	UK	2.3	0.8	0.5	0.4	3.7	1.0	1.8	0.6
		E	2.1	0.8	0.5	0.4	3.4	1.0	1.6	0.6
		W	1.7	0.7	0.8	0.8	3.0	0.7	0.8	0.5
		E & W[6]	2.1	0.8	0.5	0.5	3.4	1.0	1.6	0.6
		S	4.0	0.6	..	..	7.1	0.9	3.8	0.4
		NI	2.7	0.7	..	..	4.3	1.3	3.0	..

Rates based on less than 20 cases are in italics as a warning to the user that their reliability as a measure may be affected by the small number of events.

1 *Cause of death was defined using International Classification of Diseases, Tenth Revision (ICD-10).*
2 *All data based on year of registration. Previously England and Wales were based on occurences, Scotland and Northern Ireland on registrations.*
3 *Rates for 'All Ages' are based on the European Standard Population and include the under ones.*
4 *Figures for intentional self harm only include Y10-Y34 with inquest verdict 'open' for deaths in England and Wales; Figures for Scotland and Northern Ireland include all deaths coded to Y10-Y34.*
5 *Figures for assault include Y33.9 with inquest verdict 'pending' for deaths in England and Wales; Figures for Scotland and Northern Ireland only include deaths coded to X85-Y09.*
6 *'England, Wales and Elsewhere' covers both Residents and Non-Residents, comparable with Scotland and Northern Ireland data. Separate 'England' and 'Wales' categories cover Residents Only.*

Source: Office for National Statistics; General Register Office for Scotland; Northern Ireland Statistics and Research Agency

65-74		75-84		85 and over					ICD-10
M	F	M	F	M	F				
1.3	0.9	1.1	1.0	1.6	1.0	UK	Accidental poisoning by		X40-X49
1.1	0.8	0.8	1.1	1.5	1.1	E	and exposure to noxious		
2.3	1.4	1.3	1.8	..	2.1	W	substances		
1.2	0.9	0.9	1.2	1.5	1.2	E & W[6]			
2.9	1.2	3.5	..	3.7	..	S			
1.7	..	3.0	..	..	..	NI			
5.0	3.7	24.4	26.0	143.3	170.2	UK	Accidental exposure to		X59
5.4	3.8	25.8	27.9	150.8	179.8	E	unspecified factor		
0.8	3.5	23.3	24.0	133.9	191.0	W			
5.1	3.8	25.8	27.7	149.8	180.8	E & W[6]			
4.3	1.6	3.5	1.7	29.4	23.5	S			
6.6	8.6	42.7	49.4	253.8	265.9	NI			
11.4	3.8	13.2	4.5	18.7	4.7	UK	Intentional self-harm,		X60-X84,
11.3	3.9	13.3	5.0	20.7	5.2	E	and injury/poisoning of		Y10-Y34,[4]
16.2	5.6	15.6	1.8	14.9	4.3	W	undetermined intent with		with
11.7	4.0	13.4	4.8	20.4	5.1	E & W[6]	inquest verdict 'open'		verdict
15.4	4.0	15.0	2.9	14.7	2.9	S			'open'
11.6	2.9	9.1	2.0	..	5.4	NI			
1.0	0.6	0.6	0.3	1.3	0.8	UK	Assault and other		X85-Y09,
1.1	0.6	0.7	0.4	1.5	0.8	E	specified events of		Y33.9[5]
..	0.7	..	..	..	..	W	undetermined intent with		with
1.0	0.6	0.6	0.3	1.5	0.8	E & W[6]	inquest verdict 'pending'		verdict
1.0	0.4	..	...	..	..	S			'pending'
..	1.4	..	..	..	5.4	NI			

7

Table 7.3

Deaths related to drug poisoning: by age and sex,[1] 2006

United Kingdom

Death rates per 100,000 population

ICD-10			All Ages[2] (standardised)		1-14		15-44		45-64		65-74		75-84		85 and over	
			M	F	M	F	M	F	M	F	M	F	M	F	M	F
F11-F16,F18-F19,	Drug-related	United Kingdom	7.5	3.0	0.0	0.1	13.1	3.9	6.5	4.5	2.2	2.3	3.5	2.9	4.5	3.4
X40-X44, X60-X64	poisoning	England	6.5	2.7	0.0	0.0	11.3	3.3	5.9	4.0	2.1	2.2	3.6	3.2	5.3	3.7
X85, Y10-Y14	deaths	Wales	7.4	3.3	..	0.4	14.1	4.1	5.0	4.6	3.1	3.5	..	2.8	..	4.3
		England, Wales and Elsewhere[3]	6.6	2.7	0.0	0.1	11.5	3.4	5.8	4.1	2.2	2.3	3.4	3.1	4.9	3.7
		Scotland	17.1	5.7	..	..	32.1	8.8	13.0	7.0	2.9	2.4	5.3	1.7	0.0	..
		Northern Ireland	6.0	4.7	..	0.6	9.1	5.4	8.1	8.8	1.7	1.4	..	..	..	..

Rates based on less than 20 cases are in italics as a warning to the user that their reliability as a measure may be affected by the small number of events.

1 All data based on year of registration. Previously England and Wales were based on occurences, Scotland and Northern Ireland on registrations.
2 Rates for 'All Ages' are based on the European Standard Population and include the under 1s.
3 'England, Wales and Elsewhere' covers both Residents and Non-Residents, comparable with Scotland and Northern Ireland figures. The separate 'England' and 'Wales' categories cover Residents Only.

Source: Office for National Statistics; General Register Office for Scotland; Northern Ireland Statistics and Research Agency

Table 7.4

Alcohol-related deaths: by age and sex,[1] 2006

United Kingdom

Death rates per 100,000 population

ICD-10			All Ages[2] (standardised)		1-14		15-44		45-64		65-74		75-84		85 and over	
			M	F	M	F	M	F	M	F	M	F	M	F	M	F
F10, I42.6, K70,	Alcohol-	United Kingdom	18.4	9.2	..	0.0	8.4	4.3	44.5	21.5	39.5	20.3	25.1	16.6	17.9	10.5
K73, K74, X45	related deaths	England	16.2	8.2	..	..	7.4	4.0	39.1	18.8	34.6	18.0	24.5	17.0	18.2	10.0
		Wales	17.0	9.5	..	..	7.2	4.5	43.7	22.2	33.8	21.0	19.4	15.7	14.9	10.7
		England, Wales and Elsewhere[3]	16.3	8.3	..	..	7.4	4.0	39.5	19.0	34.7	18.3	24.2	16.9	18.0	10.0
		Scotland	38.5	17.9	..	0.3	18.6	7.6	92.6	45.8	90.2	37.6	31.8	16.1	22.1	13.2
		Northern Ireland	20.6	8.7	..	..	10.2	3.0	51.4	20.5	33.2	27.4	36.6	7.9	..	21.7

Rates based on less than 20 cases are in italics as a warning to the user that their reliability as a measure may be affected by the small number of events.

1 All data based on year of registration. Previously England and Wales were based on occurences, Scotland and Northern Ireland on registrations.
2 Rates for 'All Ages' are based on the European Standard Population and include the under ones.
3 'England, Wales & Elsewhere' covers both Residents and Non-Residents, comparable with the Scotland and Northern Ireland data. The separate 'England' and 'Wales' categories cover Residents Only.

Source: Office for National Statistics; General Register Office for Scotland; Northern Ireland Statistics and Research Agency

7

Table 7.5

Trends in period life expectancy at birth,[1] 1981-2005 (selected years)

United Kingdom   Years

		1981	1991	2001	2002	2003	2004	2005
Males								
	United Kingdom	70.8	73.2	75.6	75.9	76.2	76.5	76.9
	England	71.1	73.4	75.9	76.1	76.5	76.8	77.2
	Wales	70.4	73.1	75.3	75.5	75.8	76.1	76.6
	Scotland	69.1	71.4	73.3	73.5	73.8	74.2	74.6
	Northern Ireland	69.2	72.5	75.2	75.6	75.8	76.0	76.1
Females								
	United Kingdom	76.8	78.7	80.4	80.5	80.7	80.9	81.3
	England	77.0	78.9	80.6	80.7	80.9	81.1	81.5
	Wales	76.4	78.8	80.0	80.1	80.3	80.6	80.9
	Scotland	75.3	77.1	78.8	78.9	79.1	79.3	79.6
	Northern Ireland	75.5	78.4	80.1	80.4	80.5	80.8	81.0

1 Period life expectancy at a specific age is the average number of further years a person would live, having reached that age in the specified year, if
   the mortality rates for subsequent ages in that year applied to them throughout the rest of their life.
2 Figures are based on deaths and populations in a three-year period surrounding the year shown.

Source: Office for National Statistics; General Register Office for Scotland; Northern Ireland Statistics and Research Agency

Table 7.6

Period life expectancy at specific ages,[1,2] 2005[3]

United Kingdom   Years

		At age					
		0	1	15	45	65	80
Males							
	United Kingdom	76.9	76.3	62.5	33.9	16.9	7.6
	England	77.2	76.6	62.8	34.1	17.1	7.6
	Wales	76.6	75.9	62.1	33.6	16.7	7.6
	Scotland	74.6	74.0	60.2	32.1	15.8	7.2
	Northern Ireland	76.1	75.6	61.8	33.4	16.6	7.3
Females							
	United Kingdom	81.3	80.6	66.8	37.6	19.7	9.0
	England	81.5	80.9	67.0	37.8	19.9	9.1
	Wales	80.9	80.3	66.4	37.2	19.5	8.9
	Scotland	79.6	78.9	65.1	36.0	18.6	8.5
	Northern Ireland	81.0	80.4	66.5	37.3	19.5	8.8

1 Period life expectancy at a specific age is the average number of further years a person would live, having reached that age in the specified year, if
   the mortality rates for subsequent ages in that year applied to them throughout the rest of their life.
2 All countries deaths data by date of registration.
3 Figures for 2005 are based on deaths and populations in the three years 2004-06.

Source: Office for National Statistics; General Register Office for Scotland; Northern Ireland Statistics and Research Agency

7

Additional notes

Table 7.1 – Standardised Mortality Ratio (SMR)

The SMR expresses the number of deaths in each country as a percentage of the number that would have occurred if that country's population had experienced the sex/age specific mortality rates of the UK that year. The SMR of the reference area (the UK as a whole) is always 100.

Tables 7.2 – 7.4 – Age-standardised death rates

Age-standardised death rates are summary measures that allow comparison of mortality in populations with different age distributions. The death rates presented here represent what the crude rate would have been if the population had the same age distribution as the European standard population.

Tables 7.5 and 7.6 – Life expectancy

Life expectancy at birth for an area is an estimate of the average number of years a new-born baby would survive if he or she experienced the particular area's age-specific mortality rates for that time period throughout his or her life. The figure reflects mortality among those living in the area at that time, rather than mortality among those born in each area. It is not therefore the number of years a baby born in the area in each time period could actually expect to live, both because the death rates of the area are likely to change in the future and because many of those born in the area will live elsewhere for at least some part of their lives.

Health and care resources

This chapter contains data about healthcare resources such as hospital beds, care home places and the health service workforce. Because of differences between the four countries in legislation, the organisation of health and social care services, and statistical definitions used, the range of measures available for cross-UK comparison on this topic is limited. Important issues of comparability are referred to in the text and footnotes below where appropriate.

The highest availability of general and acute beds was in Scotland where there were 3.4 beds per 1,000 population, while England had 2.1 beds of this type per 1,000 population. Scotland had 1.2 beds for people with mental illness per 1,000 population, almost double the UK rate of 0.7 beds per 1,000. However, comparisons between countries have to be treated with caution because of differences in the classification of services.

Available beds

In the financial year 2005-06 there were 226,000 available hospital beds in the UK, that is 3.8 per 1,000 population (Table 8.1). Of these, 2.3 were general and acute beds, 0.7 for people with mental illness beds, 0.5 for geriatric specialties and 0.2 beds for maternity patients per 1,000 population.

Care home places

Of the registered care homes in England, 7 per cent of places were Local Authority homes and 14 per cent of places were voluntary homes (Table 8.2). The proportion of home places that were Local Authority in Scotland was double that of England at 14 per cent, and over a third, 34 per cent, were Local Authority in Northern Ireland.

Table 8.1

Average daily available hospital beds[1] per thousand resident population, 2005-06

United Kingdom   Rates, thousands

	Sector							Total available beds (thousands)
	General & acute	Maternity	Mental illness	Learning disability	Geriatrics	Other	All beds	
United Kingdom	2.3	0.2	0.7	0.1	0.5	0.0	3.8	226.0
England	2.1	0.2	0.6	0.1	0.5	0.0	3.5	175.6
Wales	3.2	0.2	0.8	0.1	0.5	0.0	4.7	13.8
Scotland [P]	3.4	0.2	1.2	0.1	0.6	0.0	5.6	28.2
Northern Ireland	2.6	0.4	0.6	0.3	0.6	0.2	4.8	8.2

P   Data are provisional.

1   Average daily available beds during the year in which wards are open overnight. Hospitals may also have a number of beds in wards which are only open during the day.

Source: Information Centre for Health and Social Care; Welsh Assembly Government; Department of Health; Information Services Division, NHS in Scotland; Regional Information Branch, Department of Health, Social Services and Public Safety, Northern Ireland

Table 8.2

Places available in care homes[1]: by type of care home, at 31 March 2006

United Kingdom   Percentages, numbers

| | Percentage of places available in Registered Homes | | | |
	Local authority homes[2]	Voluntary homes[3]	Other[4]	Total number of places available
England	7	14	79	441,335
Wales[5]	:	:	:	26,679
Scotland	14	17	68	43,489
Northern Ireland	34	26	40	6,557

1   Scotland figures for places available exclude children's homes. All data include residential places in homes registered as both residential and nursing.
2   England figures relate to local authority staffed homes. Wales relate to local authority staffed homes for adults and children. Northern Ireland relate to places available in statutory homes operated by the Health and Social Services Trusts for both adults and children.
3   England figures include dual registered voluntary homes. Wales include all voluntary homes for adults and children, regardless of size. Northern Ireland refer to homes for adults and children.
4   Figures for England include independent small homes (fewer than four places) and private homes. Wales include all private homes for adults and children. Scotland relate to private homes only. Northern Ireland relate to all private homes and dual registered.
5   The figures for Wales include places in small homes, children's homes and homes for people with substance misuse problems.

Source: Commission for Social Care Inspection; Care and Social Services Inspectorate for Wales; Scottish Government; Department of Health, Social Services and Public Safety, Northern Ireland

Health sector staff

The proportions of staff classified as 'medical and clinical', 'infrastructure support' and 'support to infrastructure' varied between the four countries. In England 82 per cent of NHS staff were 'medical and clinical' and 18 per cent were 'infrastructure support staff' (Table 8.3). This compares with Northern Ireland where only 63 per cent were classed as 'medical and clinical'.

The smallest proportion of staff employed as 'support to

infrastructure clinical and other direct care staff' was at 4 per cent in Scotland, compared with 30 per cent in England.

In 2006 GP practices in England, Scotland and Wales had an average of four general practitioners (GPs) working in them (number of general practitioners divided by number of practices), while Northern Ireland had approximately three GPs per practice (Table 8.4). Scotland had the highest proportion of female GPs, at 44 per cent. In Wales the proportion was slightly lower with 36 per cent being female. The country with the largest list size, that is the average number of patients per

Table 8.3

NHS Hospital and Community Health Service staff by type of staff[1] as at 30 September 2006

United Kingdom   Percentages, thousands

	Medical and dental	Nursing, midwifery and health visiting[2]	Scientific, therapeutic and technical	Support to infrastructure, clinical and other direct care staff[3]	All medical and clinical staff	NHS infrastructure support staff	All staff (000's)
England	9	32	11	30	82	18	999.6
Wales[4]	8	40	14	15	77	23	70.6
Scotland	10	44	13	4	71	29	128.8
Northern Ireland	8	30	14	11	63	37	44.6

1   Directly employed whole time equivalents. Excludes GPs. Northern Ireland excludes bank staff.
2   Nursing, Midwifery and Health Visiting excludes student nurses. Northern Ireland does not have any healthcare assistants and excludes Practice Nurses.
3   Includes qualified ambulance staff. In Northern Ireland it is not possible to seperately identify Administrative and Other Support to Direct Care staff. These staff have been classified as NHS Infrastructure Support Staff.
4   Data are provisional.

Source: Information Centre for Health and Social Care; Welsh Assembly Government; Information Services Division, NHS in Scotland; Department of Health, Social Services and Public Safety, Northern Ireland

Table 8.4

General Practioners, dentists and opticians, as at 30 September 2006

United Kingdom   Numbers, percentages

	General medical services [1]						General dental services [2]			
	Number of practices	Number of general medical practitioners (GPs) [3]	Percentage who were female	Average list size per GP	Number of practice staff (whole-time equivalents) [4]	Percentage who were direct care practice staff [4,5]	Number of dentists [6]	Percentage of population registered with NHS dentist [6]	Average registrations per dentist	Number of opticians [7]
England	8,325	33,091	41	1,610	76,977	26	21,111	49	1,171	8,946
Wales	496	1,882	36	1,650	4,224	24	1,109	48	1,369	673
Scotland	1,032	4,132	44	1,310	..	..	2,842	56	1,124	1,159
Northern Ireland	363	1,110	37	1,631	..	..	782	52	1,163	557

1 Wales Practice Staff at 30 September 2005.
2 England dental data as at 31 March 2007.
3 Figures for GPs include unrestricted principals, PMS contracted GPs and PMS salaried GPs. For Northern Ireland this includes Unrestricted Principals only. Figures for General Dental Practitioners include principals, assistants and vocational dental practitioners. Figures for Northern Ireland include principal dentists only. Salaried dentists, Hospital Dental Services and community dental services are excluded.
4 Practice Staff includes Practice Nurses, Direct Patient Care, Admin & Clerical and Other.
5 Figures relate to practice nurses, physiotherapists, chiropodists, counsellors, dispensers and complementary therapists.
6 For Northern Ireland, this figure is calculated using 2006 mid-year estimates. For Wales, population is at 31 March 2006.
7 Optometrists and opthalmic medical practitioners contracted to perform NHS sight tests at 31 December 2005 (provisional for optometrists in Scotland). For England and Wales, data as at 31 December 2006.

Source: Information Centre for Health and Social Care; Welsh Assembly Government; Information Services Division, NHS in Scotland; Central Services Agency, Northern Ireland

GP, was Wales with 1,650 patients registered per GP. Scotland had the smallest list size of 1,310 patients per GP.

More than half the population in Scotland and Northern Ireland are registered with an NHS Dentist. Scotland had the highest proportion with 56 per cent of the population being registered. Wales had the largest number of people registered per dentist at 1,369 and Scotland had the lowest with 1,124 registrations per dentist.

Expenditure on health and personal social services

The total UK expenditure on health and personal social service for 2006-07 was £119 billion, an average of £1,963 per person (Table 8.5). The highest expenditure per head was in Scotland at £2,313 and the lowest was in England at £1,915.

Table 8.5

Total expenditure[1] on services by Health and Personal Social Services, 2006-07

United Kingdom   Numbers, rates

	£ millions	£ per head	Percentage of total UK Health and Personal Social Services expenditure	Population (000's)
England	97,196	1,915	82	50,762.9
Wales	6,254	2,109	5	2,965.9
Scotland	11,834	2,313	10	5,116.9
Northern Ireland	3,651	2,096	3	1,741.6
UK identifiable expenditure	118,935	1,963	100	60,587.3

1 Total expenditure on services (TES) in this period was £118,935 million. TES is the spending aggregate that is allocated to function and covers most expenditure by the public sector that is included in Total Managed Expenditure (TME).

Source: HM Treasury

Additional notes

Table 8.1 – Available beds

The 'total available beds' figure is the average daily number of open and staffed beds in wards that are open during the day only in NHS hospitals in England. These beds could be in a separate day-case unit or a designated ward for day-cases that was not open overnight. Beds on wards open overnight that were used for day-case patients would count as overnight beds and not day only beds; such beds are excluded from this statistic.

Available beds exclude healthy newborn babies except in Northern Ireland.

There is no national definition of the 'acute' sector and such definitions that are used in this table will vary between the countries.

Table 8.3 NHS and community health service staff

General medical practitioners (family GPs), general dental practitioners, the staff employed by practitioners, pharmacists in general pharmaceutical services and staff working in other contracted out services are not included in the figures. Medical and dental staff that are included are those holding permanent, paid (whole-time, part-time, sessional) and/or honorary appointments in NHS hospitals and Community Health services. Figures include clinical assistants and hospital practitioners. Bank staff maintain service delivery by covering staffing shortfalls and fluctuating workloads and, as a consequence, their input to the service is difficult to measure.

Previously there has been much confusion over non-medical staff groups. To address this issue the health service has now classified all staff into three areas:

1. Clinical staff – professionally qualified staff treating patients.

2. Support to clinical staff – staff providing direct support to clinical staff, often with direct patient care, who free up the time of clinical staff allowing them more time to treat patients.

3. Staff supporting NHS infrastructure – staff essential to the day-to-day running of the organisations.

Unqualified and trainee nurses, health professionals and scientific staff are included under 'Support to clinical staff' as are ambulance staff. Formerly all ambulance, paramedics and support workers were included in the figures for other management and support staff.

Occasional sessional staff in Community Health medical and dental services for which no whole-time equivalent is collected is not included. Nursing, midwifery and health visiting staff included healthcare assistants, and excluded nurse teachers and student nurses. Scientific, therapeutic and technical staff incorporating PAMs. Administration and estates comprise administration and clerical, senior managers and works staff. Other staff are ancillary, ambulance staff and support staff. All direct care staff are in medical and dental, nursing, midwifery and health visiting, and scientific, therapeutic and technical groups.

Table 8.4 General practitioners and dentists

The figures for general practitioners (GPs) include unrestricted principals and equivalents (UPEs), personal medical service (PMS), contracted GPs and PMS salaried GPs. An unrestricted principal is a practitioner who provides the full range of general medical services and whose list is not limited to any particular group of people. In a few cases, they may be relieved of the liability for emergency out-of-hours calls from patients that are not their own. Most people have an unrestricted principal as their GP. Doctors may also practice in the general medical services as restricted principals, assistants, associated or GP registrars.

A PMS contracted doctor is a practitioner who provides the full range of services through the PMS pilot contract and like unrestricted principals they have a patient list. A PMS salaried doctor is employed to work in a PMS pilot, provides the full range of services and has a list of registered patients.

Other types of general medical practitioners include GP retainers, restricted principals, assistants, associates (Scotland only), GP registrars, salaried doctors (paragraph 52 SFA) and PMS other.

The figures for general dental practitioners include principals, assistants and vocational dental practitioners in the general dental service and, in England and Wales, the personal dental service. Dentists working in the general dental service may practise under the NHS or privately – most dentists do a mixture of NHS and private work. Salaried dentists are excluded. Neither the hospital dental service nor the community dental services are included.

Table 8.5 – Total expenditure on services

The key concept to understand in the derivation of the public expenditure by function series is Total Expenditure on Services (TES). This is the spending aggregate that is allocated to function and covers most expenditure by the public sector that

8

is included in Total Management Expenditure (TME) (about 95 per cent).

TES includes central government spending but excludes the part of this that is finance to local authorities and public corporations. This central government expenditure is then combined with actual spending by local authorities and corporations to give total public sector expenditure. TES is a near-cash measure of spending in that it includes all non-cash items such as depreciation and cost of capital charges.

Chapter 9

Health and the environment

This chapter contains statistics about selected aspects of the environment that affect health, including the cleanliness of drinking and bathing water and air quality.

Drinking and bathing water

The quality of drinking water is regularly assessed by sampling water leaving treatment works, in reservoirs and at consumers' taps. Samples are assessed according to guidelines for the minimum acceptable standard of drinking water quality. Prior to 2004 all results presented here show the percentages of samples with a higher concentration of bacteria and organisms than is acceptable (that is those that exceed the Prescribed Concentration Value or PCV). Due to a change in regulations, figures from 2004 onwards are not directly comparable with those prior to 2004. Additionally, post 2004, figures for supply zones are the mean zonal compliance figures[1] and are not the percentage of samples exceeding the PCV.

---

1 Calculation of Mean Zonal Compliance is described in the Drinking Water Inspectorate's Annual Report available at www.dwi.gov.uk

Figure 9.1

Determinations exceeding Prescribed Concentration or Value,[1] 2006

United Kingdom

Percentages

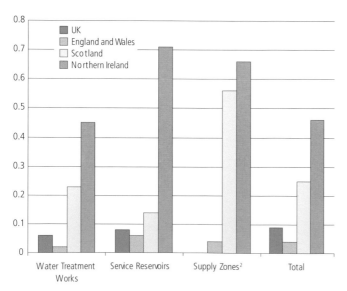

1 The Prescribed Concentration or Value (PCV) is the numerical value assigned to water quality standards, defining the maximum or minimum legal concentration or value of a parameter. Figures represented here include relaxed PCVs.
2 Figures for supply zones are the mean zonal compliance figures. Calculation methods of these figures are detailed in the Drinking Water Inspectorate's annual report at www.dwi.gov.uk. No UK wide calculation is made for supply zones.

Source: Drinking Water Inspectorate, Department for the Environment, Food and Rural Affairs

Among samples taken at all sites in the UK between 1995 and 2006, the percentage exceeding the PCV has decreased, although it should be noted that the figures for 2004 onwards are not directly comparable to previous years due to changes in the regulations and the way water supply companies monitor water quality. In particular, in reservoirs the percentage not complying has decreased from 0.12 per cent in 2004 to 0.08 per cent in 2006 (Figure 9.1, Table 9.1). (The figure for 1995, prior to changes to the methodology was 0.58.)

The greatest improvements in the quality of drinking water between 2004 and 2006 occurred in Northern Ireland, where the total percentage of samples exceeding the PCV decreased from 0.78 per cent to 0.45 per cent. In service reservoirs, Scotland had the greatest improvements in drinking water quality between 2004 and 2006, with the number of samples exceeding the PCV decreasing from 0.35 per cent to 0.14 per cent. Northern Ireland had an increase in the number of samples from water treatment works exceeding the PVC from 0.17 per cent in 2004 to 0.45 per cent in 2006.

Bathing waters, as defined by the EC Directive on Bathing Water (Article 1, 76/160/EEC), are waters where *'bathing is not prohibited and is traditionally practiced by a large number of bathers'*. Bathing waters are regularly tested for a number of parameters. Annual testing occurs during the *'bathing season'*, which in Northern Ireland is June to mid September. The parameters include the microbiological determinants: total and faecal coliforms and faecal streptococci. To comply with the EC directive's mandatory standard for microbiological water quality, 95 per cent of the samples must comply with the standards set for total and faecal coliforms. The data presented here show the percentage of bathing waters that comply.

In England, Scotland and Wales the percentage of bathing waters complying with the standard for cleanliness has increased between 1996 and 2006. In 2006, all of the UK countries with the exception of Wales had 100 per cent of bathing waters complying with the mandatory standard for cleanliness. Wales had 99 per cent, compared with 93 per cent in 1996 (Table 9.2). For England 100 per cent of bathing water in 2006 compared with 89 per cent in 1996 complied with mandatory standards of cleanliness.

There have been a greater number of fluctuations in the percentage of bathing waters complying with the mandatory requirements of the directive complying in Scotland and Northern Ireland between 1995 and 2005 owing to the relatively small number of identified bathing waters. In 2006, 100 per cent of Scotland's bathing water complied with the standards as did 100 per cent of Northern Ireland's.

Air pollution

Nitrogen dioxide concentrations throughout the UK have been assessed at urban background and roadside locations. Nitrogen dioxide, PM10 and sulphur dioxide levels are presented here by location across the UK in units of micrograms per cubic meter (ugm^{-3}).

Map 9.1 shows that the area with the highest concentration of nitrogen dioxide is London, with 35 or more micrograms of nitrogen dioxide per cubic meter. Other areas of high concentrations (between 25.0 and $34.9ugm^{-3}$) are clustered around major roads and cities. Northern Ireland, West Wales and the Scottish Highlands have the lowest concentrations of nitrogen dioxide with less than five micrograms per cubic meter.

PM10 is defined as the mass of particles in the atmosphere with a size less than ten micrometers diameter and have been assessed at urban background and roadside locations.

Map 9.2 shows the area with the highest concentration of PM10 is London, with 25 or more micrograms per cubic meter. There are clusters of between 20.0 to 30.0 ugm^{-3} around major towns and cities and the concentration for England as a whole is 15-20 ugm^{-3}. In Cornwall, Wales, Scotland and Northern Ireland the PM10 concentration is 10-15 ugm^{-3}. Concentration is lowest in the highlands of Scotland at less than 10 ugm^{-3}.

Map 9.3 shows that a small number of areas around the Midlands and Humberside had the highest concentrations of sulphur dioxide. The majority of England and Wales and some parts of Scotland had levels of between 1.0 and $3.9ugm^{-3}$ and the remainder of the UK had concentrations of less than one microgram per cubic meter.

Table 9.1

Trends in drinking water quality, 1996-2006

United Kingdom

Number, percentages

	Total number of determinations[1]											
	1995	1996	1997	1998	1999	2000	2001	2002	2003	2004	2005	2006
United Kingdom												
Water treatment works	527,350	518,149	505,378	479,871	471,331	450,174	425,403	471,058	456,334	490,424	482,965	511,548
Service reservoirs	698,464	690,696	685,117	669,853	660,877	652,271	639,782	640,149	631,975	616,961	611,481	605,130
Supply zones [10]	2,524,559	2,395,667	2,301,672	2,159,933	2,117,605	2,051,014	2,231,464	2,311,406	2,246,106	1,393,271	1,445,026	1,466,749
Total	3,750,373	3,604,512	3,492,167	3,309,657	3,249,813	3,162,359	3,296,649	3,422,613	3,334,415	2,500,656	2,539,472	2,583,427
England and Wales												
Water treatment works [3,4]	410,922	404,625	392,406	373,285	367,577	347,097	328,891	374,592	368,578	387,158	382,679	403,631
Service reservoirs [4]	519,380	520,438	514,818	504,767	497,261	492,307	490,284	486,601	482,201	467,765	462,197	456,952
Supply zones [4,5]	2,223,949	2,129,987	2,073,513	1,929,228	1,920,059	1,844,891	2,004,739	2,112,368	2,045,473	1,182,689	1,233,977	1,240,138
Total [6]	3,154,251	3,055,050	2,980,737	2,807,280	2,784,897	2,684,295	2,823,914	2,973,561	2,896,252	2,037,612	2,078,853	2,100,721
Scotland												
Water treatment works [4,7]	92,534	93,692	92,748	86,938	84,394	84,555	78,460	79,168	70,650	83,227	79,650	78,057
Service reservoirs [4,8]	129,908	131,550	132,326	127,114	125,572	122,650	113,084	116,890	113,164	112,680	112,820	112,350
Supply zones [4,11]	230,679	217,161	178,608	179,903	143,048	151,717	172,755	148,349	155,427	152,318	153,291	170,552
Total	453,121	442,403	403,682	393,955	353,014	358,922	364,299	344,407	339,241	348,225	345,761	360,959
Northern Ireland[3]												
Water treatment works [4,9]	23,894	19,832	20,224	19,648	19,360	18,522	18,052	17,298	17,106	20,039	20,636	29,860
Service reservoirs [4]	49,176	38,708	37,973	37,972	38,044	37,314	36,414	36,658	36,610	36,516	36,464	35,828
Supply zones [4]	69,931	48,519	49,551	50,802	54,498	54,406	53,970	50,689	45,206	58,264	57,758	56,059
Total	143,001	107,059	107,748	108,422	111,902	110,242	108,436	104,645	98,922	114,819	114,858	121,747

1　Determinations are analyses for specific parameters or values, including the substances, organisms and properties listed in Schedule 2 and Regulation 3 of the regulations.

2　The Prescribed Concentration or Value (PCV) is the numerical value assigned to water quality standards, defining the maximum or minimum legal concentration or value of a parameter. Figures presented here include relaxed PCVs.

3　Figures in 1995 for Northern Ireland cover the 15 month period October 1994-December 1995.

4　Figures for 2004 onwards not directly comparable to previous years due to implementation of Water Supply (Water Quality) Regulations 2000 (England) - Water Supply (Water Quality) Regulations 2001 (Wales) - Water Supply (Water Quality) Regulations 2001 (Scotland) - Water Supply (Water Quality) Regulations (Northern Ireland) 2002. The 2001/2 Regulations introduced new and revised standards and changed the way water supply companies monitor water quality. A feature of the 2000/1/2 Regulations is the introduction of European Union (EU), national and indicator parameters. Only EU and N parameters have a PCV (see 1 above). Indicator parameters have no PCV, but exceedences of the value trigger investigation. Figures listed in these tables are tests of EU and National parameters only, as these are mandatory parameters, and the closest for comparison with previous years' data.

5　Test in supply zones and supply points. A feature of the 2000/1/2 Regulations, certain zonal parameters may be tested at treatments works or services reservoirs nominated as supply points.

6　Overall reduction in tests from 2004 onwards due to 2000 Regulations, 'indicator parameters' and monitoring differences.

7　Figures for Scotland do not include determinations for cryptosporidium.

8　Regulations require that 95% of samples taken from service reservoirs shall not contain coliforms. Figures identify all samples from service reservoirs which contain coliforms as failing PCV.

9　Samples taken at water treatment works (NI) include turbidity from 2006. Sample numbers and failures for the turbidity parameter are not included in water treatment works figures prior to 2006.

10　The mean zonal compliance figure for supply zones for the UK is not calculated.

11　The mean zonal compliance figure for Scotland in 2004 was not calculated.

Source: Drinking Water Inspectorate, Department for the Environment, Food and Rural Affairs

				Percentage of determinations exceeding Prescribed Concentration Value (PCV) [2]								
1995	1996	1997	1998	1999	2000	2001	2002	2003	2004	2005	2006	
												United Kingdom
0.35	0.32	0.36	0.27	0.16	0.14	0.09	0.08	0.08	0.10	0.09	0.06	Water treatment works
0.58	0.44	0.49	0.37	0.24	0.21	0.16	0.17	0.11	0.12	0.10	0.08	Service reservoirs
0.79	0.50	0.45	0.43	0.35	0.30	0.25	0.22	0.22	-	-	-	Supply zones [10]
0.69	0.46	0.44	0.39	0.30	0.26	0.21	0.19	0.18	0.12	0.10	0.09	Total
												England and Wales
0.10	0.09	0.11	0.09	0.07	0.08	0.06	0.04	0.05	0.04	0.03	0.02	Water treatment works [3,4]
0.21	0.16	0.21	0.14	0.13	0.12	0.10	0.09	0.06	0.06	0.05	0.06	Service reservoirs [4]
0.71	0.37	0.29	0.27	0.22	0.20	0.17	0.15	0.15	0.06	0.04	0.04	Supply zones [4,5]
0.55	0.30	0.25	0.22	0.18	0.17	0.15	0.13	0.12	0.06	0.05	0.04	Total [6]
												Scotland
1.43	1.30	1.43	1.06	0.54	0.40	0.22	0.26	0.24	0.39	0.38	0.23	Water treatment works [4,7]
1.99	1.48	1.58	1.29	0.68	0.50	0.34	0.42	0.26	0.35	0.23	0.14	Service reservoirs [4,8]
1.26	1.44	1.92	1.66	1.45	1.00	0.81	0.72	0.86	1.16	0.58	0.56	Supply zones [4,11]
1.51	1.42	1.70	1.41	0.96	0.69	0.54	0.51	0.53	0.43	0.36	0.25	Total
												Northern Ireland [3]
0.50	0.30	0.30	0.22	0.14	0.17	0.13	0.12	0.13	0.17	0.11	0.45	Water treatment works [4,9]
0.70	0.60	0.55	0.40	0.29	0.52	0.34	0.46	0.26	0.19	0.29	0.21	Service reservoirs [4]
1.60	1.80	1.88	2.04	1.90	1.80	1.62	1.45	1.25	1.35	0.98	0.66	Supply zones [4]
1.11	1.09	1.11	1.14	1.05	1.09	0.94	0.88	0.69	0.78	0.52	0.45	Total

Table 9.2

Trends in bathing water cleanliness, 1995-2006

United Kingdom

Numbers, percentages

	1996	1997	1998	1999	2000	2001	2002	2003	2004	2005	2006
Identified coastal bathing waters											
England	377	383	389	391	396	397	398	403	404	405	404
Wales	56	64	68	70	75	75	75	78	78	80	80
Scotland	23	23	23	58	58	58	58	58	58	58	61
Northern Ireland	16	16	16	16	16	16	16	16	16	16	16
Percentage complying with mandatory standards of cleanliness[1]											
England	89	88	90	90	95	98	99	99	98	99	100
Wales	93	94	94	99	99	93	100	99	100	100	99
Scotland	91	78	52	88	84	84	84	95	93	95	100
Northern Ireland	100	88	94	100	100	81	94	100	88	94	100

1   There are a small number of designated coastal bathing waters in Scotland, Wales and Northern Ireland which can cause greater fluctuations in percentage compliance.

Source: Department for the Environment, Food and Rural Affairs

Map 9.1

Estimated annual mean nitrogen dioxide concentration[1], 2006

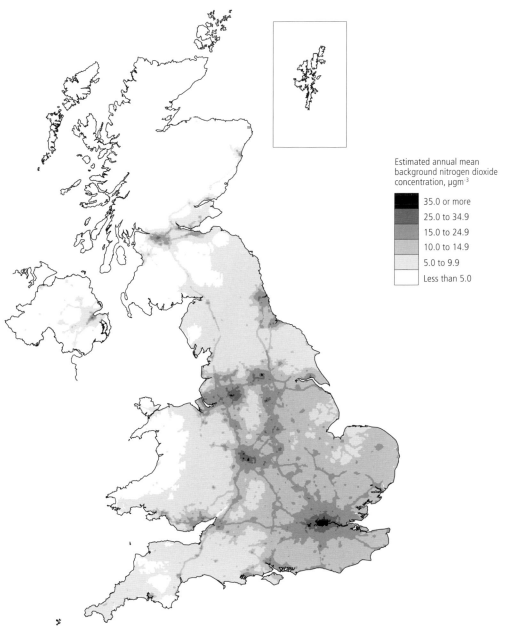

Estimated annual mean
background nitrogen dioxide
concentration, μgm^{-3}

■	35.0 or more
■	25.0 to 34.9
■	15.0 to 24.9
■	10.0 to 14.9
□	5.0 to 9.9
□	Less than 5.0

1   *In units of micrograms per cubic metre.*

Source: Produced by NetCen on behalf of DEFRA

Map 9.2

Estimated annual mean PM$_{10}$ concentration[1], 2006

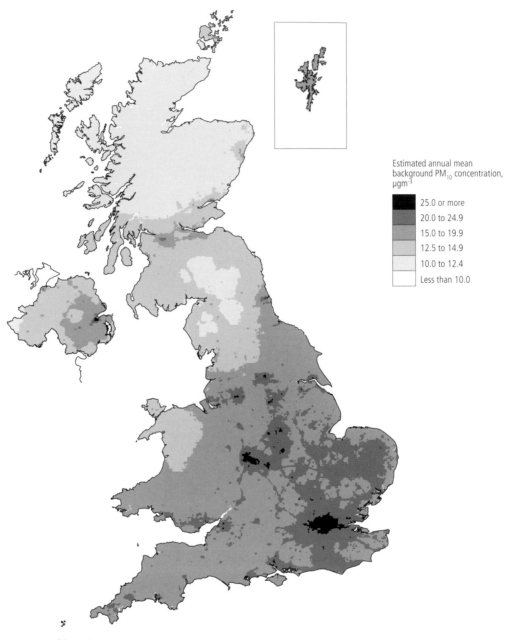

Estimated annual mean
background PM$_{10}$ concentration,
µgm^{-3}

- 25.0 or more
- 20.0 to 24.9
- 15.0 to 19.9
- 12.5 to 14.9
- 10.0 to 12.4
- Less than 10.0

1   In units of micrograms per cubic metre.

Source: Produced by NetCen on behalf of DEFRA

Map 9.3

Estimated annual mean sulphur dioxide concentration[1], 2006

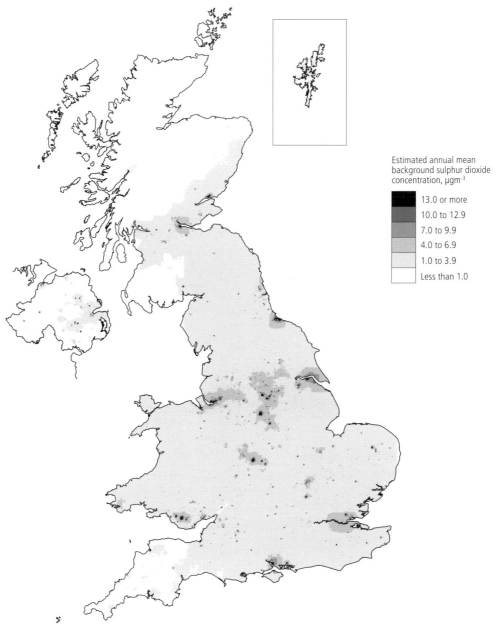

Estimated annual mean
background sulphur dioxide
concentration, μgm[-3]

■	13.0 or more
■	10.0 to 12.9
■	7.0 to 9.9
■	4.0 to 6.9
■	1.0 to 3.9
□	Less than 1.0

1   *In units of micrograms per cubic metre.*

Source: Produced by NetCen on behalf of DEFRA

Additional notes

Table 9.1 – Drinking water

Assessment is done through regular sampling of water leaving treatment works and in-service reservoirs for microbiological parameters and at consumers taps in discrete water supply zones (which contain less than 50,000 people resident) for a more extensive set of parameters. In the UK, local authorities check the quality of private water supplies and may also check the quality of public water supplies within all areas.

The water samples are assessed according to guidelines for the minimum acceptable standard of drinking water quality, referred to as Prescribed Concentration Values (or PCVS).

The Prescribed Concentration Value (PCV) is the numerical value assigned to drinking water standards defining the maximum or minimum concentration or value of a parameter.

Table 9.2 – Bathing water

The objective of the 1976 Bathing Water Directive (76/160/ EEC) is to protect public health and the environment from faecal pollution at bathing waters. The Directive sets a mandatory level for water cleanliness and at least 95 per cent of samples tested for faecal coliforms must have levels lower than this for the waters to be passed as identified bathing waters.

Maps 9.1–9.3 – Air pollution – Nitrogen dioxide, PM10 and sulphur dioxide concentrations

The Air Quality Strategy for England, Scotland, Wales and Northern Ireland sets out health-based standards for eight main air pollutants and objectives for their achievement throughout the UK. Standards for air pollution are concentrations over a given time period that are considered to be acceptable in the light of what is known about the effects of each pollutant on health and on the environment. They can also be used as a benchmark to see if air pollution is getting better or worse. An exceedence of a standard is a period of time (which is defined in each standard) where the concentration is higher than that set down by the standard. The objectives adopted in the UK, listed below, are based on the Air Quality Regulations 2000 and (Amendment) Regulations 2002.

Nitrogen Dioxide (provisional objective)	200 µg/m³ Not to be exceeded more than 18 times per year	1 Hour Mean	31 December 2005
	40 µg/m³	Annual Mean	31 December 2005

Particles (PM₁₀)	50 µg/m³ Not to be exceeded more than 7 times per year	24 Hour Mean	31 December 2010
	18 µg/m³	Annual Mean	31 December 2010

These 2010 Air Quality Objectives for PM 10 apply in Scotland only, as set out in the Air Quality (Scotland) Amendment Regulations 2002.

Sulphur Dioxide	266 µg/m³ Not to be exceeded more than 35 times per year	15 Minute Mean	31 December 2005
	350 µg/m³ Not to be exceeded more than 24 times per year	1 Hour Mean	31 December 2004
	125 µg/m³ Not to be exceeded more than 3 times per year	24 Hour Mean	31 December 2004
	(V) 20 µg/m³	Annual Mean	31 December 2000
	(V) 20 µg/m³	Winter Mean (01 October – 31 March)	31 December 2000

International comparisons

Chapter 10

DATA

Download data by clicking the online pdf

www.statistics.gov.uk/downloads/theme_health/ukhs3/

This chapter compares selected demographic and health measures for the UK and its constituent countries with other countries in Europe. There are a number of difficulties involved in comparing data internationally, for example differences in methods of data collection, differences in the social and ethnic characteristics of the populations, and differences between national healthcare systems.

As far as possible, these figures have been based on data published by Eurostat (the statistical agency of the European Union (EU)). Because of efforts which have been made within the EU to collect good quality comparative statistics, and because many European countries are relatively similar to the UK in their population characteristics, comparison within

Table 10.1

Population by age group, 2006[1]

European Union

Numbers and percentages

	Total Population	Age (years)					
		0-14	15-24	25-49	50-64	65-79	80 and over
		Thousands					
European Union (27 countries)	**492,852.3**	**78,626.9**	**62,615.6**	**179,606.7**	**89,355.2**	**62,219.7**	**20,424.6**
Austria	8,265.9	1,312.6	1,020.5	3,116.4	1,454.3	1,000.7	361.1
Belgium	10,511.3	1,796.1	1,269.7	3,739.0	1,897.4	1,343.1	465.8
Bulgaria	7,718.7	1,047.0	1,047.3	2,741.0	1,554.8	1,074.2	254.2
Cyprus	766.4	141.1	121.0	284.5	127.2	72.2	20.0
Czech Republic	10,251.0	1,501.3	1,352.0	3,785.4	2,155.8	1,134.8	321.5
Denmark	5,427.4	1,015.8	605.5	1,903.9	1,079.0	600.1	222.8
Estonia	1,344.6	202.4	210.2	466.1	240.5	180.9	44.0
Finland	5,255.5	906.9	654.8	1,744.7	1,107.8	628.7	212.4
France	62,886.1	11,693.1	8,137.7	21,614.7	11,232.1	7,299.2	2,907.9
Germany	82,437.9	11,649.8	9,689.5	30,085.4	15,143.0	12,189.2	3,680.8
Greece	11,125.1	1,593.5	1,329.5	4,182.8	1,958.7	1,658.5	401.0
Hungary	10,076.5	1,553.4	1,302.6	3,606.8	2,022.9	1,240.1	350.5
Ireland	4,209.0	861.7	638.7	1,589.9	650.3	354.0	113.2
Italy	58,751.7	8,283.9	6,071.9	22,023.9	10,779.5	8,583.8	3,008.5
Latvia	2,294.5	328.5	360.5	815.0	404.7	311.9	73.6
Lithuania	3,403.2	560.3	530.2	1,229.9	560.8	421.4	100.3
Luxembourg	459.5	85.4	53.4	176.0	78.5	50.7	15.2
Malta	404.3	69.2	58.4	141.3	80.9	42.4	11.9
Netherlands	16,334.2	2,984.5	1,955.7	5,957.9	3,105.4	1,743.4	587.0
Spain	43,758.2	6,341.6	5,189.5	17,659.2	7,259.3	5,384.3	1,924.1
Poland	38,157.0	6,189.1	6,185.3	13,748.6	6,958.1	4,044.9	1,030.8
Portugal	10,569.5	1,644.2	1,293.0	3,946.6	1,875.5	1,395.2	414.8
Romania	21,610.2	3,359.7	3,294.9	7,994.5	3,762.7	2,653.6	544.4
Slovenia	2,003.3	283.2	261.6	760.3	385.2	248.8	64.0
Slovakia	5,389.1	894.3	855.6	2,045.5	961.0	501.4	131.1
Sweden	9,047.7	1,560.7	1,125.6	3,013.3	1,782.5	1,078.2	487.1
United Kingdom	**60,587.3**	**10,737.4**	**8,020.1**	**21,308.7**	**10,833.1**	**6,988.4**	**2,699.4**
England	50,762.9	9,006.8	6,706.0	17,957.5	9,017.0	5,808.8	2,276.9
Wales	2,965.9	520.8	398.6	951.2	570.5	377.2	147.7
Scotland	5,116.9	856.1	667.8	1,795.3	959.8	624.3	213.8
Northern Ireland	1,741.6	353.9	257.7	604.7	286.0	178.2	61.1

1 UK constituent countries data are 2006 mid-year population estimates; all other figures as at 1 January 2006.

Source: Eurostat; Office for National Statistics

Europe tends to be more informative than possible comparisons with a broader group of countries worldwide.

Population

In 2006, 36.4 per cent of the population of the EU were aged between 25 and 49 years. There were 16.0 per cent aged 14 years or under and 4.1 per cent of the population were aged

80 years or over. The age distribution in the UK was broadly similar to that in the EU as a whole (Table 10.1).

Ireland had the highest proportion of children aged 14 or under (20.5 per cent). Bulgaria had the lowest proportion at 13.6 per cent. Sweden had the highest proportion of people aged 80 or over at 5.4 per cent, followed by Italy at 5.1 percent and Wales with 5.0 per cent.

Age (years)						Total	
0-14	15-24	25-49	50-64	65-79	80 and over	Population	
Percentages							
16.0	**12.7**	**36.4**	**18.1**	**12.6**	**4.1**	**492,852.3**	**European Union (27 countries)**
15.9	12.3	37.7	17.6	12.1	4.4	8,265.9	Austria
17.1	12.1	35.6	18.1	12.8	4.4	10,511.3	Belgium
13.6	13.6	35.5	20.1	13.9	3.3	7,718.7	Bulgaria
18.4	15.8	37.1	16.6	9.4	2.6	766.4	Cyprus
14.6	13.2	36.9	21.0	11.1	3.1	10,251.0	Czech Republic
18.7	11.2	35.1	19.9	11.1	4.1	5,427.4	Denmark
15.1	15.6	34.7	17.9	13.5	3.3	1,344.6	Estonia
17.3	12.5	33.2	21.1	12.0	4.0	5,255.5	Finland
18.6	12.9	34.4	17.9	11.6	4.6	62,886.1	France
14.1	11.8	36.5	18.4	14.8	4.5	82,437.9	Germany
14.3	12.0	37.6	17.6	14.9	3.6	11,125.1	Greece
15.4	12.9	35.8	20.1	12.3	3.5	10,076.5	Hungary
20.5	15.2	37.8	15.5	8.4	2.7	4,209.0	Ireland
14.1	10.3	37.5	18.3	14.6	5.1	58,751.7	Italy
14.3	15.7	35.5	17.6	13.6	3.2	2,294.5	Latvia
16.5	15.6	36.1	16.5	12.4	2.9	3,403.2	Lithuania
18.6	11.6	38.3	17.1	11.0	3.3	459.5	Luxembourg
17.1	14.4	34.9	20.0	10.5	3.0	404.3	Malta
18.3	12.0	36.5	19.0	10.7	3.6	16,334.2	Netherlands
14.5	11.9	40.4	16.6	12.3	4.4	43,758.2	Spain
16.2	16.2	36.0	18.2	10.6	2.7	38,157.0	Poland
15.6	12.2	37.3	17.7	13.2	3.9	10,569.5	Portugal
15.5	15.2	37.0	17.4	12.3	2.5	21,610.2	Romania
14.1	13.1	38.0	19.2	12.4	3.2	2,003.3	Slovenia
16.6	15.9	38.0	17.8	9.3	2.4	5,389.1	Slovakia
17.3	12.4	33.3	19.7	11.9	5.4	9,047.7	Sweden
17.7	**13.2**	**35.2**	**17.9**	**11.5**	**4.5**	**60,587.3**	**United Kingdom**
17.7	13.2	35.4	17.8	11.4	4.5	50,762.9	England
17.6	13.4	32.1	19.2	12.7	5.0	2,965.9	Wales
16.7	13.0	35.1	18.8	12.2	4.2	5,116.9	Scotland
20.3	14.8	34.7	16.4	10.2	3.5	1,741.6	Northern Ireland

1   UK constituent countries data are 2006 mid-year population estimates; all other figures as at 1 January 2006.

Source: Eurostat; Office for National Statistics

Fertility

The Total Fertility Rate (TFR) is the average number of children that would be born alive to a woman during her lifetime if current age and specific fertility rates were to continue. In both 2000 and 2005 the TFR for the EU was 1.5. The total fertility rate for the UK was slightly higher than the EU average, at 1.6 in 2000 and 1.8 in 2005 (Figure 10.1).

France and Ireland had the highest TFR in 2000 and 2005 with a rate of 1.9 for both countries in both years. In 2000, the Czech Republic had the lowest TFR at 1.1, increasing to 1.3 by 2005. The TFR in Poland had declined from 1.4 in 2000 to 1.2 in 2005, the lowest rate in the EU.

Life expectancy

Life expectancy is the number of years a person would be expected to live if current age-specific mortality rates continued.

In 2005 life expectancy in the EU was 75.8 years for males and 81.9 years for females (Figure 10.2). Sweden had the highest male life expectancy at 78.5 years, followed by Italy (77.6 years) and Ireland (77.3 years) compared to the lowest male life expectancy which was in Lithuania at 65.3 years. For women, France had the highest life expectancy at 83.8 years, followed by Spain (83.7 years) and Italy (83.2 years) compared to the lowest female life expectancy which was in Romania at 75.7 years.

Figure 10.1

Total fertility rate, 2000 and 2005

European Union

Number of children per woman

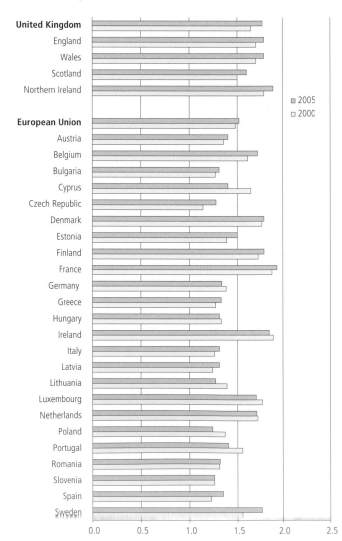

Source: Eurostat

Figure 10.2

Life expectancy at birth, 2005

European Union

Years

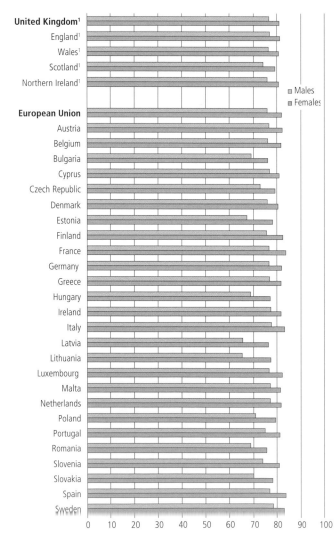

1 Data for UK is for period 2003-2005.

Source: Eurostat

Scotland had the lowest male life expectancy of the UK countries at 74.2 years; this was the only UK male life expectancy lower than the overall figure for the EU. All female life expectancies for the UK were lower than the overall EU life expectancy.

Infant mortality

The infant mortality rate is the number of deaths under one year old per 1,000 live births. In the EU as a whole, the infant mortality rate declined from 4.8 per 1,000 live births in 2002 to 4.5 per 1,000 live births in 2005 (Table 10.2). Romania had the highest infant mortality rate in 2005 at 15.0 per 1,000 live births, followed by Bulgaria with a rate of 10.4 per 1,000, Latvia with 7.8 per 1,000 and Slovakia with a rate of 7.2 per 1,000. Over the period 2002 to 2005 Bulgaria had the largest decrease in the infant mortality rate, from 13.3 per 1,000 live births to 10.4.

Wales was the only country in the UK with an infant mortality rate lower than the average for the EU, at 4.3 per 1,000 live births in 2005.

Mortality by cause

Age-standardised death rates are summary measures that allow comparison of mortality in populations with different age distributions.

For purposes of comparison with other European countries, the mortality data for the UK which are presented here are based on the WHO Health for All database, which uses codes and groupings available for all the EU countries but does not take account of national differences in classification practice. These figures on mortality are consequently not directly comparable with routine ONS mortality publications, or with data presented elsewhere in this report.

In 2005, Latvia had the highest age-standardised male all causes mortality rate at 1609.7 deaths per 100,000 (Table 10.3). This was more than double the mortality rate for deaths of all causes in Ireland, which was the lowest in Europe at 742.7 deaths per 100,000. The male death rate for the UK of 752.8 deaths per 100,000 was the third lowest out of the 19 countries where data were available.

Male death rates from cancer were highest in Hungary and lowest in Cyprus. The rate of trachea, bronchus and lung cancer in Hungary was 112.6 per 100,000 population, almost three times the Cyprus rate of 37.7 per 100,000. The rate for all cancers was more than double; 330.8 for Hungary compared with 149.6 per 100,000 population for Cyprus.

The UK male rate from deaths from malignant neoplasms was

Table 10.2

Trends in infant mortality rates[1]

European Union				Rates
	2002	2003	2004	2005
European Union (27 countries)	4.8	:	4.6	4.5
Austria	4.1	4.5	4.5	4.2
Belgium	4.4	:	4.7	4.4
Bulgaria	13.3	12.3	11.6	10.4
Cyprus	4.7	4.1	3.5	4.0
Czech Republic	4.1	3.9	3.7	3.4
Denmark	4.4	4.4	4.4	4.4
Estonia	5.7	7.0	6.4	5.4
Finland	3.0	3.1	3.3	3.0
France	4.2	4.2	4.0	3.8
Germany	4.2	4.2	4.1	3.9
Greece	5.1	4.0	4.1	3.8
Hungary	7.2	7.3	6.6	6.2
Ireland	5.1	5.1	4.8	4.0
Italy	4.3	3.9	4.1	4.7
Latvia	9.8	9.4	9.4	7.8
Lithuania	7.9	6.7	7.9	6.8
Luxembourg	5.1	4.9	3.9	2.6
Malta	5.9	5.7	5.9	6.0
Netherlands	5.0	4.8	4.4	4.9
Poland	7.5	7.0	6.8	6.4
Portugal	5.0	4.1	3.8	3.5
Romania	17.3	16.7	16.8	15.0
Slovenia	3.8	4.0	3.7	4.1
Slovakia	7.6	7.9	6.8	7.2
Spain	4.1	3.9	4.0	3.8
Sweden	3.3	3.1	3.1	2.4
United Kingdom	5.3	5.3	5.1	5.1
England	5.3	5.3	5.1	5.0
Wales	4.7	4.1	5.1	4.3
Scotland	5.3	5.1	4.9	5.2
Northern Ireland	4.6	5.2	5.3	6.1

1 Deaths under one year per 1,000 births.

Source: Eurostat; Office for National Statistics

216.9 per 100,000 population, over 30 per cent lower than the rate for Hungary. However, the UK male rate for ischaemic heart disease was 150.4 deaths per 100,000 population, twice that of Portugal which at 71.9 had the lowest rate in Europe.

In 2005 Bulgaria had the highest all causes female age-standardised death rate at 823.2 deaths per 100,000 population (Table 10.4). The lowest rate of female deaths from all causes was in Spain, at 419.7 deaths per 100,000 population. The age-standardised mortality rate for females in the UK was 538.8 deaths per 100,000.

10

Table 10.3

Age-standardised death rates[1] for males: selected causes of death, 2005

European Union

Rates per 100,000 population

	Selected Causes						
	Malignant neoplasm	Trachea, bronchus & lung cancer	Ischaemic heart disease	Cerebro-vascular diseases	Bronchitis, emphysema & asthma	Transport accidents	All causes
European Union (27 countries)	:	:	:	:	:	:	:
Austria	215.7	53.0	146.7	46.0	33.8	14.1	773.2
Belgium	:	:	:	:	:	:	:
Bulgaria	225.5	71.9	219.5	229.4	25.5	16.9	1362.9
Cyprus	149.6	37.7	121.5	47.6	19.4	39.0	763.9
Czech Republic	:	:	:	:	:	:	:
Denmark	:	:	:	:	:	:	:
Estonia	307.9	84.8	388.5	147.6	23.8	23.2	1470.3
Finland	:	:	:	:	:	:	:
France	:	:	:	:	:	:	:
Germany	215.3	57.5	141.5	49.1	28.2	9.8	775.9
Greece	217.5	74.6	110.4	94.7	9.8	23.8	757.1
Hungary	330.8	112.6	347.2	133.3	57.0	23.3	1373.0
Ireland	211.6	52.4	153.6	47.6	37.0	9.4	742.7
Italy	:	:	:	:	:	:	:
Latvia	296.7	86.9	432.9	219.4	22.8	31.5	1609.7
Lithuania	289.1	82.6	490.6	139.1	46.6	39.9	1571.2
Luxembourg	216.2	64.0	94.7	56.2	34.2	11.8	776.6
Malta	183.4	52.9	198.8	62.2	44.9	6.8	760.8
Netherlands	240.1	73.2	86.8	46.6	42.2	7.1	767.0
Poland	295.6	103.7	163.1	101.5	33.6	23.6	1175.8
Portugal	215.6	48.4	71.9	109.0	28.3	20.4	891.0
Romania	:	:	:	:	:	:	:
Slovenia	272.4	79.3	116.6	76.9	36.5	19.5	978.5
Slovakia	304.1	83.4	342.2	92.1	27.9	22.2	1282.7
Spain	232.7	71.7	81.7	51.4	44.8	16.8	751.7
Sweden	:	:	:	:	:	:	:
United Kingdom	216.9	54.9	150.4	56.4	39.5	8.7	752.8

1   Rates are standardised using the European Standard Population.

Source: Eurostat

As for males, the female death rates for all cancers and for trachea, bronchus and lung cancer were highest in Hungary. Breast cancer death rates were highest in Ireland at 30.9 per 100,000 population; this was closely followed by the Netherlands with a rate of 29.8, and the UK with a rate of 28.5.

The UK had the highest rate of deaths among females from bronchitis, emphysema and asthma at 26.0 per 100,000 population followed by Hungary at 24.1 and Ireland at 23.3. Greece had the lowest rate for deaths among females from bronchitis, emphysema and asthma at 4.3 per 100,000 population.

Self-assessed health

Information on self-assessed health is taken from Organisation for Economic Co-operation and Development health data and is presented for the countries of the EU where available. Survey respondents assessed their health in general according to a five-point scale, ranging from very bad to very good. It should be noted that self-assessed health is a subjective measure and differences between countries may be affected by cultural factors and different expectations of health.

Portugal reported the highest incidence of bad or very bad health in 2003 at 22.5 per cent. This was over 11 times higher

Table 10.4

Age-standardised death rates[1] for females: selected causes of death, 2005

European Union   Rates per 100,000 population

	Selected Causes								
	Malignant neoplasm	Trachea, bronchus & lung cancer	Cancer of the cervix	Malignant neoplasm of breast	Ischaemic heart disease	Cerebro-vascular diseases	Bronchitis, emphysema & asthma	Transport accidents	All causes
European Union (27 countries) :	:	:	:	:	:	:	:	:	:
Austria	132.5	17.2	3.2	24.7	85.5	36.6	13.7	4.1	481.7
Belgium	:	:	:	:	:	:	:	:	:
Bulgaria	128.6	11.8	6.9	23.6	117.3	169.9	9.4	5.1	823.2
Cyprus	99.2	11.6	1.2	20.8	51.2	49.7	7.6	19.8	535.3
Czech Republic	:	:	:	:	:	:	:	:	:
Denmark	:	:	:	:	:	:	:	:	:
Estonia	136.8	12.5	6.8	24.0	192.1	104.8	4.9	7.2	687.5
Finland	:	:	:	:	:	:	:	:	:
France	:	:	:	:	:	:	:	:	:
Germany	134.7	18.2	2.7	26.2	75.6	41.7	12.2	3.2	495.4
Greece	113.0	11.1	1.2	21.7	48.8	101.0	4.3	6.4	530.8
Hungary	172.7	32.0	6.5	27.4	201.4	90.7	24.1	6.5	754.7
Ireland	158.3	28.4	3.7	30.9	77.1	38.3	23.3	3.7	506.4
Italy	:	:	:	:	:	:	:	:	:
Latvia	136.8	10.6	6.5	23.7	198.6	162.8	4.5	9.8	774.8
Lithuania	139.3	8.5	9.8	24.3	267.4	110.7	9.5	11.2	738.2
Luxembourg	123.2	20.4	1.3	20.9	44.1	48.5	11.9	8.9	486.2
Malta	119.9	6.8	1.0	28.1	110.6	63.3	8.1	2.2	527.2
Netherlands	156.7	29.9	2.2	29.8	38.9	40.6	19.4	2.4	506.2
Poland	155.3	21.3	7.8	21.3	78.3	75.8	8.3	6.1	626.1
Portugal	111.4	8.3	3.1	19.7	38.7	84.3	8.9	4.8	530.6
Romania	:	:	:	:	:	:	:	:	:
Slovenia	148.1	19.3	2.7	26.9	53.8	53.2	9.8	6.6	552.6
Slovakia	146.8	11.9	6.8	22.1	222.9	63.1	7.7	5.8	718.1
Spain	103.3	8.3	2.1	18.5	35.7	40.6	9.2	4.1	419.7
Sweden	:	:	:	:	:	:	:	:	:
United Kingdom	156.7	30.7	2.6	28.5	72.4	54.6	26.0	2.3	538.8

1 Rates are standardised using the European Standard Population.

Source: Eurostat

than Ireland, which recorded the lowest incidence of bad or very bad health at 1.9 per cent (Fig 10.3). Poland had the second highest proportion of bad or very bad health (17.7 per cent) followed by Hungary (14.6 per cent). In the UK the percentage of people reporting bad or very bad health was 5.0 per cent in 2003.

Smoking

In all countries except Sweden, the proportion of men who were daily smokers was higher than the proportion of women (Figure 10.4). Latvia reported the highest percentage of male smokers – over half of all men smoked daily (50.6 per cent) –

followed by men in Estonia (49.8 per cent), Slovenia (47.1 per cent) and Lithuania (44.0 per cent). The country with the lowest proportion was Sweden where only 16.5 per cent of men were smokers. Finland had the second lowest proportion of men who smoked at 21.6 per cent, followed by Ireland at 23.9 per cent. In the UK 27.7 per cent of men smoked daily, the sixth lowest of the 26 countries where data was available.

Austria had the highest proportion of women who were daily smokers (32.2 per cent), followed by Denmark (31.9 per cent) and the UK (25.7 per cent). Portugal had the lowest proportion of women who smoked daily, at 6.8 per cent

10

Figure 10.3

Proportion of adults with 'bad' or 'very bad' health, 2003

European Union

Percentages

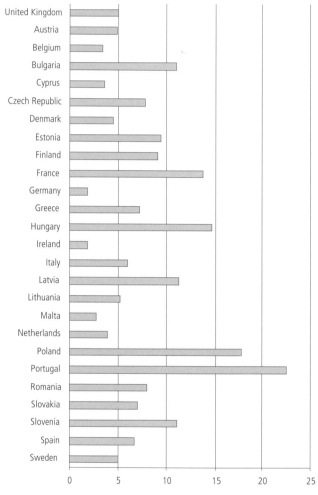

Source: Eurostat

Figure 10.4

Percentage of daily smokers among adults aged 16 or over, 2003

European Union

Percentages

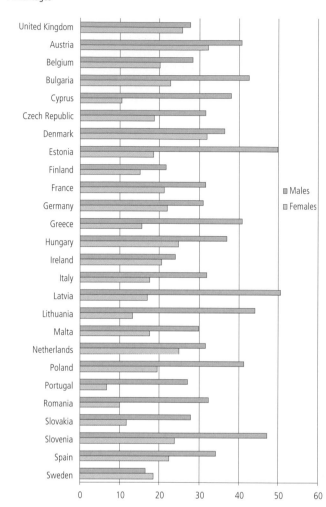

Source: Eurostat

The upper age limit of survey samples for the European surveys used to produce estimates of daily smoking prevalence differ by country. As age has an important influence on smoking prevalence, the comparisons presented here are for illustrative purposes only.

Obesity

The body mass index (BMI) is the most commonly used measure of obesity. It is defined as weight in kilograms divided by the square of the height in meters. Adults with a BMI of between 25 and 30 inclusive are deemed to be overweight and those with a BMI over 30 are defined as obese.

With the exception of the UK, the data presented here are based on self-reported height and weight information. This is not as reliable as data obtained from health examinations, which is presented for the UK. Differences between countries may therefore be at least partly due to differences in reporting.

In 2003, Malta had the highest proportion of obese adults with 23 per cent of the adult population having a BMI of 30 or more (Figure 10.5). The UK had the next largest proportion (22.7 per cent) followed by Germany (20.3 per cent).

Italy had the lowest incidence of adult obesity, with only 8.1 per cent of the population reporting a BMI of over 30. Austria had the next lowest proportion of obese adults at 8.6 per cent.

Figure 10.5

Percentage of adult population who are obese,[1,2] 2003

European Union

Percentages

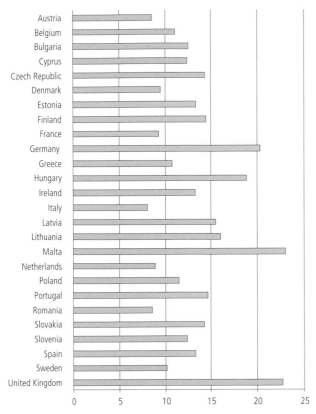

1 Obesity rates are defined as the percentage of the population with a Body Mass Index (BMI) over 30. The BMI is a single number that evaluates an individual's weight status in relation to height.
2 For the UK, figures are based on health examinations, rather than self-reported information. Obesity estimates derived from health examinations are generally higher and more reliable than those derived from self reported information.

Source: Eurostat

Additional notes

Figure 10.1 – Total fertility rate (TFR)

The sum of the single year age-specific fertility rates of all women aged 15–44 years in a population at one point in time. The TFR estimates the number of children a woman would have if exposed to the age-specific fertility rates for the current year, throughout her child-bearing years.

Table 10.2 – Life expectancy

Life expectancy at birth for an area is an estimate of the average number of years a new-born baby would survive if he or she experienced the particular area's age-specific mortality rates for that time period throughout his or her life. The figure reflects mortality among those living in the area at that time, rather than mortality among those born in each area. It is not therefore the number of years a baby born in the area in each time period could actually expect to live, both because the death rates of the area are likely to change in the future and because many of those born in the area will live elsewhere for at least some part of their lives.

Tables 10.3 and 10.4 – Age- standardised death rates

Age-standardised death rates are summary measures that allow comparison of mortality in populations with different age distributions. The death rates presented here represent what the crude rate would have been if the population had the same age distribution as the European standard population.

Topic links with other ONS publications

Some of the contents of this volume have previously appeared in other ONS publications, in a more or less identical form. Other information is similar to material which has appeared elsewhere, but differs in one or more aspects – such as age groups, definitions or time periods – because of differences in the focus and scope of the different publications. This appendix provides a brief cross-reference between *UK Health Statistics* and three key publications, *Focus on Health*, *Social Trends 38* and *Regional Trends 40*.

The following table shows, for each table or figure in *UK Health Statistics*, the most relevant tables, figures or maps in each of these three publications, where appropriate. Items in *UK Health Statistics* for which there is no direct equivalent in any of the three publications are excluded.

Focus on Health

Focus on Health describes the health of people living in the UK across six key dimensions: health status, risk factors, ill-health, preventive, curative and long-term care services and mortality. Emphasis is placed on trends over time.

On most health topics, *Focus on Health* contains greater non-geographical detail than *UK Health Statistics*, for example analyses of health by age, sex, socioeconomic classification and ethnicity. The range of specific health topics covered by *Focus on Health* is also wider. There is extensive descriptive text on some topics. Figures are in most cases presented for the UK as a whole, Great Britain, or England only.

Bajekal M, Osborne V, Yar M and Meltzer H (eds.) (2006) *Focus on Health*, 2006 edition, Palgrave Macmillan: Basingstoke.

Also available on the National Statistics website at:

www.statistics.gov.uk/focuson/health/

Social Trends

An established reference source, *Social Trends* draws together social and economic data from a wide range of government departments and other organisations; it paints a broad picture of British society today, and how it has been changing.

Because of its wide-ranging content, there is material in *Social Trends* relating to most chapters of *UK Health Statistics*. The level of detail is relatively limited. Figures are in most cases presented for the UK as a whole, Great Britain, or England only, depending on the availability of data.

The most recent edition – *Social Trends 38* – was published on 8 April 2008.

Self A and Zealey L (eds.) (2008) *Social Trends 38*, Palgrave Macmillan: Basingstoke.

Also available on the National Statistics website at:

www.statistics.gov.uk/socialtrends38

Regional Trends

Regional Trends is a comprehensive source of official statistics for the Statistical Regions of the UK (Scotland, Wales, Northern Ireland and the Government Office Regions within England). It includes a wide range of demographic, social, industrial and economic statistics, covering aspects of life in the regions.

Figures in *Regional Trends* are in most cases presented for the UK as a whole or for Great Britain, for the constituent countries, and for the Government Office Regions of England. Some data are presented for NHS regions or other administrative areas.

The most recent edition – *Regional Trends 40* – was published on 8 May 2008.

Sly F (eds.) (2008) *Regional Trends 40*, 2008 edition, Palgrave Macmillan: Basingstoke.

This edition is also available on the National Statistics website at:

www.statistics.gov.uk/RegionalTrends40

UK Health Statistics No. 3		Focus on Health	Social Trends 38	Regional Trends 40
1: People and work				
Table 1.1	Population by age and sex, 2006		Table 1.2	Table 3.2
Table 1.3	Population by ethnic group, 2005		Table 1.5	Table 3.6
Table 1.4	Size of households, 2007		Table 2.1	
Table 1.5	Composition of households, 2007			Table 3.17
Table 1.6	Adult popn of working age: by sex and socioeconomic classification, 2005		Figure 1.6	
Table 1.7	Population of working age by highest qualification, 2005		Table 4.5	
Table 1.8	Unemployment and economic activity, 2006		Figure 4.1, 4.14	Table 5.1, 5.3, 5.14
2: Pregnancy and childbirth				
Table 2.1	Age specific fertility rates, total fertility rate (TFR), and percentage of live births outside marriage, 2006		Table 2.13	
Table 2.2	Trends in total fertility rate, 1971–2006		Table 2.13	
Table 2.3	Conceptions: by age and outcome, 2004–05	Figure 6.7	Table 2.18	
Table 2.4	Legal abortions by age, 2006		Figure 2.19	
Table 2.5	Live births by birthweight and mothers age, 2006			Table 3.10
Table 2.7	Trends in infant, neonatal and perinatal mortality rates, 1971–2006	Figure 13.6	Figure 7.5	Table 7.2
3: General health and morbidity				
Table 3.1	Self-assessed 'good' or 'fairly good' health: by age and sex, 2006	Figure 2.1, 2.2, 2.12, 2.16	Table 7.3	
Table 3.2	Healthy life expectancy and disability-free life expectancy at birth and age 65: by country and sex, 2004		Table 7.2	
Table 3.3	General practice consultations by age and sex, 2006	Figure 11.1		
Table 3.4	Trends in road accident casualties: by severity, 1994–2006		Table 12.16	Table 10.14
Table 3.5	Newly diagnosed cases of cancer: by sex and by cancer site, 2004		Figure 7.15	
Table 3.9	Notifications of selected communicable diseases, 1996 and 2006	Figure 10.2, 10.3	Figure 7.6, 7.7	
Table 3.10	New diagnoses of sexually transmitted infections: by sex and condition, 2000–2006	Table 6.13	Map 7.21	
Table 3.11	Trends in new diagnoses of HIV and deaths of HIV-infected individuals, 1985–2006			
Table 3.12	Trends in diagnosed HIV-infected patients: by probable route of infection, 1997–2006		Figure 7.22	Table 7.6
4: Health-related behaviour				
Table 4.1	Cigarette smoking among adults aged 16 and over: by sex, 2006	Figure 4.1, 4.2	Figure 7.13	Table 7.8
Table 4.2	Trends in cigarette smoking among 11 to 16 year olds: by age and sex, 1990–2006	Figure 4.3, 4.4		
Table 4.3	Changes to smoking habits during pregnancy, 2005	Table 10.6		
Table 4.4	Maximum daily alcohol consumption last week among adults aged 16 and over: by sex, 2006	Figure 4.6, 4.7	Table 7.11	Table 7.9
Table 4.5	Trends in alcohol consumption among 11 to 16 year olds: by age and sex, 1990–2006	Figure 4.8–4.12		
Table 4.6	Proportion of people meeting physical activity recommendations: by age and sex, 2005–06	Table 5.17, Figure 5.19		
Table 4.7	Purchases of and expenditure on selected foods, 2004–2006		Table 7.9	Figure 8.12
Table 4.8	Energy and nutrient intakes, 2004–2006	Figure 5.8–5.10		

UK Health Statistics No. 3		Focus on Health	Social Trends 38	Regional Trends 40
5: Preventative healthcare				
Table 5.3	Immunisation against influenza among the elderly population (65+), 2005–06	Figure 10.4		
Table 5.4	Current use of contraception: by country, 2006–07	Table 6.8, 6.9		
Table 5.5	Cervical and breast cancer screening: by age, 2005–06			Table 7.5
6: Use of services				
Table 6.1	Hospital inpatient and day case activity, 2005–06		Table 8.13	Table 7.11
Table 6.2	Hospital outpatient activity, outpatient attendances by sector, 2006–07		Figure 8.12	Table 7.11
Table 6.6	Children and young people on child protection registers: by age and category as at 31st March 2006			Table 7.15
Table 6.7	Prescriptions dispensed, numbers and cost, 2006			Table 7.12
7: Mortality and life expectancy				
Table 7.1	Age specific death rates: by sex, 2006	Table 13.2 Figure 13.3	Table 1.9	Table 3.11
Table 7.2a	Deaths by underlying cause, ICD-10 chapter, age and sex, 2006	Appendix Table 13B	Figure 7.4	
Table 7.4	Alcohol-related deaths: by age and sex, 2006	Table 4.14	Figure 7.12	
Table 7.6	Period life expectancy at specific ages, 2005		Figure 7.1	
8: Health and care resources				
Table 8.1	Average daily available hospital beds per 1,000 resident population, 2005–06			Table 7.11
Table 8.2	Places available in residential care homes: by type of care home as at 31st March 2006			Table 7.14
Table 8.4	General Practitioners, dentists and opticians, as at 30 September 2006		Table 8.11	Table 7.13
Table 8.5	Total expenditure on services by Health and Personal Social Services, 2006–07		Figure 8.3	
9: Health and the environment				
Table 9.2	Trends in bathing water cleanliness, 1995–2006		Table 11.14	Table 11.18 (web only)
Map 9.1	Air quality: Nitrogen dioxide concentrations		Figure 11.12	Map 11.4
Map 9.2	Air quality: PM10 concentrations		Figure 11.12	
Map 9.3	Air quality: sulphur dioxide concentrations		Figure 11.12	Map 11.3
10: International comparisons				
Table 10.1	Population: by age group, 2006		Table 1.4	Table 3.2
Table 10.2	Trends in infant mortality rates, 2002–2005			Table 7.2